Dreamweaver® 4

VIRTUAL CLASSROOM

Robert Fuller and Laurie Ann Ulrich

OSBORNE

New York   Chicago   San Francisco
Lisbon   London   Madrid   Mexico City
Milan   New Delhi   San Juan
Seoul   Singapore   Sydney   Toronto

Osborne/**McGraw-Hill**
2600 Tenth Street
Berkeley, California 94710
U.S.A.

To arrange bulk purchase discounts for sales promotions, premiums, or fund-raisers, please contact Osborne/**McGraw-Hill** at the above address. For information on translations or book distributors outside the U.S.A., please see the International Contact Information page immediately following the index of this book.

Dreamweaver® 4 Virtual Classroom

Brainsville.com™
The better way to learn.

1234567890 QPD QPD 01987654321

Book p/n 0-07-213107-1 and CD p/n 0-07-213106-3
parts of
ISBN 0-07-213108-X

Publisher	**Acquisitions Coordinator**	**Production Manager**
Brandon A. Nordin	Alissa Larson	epic/Eric Houts
Vice President &	**Technical Editor**	**Computer and Series Designer**
Associate Publisher	Mike Parisi	epic/Andrea Reider
Scott Rogers		
	Copy Editor	**Illustrators**
Editorial Director	Lunaea Weatherstone	Lyssa Seiben-Wald
Roger Stewart		Beth Young
	Proofreader	Michael Mueller
Project Editors	Paul Tyler	
Jody McKenzie		**Cover Design**
Jenn Tust	**Indexer**	Ted Holladay
	David Heiret	

This book was composed with QuarkXPress™.

Dedication

To my family:

Noni and Papa, Mom and Dad, Aunt Nan and Uncle Dick, Aunt Jean and Uncle Bud, Jeannie and Tom, Mike and Cheryl, Ann and Vaughn, Deborah and Melanie, David and Tina, Christopher, Michelle, Suzy, Lori and Lance, Patrick, Tomas, Meghan, Joshua, Sarah, Lee, and Tyler.

In those last few moments just before the sun rises, when I find myself alone, my thoughts turn to each of you and I wish that I was home again.

—Robert Fuller

About the Authors

Robert Fuller is a visual artist who turned his attention to Web-based media in 1995. He survived Silicon Alley, where he was senior Web developer for a very pretentious "pre-IPO Internet start-up" (but resigned because they were much too full of themselves). He now divides his time between writing, teaching Web design, and discussing catnip appreciation with his best friend, Jasper.

Laurie Ann Ulrich started her professional life planning to be an artist, but she discovered computers in 1981 and has been hooked on them ever since. Moving from computer systems management to running computer training centers and then to forming her own computer training and consulting firm (Limehat & Company, Inc.), Laurie has been helping businesses, nonprofit organizations, and individuals make effective use of computers for nearly 20 years. In 1998, she added Web design and Web site hosting to the list of services offered by her company, finally enabling her to combine her creative ability and technical interests. Since 1990, Laurie has trained thousands of students, written hundreds of computer training manuals, and in the last three years has sole authored, cowritten, and contributed to more than 15 nationally published computer books on topics ranging from Microsoft Office to using the Internet to plan a vacation. Her main personal and professional Web site can be found at http://www.planetlaurie.com/, and she can be reached via e-mail at laurie@planetlaurie.com.

Contents at a Glance

Contents

11 Working with Multimedia Elements 207

Acknowledgments

I want to thank Roger Stewart for giving me the opportunity to write this book. Thank you for your guidance, friendship, and unparalleled sense of humor. I am eternally grateful. I also want to thank Jody McKenzie, Jenn Tust, Alissa Larson, and Lunaea Weatherstone for everything they've done to see this project through to completion. Lastly, I need to thank Laurie Ulrich for introducing me to Roger in the first place and for not shooting me years ago when she first had the chance.

INTRODUCTION

Introduction

Who Will Enjoy this Book?

Hopefully, you will, if you're interested in learning Dreamweaver, or if you've been using Dreamweaver and want to learn more. The concepts and ideas I share in this book are intended to help you get a handle on arguably the best Web design tool available and show you how to use this tool to expand your Web design skills. Dreamweaver is a deceptively easy tool to use, but don't let this fool you. Dreamweaver is an industrial-strength application, and it's precisely this ease of use that makes it a favorite among Web design professionals.

I wrote this book with the beginning-to-intermediate user in mind. If you come to Dreamweaver with little previous HTML (Hypertext Markup Language) experience, don't be afraid. Though Dreamweaver is at its heart a tool for creating HTML documents, and HTML is the foundation on which Web pages are built, a thorough understanding of the language is not a prerequisite for using Dreamweaver effectively. In fact, using Dreamweaver is an excellent way to learn HTML, and I've done my best to point out each of the features that facilitate this process while I was writing.

WHAT MAKES THIS A VIRTUAL CLASSROOM?

The accompanying CD makes this book a "virtual classroom." Instead of just reading about the Dreamweaver features and tools covered, you can watch and listen to the author discuss them as helpful visuals appear onscreen, demonstrating software features and design techniques.

It's important to note that the CD is not a visual repetition of the book. Not everything discussed in the book is covered on the CD, and there are topics broached on the CD that are covered in more detail there than in the book. The goal for the CD is to give you the experience of sitting in on one of my Dreamweaver classes, allowing me to elaborate on certain topics that could be better expressed and explained in a full-color, moving medium. Topics in the book that wouldn't be any better explained through sound, color, and motion are not found on the CD, while topics that couldn't be effectively explained through text and black and white images *are* found on the CD.

It's entirely possible to learn a great deal from the book without ever watching the CD. I hope, however, that you'll read the book and then watch the CD to enhance what you've absorbed through your reading. This would be the closest match to the hands-on classroom training experience, because I typically discuss a topic and then show it to or demonstrate it for the class, inviting the students to work along with me on their computers so that the skills become part of each student's personal experience.

HOW THIS BOOK WORKS

Of course, you know how a book *works*: you open it, and start reading, turning pages as you go. Not too difficult, right? This book, however, has some useful features you should be aware of:

▶ **CD-ROM references** At the end of chapters containing topics covered on the CD, an "On the Virtual Classroom CD-ROM" notation and CD-ROM icon will appear, directing you to the specific CD lesson that relates to the chapter you've just read.

▶ **Tips, notes, and sidebars** Whenever I thought of something that I'd present as a quick aside during class, I turned it into a tip or a note. Tips and notes relate to the main topic in the nearby text, but are extra bits of helpful information rather than entire topics unto themselves. Sidebars delve a little deeper, discussing larger topics that relate to nearby text.

I hope you enjoy the book, and if you have any specific design questions or quandaries, I invite you to contact me via e-mail at robert@highstrungproductions.com. I answer all reader mail, attempting to do so within 24 to 48 hours of receiving it. I look forward to hearing from you!

 DREAMWEAVER 4 VIRTUAL CLASSROOM CD

This CD contains an exciting new kind of video-based instruction to help you learn Web design faster. We believe this learning tool is a unique development in the area of computer-based training. The author actually talks to you, right from your computer screen, demonstrating topics he wrote about in the book. Moving "screencams" and slides accompany his presentation, reinforcing what you're learning.

The technology and design of the presentation were developed by Brainsville.com. The content on the CD-ROM was developed by Osborne/McGraw-Hill, Robert Fuller, and Brainsville.com. Patents (pending), copyright, and trademark protections apply to this technology and the name Brainsville.com.

Please read the following directions for usage of the CD-ROM, to ensure that the lessons play as smoothly as possible.

GETTING STARTED

The CD-ROM is optimized to run under Windows 95/98/Me/NT/2000 using the RealPlayer version 8 (or later), from Real Networks. However, it will also run fine on most PowerPC Macintoshes with RealPlayer for the Mac. (Note that RealPlayer versions earlier than 8 will not work.) If you don't have the RealPlayer installed, you must install it, either by downloading it from the Internet at http://www.real.com, or by running the Setup program from the CD-ROM. To install from the Web, you should download the latest RealPlayer. You can choose the Basic player, which is free, if you don't want to purchase the full version. You typically have to look around a bit to get to the correct page. You're looking for RealPlayer "Basic."

To install RealPlayer from the CD-ROM follow these steps:

On a Windows PC:

1. Insert the CD-ROM in the drive.
2. Use Explorer or My Computer to browse to the CD-ROM.
3. Open the RealPlayer folder and then open the correct folder for your type of computer.
4. Double click on the setup program there.
5. Follow the setup instructions on screen.

On a Mac:

1. Insert the CD-ROM in the drive.
2. Open the RealPlayer folder and then open the folder containing the Mac version of the RealPlayer.
3. Run the Publishing RM8A Installer file.
4. Follow the setup instructions on screen.

RUNNING THE CD IN WINDOWS 95/98/ME/NT/2000

Minimum Requirements:

RealPlayer 8 or later
Pentium II P333 (or equivalent)
64M RAM
8X CD ROM
16-bit sound card and speakers
65,000-color video display card (video)
Windows 95, Windows 98, Windows 2000, Windows ME, or Windows NT 4.0
with at least Service Pack 4

Dreamweaver 4 Virtual Classroom CD-ROM can run directly from the CD (see
below for running it from the hard drive for better performance, if necessary) and
should start automatically when you insert the CD in the drive. If the program
does not start automatically, your system may not be set up to automatically
detect CDs. To change this, you can do the following:

1. Choose Settings, Control Panel, and click the System icon.
2. Click the Device Manager tab in the System Properties dialog box.
3. Double-click the Disk drives icon and locate your CD-ROM drive.
4. Double-click the CD-ROM drive icon and then click the Settings tab in the
   CD-ROM Properties dialog box. Make sure the Auto Insert Notification box is
   checked. This specifies that Windows will be notified when you insert a com-
   pact disc into the drive.

If you don't care about the auto-start setting for your CD-ROM, and don't mind
the manual approach, you can start the lessons manually, this way:

1. Insert the CD-ROM.
2. Double-click the My Computer icon on your Windows desktop.
3. Open the CD-ROM folder.
4. Double-click the jmenu.exe icon in the folder.
5. Follow instructions on the screen to start.

RUNNING ON A MAC

Minimum Requirements:

RealPlayer 8 or later

Mac OS 8.1 or later

32 MB RAM

Virtual Memory turned on, set to 64MB

604 PowerPC (200 MHz or better)

1. Insert the CD-ROM.

2. Open the CD-ROM folder.

3. Double-click on the ClickToStart icon. If this doesn't work, then open the RealPlayer and from the RealPlayer window open the ClickToStart file. It should begin playing.

4. Follow instructions as described by the author, or read the section below.

THE OPENING SCREEN

When the program autostarts on a PC, you'll see a small window in the middle of your screen with an image of the book. Simply click the book to launch the RealPlayer and start the lessons. On the Mac, you have to start the Virtual Classroom manually as described above.

Regardless of how you start the Virtual Classroom, the RealPlayer window should soon open and the Virtual Classroom introduction should begin running. You click on the links in the lower left region of the RealPlayer window to jump to a given lesson. The author will explain how to use the interface.

The RealPlayer will completely fill a screen that is running at 800 × 600 resolution. (This is the minimum resolution required to play the lessons). For screens with higher resolution, you can adjust the position of the player as you like on screen. If the content panel in the RealPlayer is turned on, you'll see a number of entertainment and news stations listed on the left side of the RealPlayer window. You can turn those off by going to the program's View menu and choosing Content Pane.

If you are online, you can click on the Brainsville.com logo under the index marks to jump directly to the Brainsville.com Web site for information about the additional hour of instructional material we have available. (See the description in the back of the book, or run the promotional trailer at the end of the Conclusion lesson for more details.)

IMPROVING PLAYBACK

Your Virtual Classroom CD-ROM employs some cutting-edge technologies, requiring that your computer be pretty fast to run the lessons smoothly. For example, each lesson actually runs two videos at the same time—one for the instructor's image and one for the screen cam. Many variables determine a computer's video performance, so we can't give you specific requirements for running the lessons. CPU speed, internal bus speed, amount of RAM, CD-ROM drive transfer rate, video display performance, CD-ROM cache settings and other variables will determine how well the lessons will play. Our advice is to simply try the CD. The disk has been tested on laptops and desktops of various speeds, and in general, we have determined that you'll need at least a Pentium II-class computer running in excess of 300Mhz for decent performance. (If you're doing serious Web-design work, it's likely your machine is at least this fast.)

CLOSE OTHER PROGRAMS

For best performance, make sure you are not running other programs in the background while viewing the CD-based lessons. Rendering the video on your screen takes a lot of computing power, and background programs such as automatic email checking, Web-site updating, or Active Desktop applets (such as scrolling stock tickers) can tax the CPU to the point of slowing the videos.

ADJUST THE SCREEN COLOR DEPTH TO SPEED UP PERFORMANCE

It's possible the author's lips will be out of synch with his or her voice, just like Web-based videos often look. There are a couple solutions. Start with this one: lowering the color depth to 16-bit color makes a world of difference with many computers, laptops included. Rarely do people need 24-bit or 32-bit color for their work anyway, and it makes scrolling your screen (in any program) that much slower when running in those higher color depths. Try this:

1. Right click on the desktop and choose Properties.
2. Click the Settings tab.

3. In the Colors section, open the drop-down list box and choose a lower setting. If you are currently running at 24-bit (True Color) color, for example, try 16-bit (High Color). Don't use 256 colors, since video will appear very funky if you do, and you'll be prompted by RealPlayer to increase the color depth anyway.

4. Click OK. With most computers these days, you don't have to restart the computer after making this change. The RealPlayer should run more smoothly now, since your computer's CPU doesn't have to work as hard to paint the video pictures on your screen.

If copying the files to the hard disk didn't help the synch problem, see the section below about copying the CD's files to the hard disk.

TURN OFF SCREEN SAVERS, SCREEN BLANKERS, AND STANDBY OPTIONS

When lessons are playing you're likely to not interact with the keyboard or mouse. Because of this, your computer screen might blank, and in some cases (such as with laptops) the computer might even go into a standby mode. You'll want to prevent these annoyances by turning off your screen saver and by checking the power options settings to ensure they don't kick in while you're viewing the lessons. You make settings for both of these parameters from the Control Panel.

1. Open Control Panel, choose Display, and click on the Screen Saver tab. Choose None for the screen saver.

2. Open Control Panel, choose Power Management, and set System Standby, Turn off Monitor, and Turn off Hard Disks to Never. Then click Save As and save this power setting as "Brainsville Courses." You can return your power settings to their previous state if you like, after you are finished viewing the lessons. Just use the Power Schemes drop-down list and choose one of the factory-supplied settings, such as Home/Office Desk.

COPY THE CD FILES TO THE HARD DISK TO SPEED UP PERFORMANCE

The CD-ROM drive will whir quite a bit when running the lessons from the CD. If your computer or CD-ROM drive is a bit slow, it's possible the author's lips will be out of synch with his or her voice, just like Web-based videos often look. The video might freeze or slow down occasionally, though the audio will typically keep going along just fine. If you don't like the CD constantly whirring, or you are annoyed by out-of-synch video, you may be able to solve either or both problems by copying the CD-ROM's contents to your hard disk and running the lessons from there. To do so:

1. Using My Computer or Explorer, check to see that you have at least 650M free space on your hard disk.

2. Create a new folder on your hard disk (the name doesn't matter) and copy all the contents of the CD-ROM to the new folder (you must preserve the subfolder names and folder organization as it is on the CD-ROM).

3. Once this is done, you can start the program by opening the new folder and double-clicking on the file jmenu.exe. This will automatically start the lessons and run them from the hard disk.

4. (Optional) For convenience, you can create a shortcut to the jmenu.exe file and place it on your desktop. You will then be able to start the program by clicking on the shortcut.

Update your RealPlayer

The RealPlayer software is updated frequently and posted on the Real Networks Web site. You can update your software by clicking Help, then Check for Updates, on the RealPlayer window. We strongly suggest you do this from time to time.

Make Sure Your CD-ROM Drive Is Set for Optimum Performance

CD-ROM drives on IBM PCs can be set to transfer data using the DMA (Direct Memory Access) mode, assuming the drive supports this faster mode. If you are experiencing slow performance and out-of-synch problems, check this setting. These steps are for Windows 98 and Windows ME:

1. Open Control Panel, chose System.

2. Click on the Device Manager tab

3. Click on the plus sign (+) to the left of the CD-ROM drive.

4. Right-click on the CD-ROM drive.

5. Choose Properties.

6. Click the Settings tab.

7. Look to see if the DMA check box is turned on (it will have a checkmark in it).

If selected, this increases the CD-ROM drive access speed. Some drives do not support this option. If the DMA check box remains selected after you restart Windows then this option is supported by the device.

In Windows 2000, the approach is a little different. You access the drive's settings via Device Manager as above, but click on IDE/ATAPI Controllers. Right-click the IDE channel that your CD-ROM drive is on, choose Properties, and make the settings as appropriate. (Choose the device number, 0 or 1, and check the settings. Typically it's set to "DMA if available," which is fine. It's not recommended that you change these settings unless you know what you are doing.)

TROUBLESHOOTING

This section offers solutions to common problems. (Check http://www.real.com for much more information about the RealPlayer, which is the software the Virtual Classroom CDs use to play.)

THE CD WILL NOT RUN

If you have followed the instructions above and the program will not work, you may have a defective drive or a defective CD. Be sure the CD is inserted properly in the drive. (Test the drive with other CDs to see if they run.)

REALPLAYER HANGS AT THE BEGINNING

Sometimes the RealPlayer opens up in a small window and just seems to hang. If you wait a few seconds (perhaps 15 seconds), it will sometimes start up. If not, you may have to restart the computer to get the RealPlayer to start properly again.

THE SCREEN-CAM MOVIE IN A LESSON HANGS

If the author continues to talk, but the accompanying screen-cam seems to be stuck, just click on the lesson index in the lower left region of the RealPlayer window to begin your specific lesson again. If this doesn't help, close the RealPlayer window, and start the Virtual Classroom again.

VOLUME IS TOO LOW OR IS TOTALLY SILENT

1. Check your system volume first. Click on the little speaker icon next to the clock, down in the lower-right-hand corner of the screen. A little slider pops up. Adjust the slider, and make sure the Mute checkbox is not checked.

2. Next, if you have external speakers on your computer, make sure your speakers are turned on, plugged in, wired up properly, and the volume control on the speakers themselves is turned up.

3. Note that the RealPlayer also has a volume control setting. The setting is reached by clicking on the little speaker icon in the upper-right-hand corner of the RealPlayer window.

4. The next place to look if you're still having trouble, is in the Windows volume controls. Double-click on the little speaker by the clock, and it will bring up the Windows Volume Control sliders. Make sure that the slider for "Wave" is not muted and that it's positioned near the top.

GARBLED OR WEIRD VIDEO IMAGE AND/OR REALPLAYER FREEZES

Many popular video cards use WinDraw drivers instead of DirectDraw drivers. The WinDraw driver incorrectly reports the capability of the video hardware to RealPlayer, causing RealPlayer to think that the video hardware can do things that it cannot. When the video is optimized and the video hardware cannot support the optimization, problems will occur. Problems range from poor quality or garbled video to RealPlayer becoming unresponsive and system freezes.

If you experience similar problems, try disabling the Optimized Video setting in RealPlayer.

To disable Optimized Video in RealPlayer:

1. Start RealPlayer.
2. Click the View menu and choose Preferences.
3. Click the Performance tab.
4. Click to clear the "Use optimized video display" check box in the Video card compatibility section.

5. Click OK.

6. Restart your computer.

The following cards are known to have DirectDraw problems. Regardless of the setting in RealPlayer, optimized video is automatically disabled if any of the following card and driver combinations are detected:

ATI Rage II+ PCI, ati_m64
RAGE PRO TURBO AGP 2X (English)
Matrox Millennium G200, AGPMGAXDD32.DLL Matrox
Millennium G200 AGP, mga64.dll
Matrox Millennium G200 AGP, tsirchnl.dll
Matrox Millennium II PowerDesk, MGAXDD32.DLL
Matrox Millennium II PCI, mgapdx64.drv
Diamond Viper V33", vprddle.DLL
NVIDIA GeForce 256 AGP Plus (Dell), NVDD32.DLL
Diamond Viper V330, vprdrvle.drv
Diamond Viper V550, NVDD32.DLL
NVIDIA RIVA TNT2 Ultra, NVDD32.DLL
Hercules Thriller 3D Series (v 0.81.3539), v200032.dll
Diamond Multimedia Systems, Inc.
Stealth II G460 Ver. 1.12\x0d\x0aV, stlthg46.dll
STB Lightspeed 128, with STB Vision 95, stbvisn.drv
Diamond SpeedStar A50 for Windows 98, DMSSA50x.dll

ALL STB cards that use nVidia Riva 182zx:
STB Velocity 128 3D, stbv128.drv
STB Velocity 128 (TV Support), STBV128.DRV
STB Lightspeed 128, without STB Vision 95, stbls128.drv
S3 Inc. Trio64V+, s3_2.drv
Chips And Technologies, Accelerator (new), chipsnd.drv
Cirrus Logic 7548 PCI, cirrusmm.drv

NeoMagic controllers (widely used in Dell laptops):
NeoMagic MagicGraph 128XD, NmgcDD.dll
NeoMagic MagicGraph 128XD, Nmgc.drv

NeoMagic MagicGraph 128 PCI, nmx.drv
NeoMagic MagicMedia 256AV, NmgcDD5.dll
Diamond Stealth II G460, s2g432le.dll
Diamond Stealth II G460, s2g432le.dll

(This last section courtesy Real Networks' Web site, www.real.com)

FOR TECHNICAL SUPPORT

Phone Hudson Software at (800) 217-0059

Visit http://www.real.com (lots of tips there for tweaking RealPlayer performance)

Visit http://www.brainsville.com

Introduction to Dreamweaver

As the name implies, Dreamweaver's objective is to help you turn your Web design dreams into reality. Dreamweaver accomplishes this by combining a powerful set of Web design tools with a clean, uncluttered interface that allows your creativity to flow. The interface is also easy to customize, so you can work in a format that suits your style. But don't be fooled by the simplicity of the workspace; while Dreamweaver is a simple tool to use, it is a true professional Web design and site maintenance application.

At its core, Dreamweaver is a tool for editing HTML (Hypertext Markup Language). Don't let that sentence scare you. If you don't know HTML or only know a little, that's okay. Dreamweaver lets you build your Web pages visually in a manner that is described as "What You See Is What You Get," most often appearing as the acronym WYSIWYG (pronounced wizzy-wig). This is similar to how your word processor works. When you want to make a word appear in boldface, instead of having to know what the word processor is doing behind the scenes, you just highlight the word and click the appropriate button on the toolbar. Dreamweaver tools do the same thing. When you're building a page in the Dreamweaver Document window, you see your content displayed approximately as it would appear through a Web browser such as Internet Explorer or Netscape, with a variety of formatting tools available onscreen that allow you to visually format your content quickly and easily.

After you've been using Dreamweaver awhile, and your knowledge and skills increase, you may want to have greater access to the HTML code. Dreamweaver gives you this freedom, and that's one of the reasons it is such a powerful tool. As you'll learn later in this chapter, the Code And Design view allows you to see the HTML being created as you're typing and formatting your text and inserting images. By using this and other features, your understanding of HTML will speed your growth as a Web designer and Dreamweaver user. With that said, let's get started.

> **SEE ALSO** **For an in-depth discussion of HTML, see Appendix A.**

THE DREAMWEAVER INTERFACE

The key to Dreamweaver's interface is its simplicity. The designers at Macromedia have gone out of their way to create an environment that gives you all the tools you'll need without making your desktop seem like an airplane dashboard. Figure 1-1 shows the basic elements of the Dreamweaver workspace. Each item will be discussed in the following sections.

FIGURE 1-1

This is the Dreamweaver workspace you'll see when you first open the application.

Objects Panel

Document window

Properties Inspector

Launcher

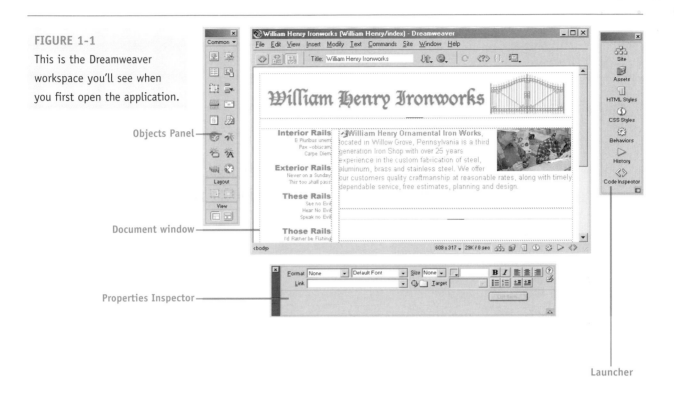

THE DOCUMENT WINDOW

The Document window, shown in Figure 1-2, is the center of the Dreamweaver workspace and is where you enter your page content. It displays your current document and responds to the formatting choices you make using other parts of the interface, such as the Properties Inspector. As mentioned before, the Document window acts as a visual representation of what your page will look like when it's displayed in a Web browser.

Along the top of the Document window sits the Title bar. Here you see the title you gave to your page and, in parentheses, the name of the folder in which your document is stored, followed by the file name of the document. While you're working on a document, there is an asterisk next to the file name to let you know you have unsaved changes.

FIGURE 1-2

The Document window displays the current document you're editing.

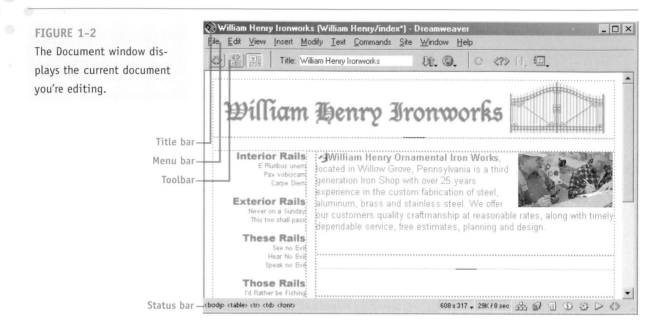

THE STATUS BAR

At the bottom of the Document window are four helpful tools that together make up the Status bar (shown next). These tools are the Tag Selector, the Window Size pop-up menu, the Download Indicator, and the Launch bar. They provide you with statistics about your document and allow quick access to other levels of the editing environment to help speed the production of your Web pages.

THE TAG SELECTOR

`<body> <table> <tr> <td> <font>` When you select an object or block of text in the Document window, the Tag Selector will display all the related HTML tags. If you click on any of these tags, the selection in the Document window will change to reflect what you've clicked. If HTML is new to you, this can be a great way to start learning how tags relate to the content they format, or *mark up*.

For more advanced users the Tag Selector makes it a snap to tweak an individual tag. When you right-click (Windows) or CTRL-click (Macintosh) any of these tags, a context menu appears giving you the ability to edit the tag directly, without having to locate it manually in the source code. Select Edit Tag to call up a small window displaying the source code ready to be modified.

THE WINDOW SIZE POP-UP MENU

One of the primary concerns when designing a Web page is making sure it displays well across multiple screen resolutions. Someone might have the resolution on their monitor set to 640 pixels × 480 pixels, while someone else's is set to 800 × 600, 1024 × 768, or even higher depending on how big their monitor is and how much screen real estate they want. That's why Dreamweaver has the Window Size pop-up menu. You'll always want to know how your design will look to different users, but you won't want to have to reset your monitor each time to check it out. The Window Size pop-up menu lets you resize the Document window to preset pixel dimensions that reflect standard monitor settings. What's more, the presets take into account the exact size of a fully expanded browser window *after* you subtract the width of the various toolbars. To access the Window Size pop-up menu (shown in Figure 1-3), click on the small drop-down arrow located to the right of the screen dimension values displayed on the Status bar.

You can add to and edit the dimension choices listed in the Window Size pop-up by choosing Edit Sizes from the bottom of the pop-up menu. Doing so will call up the Preferences dialog box, shown in Figure 1-4.

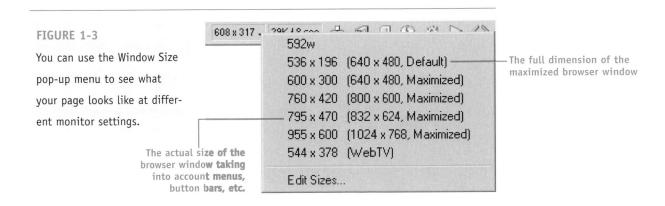

FIGURE 1-3

You can use the Window Size pop-up menu to see what your page looks like at different monitor settings.

The actual size of the browser window taking into account menus, button bars, etc.

The full dimension of the maximized browser window

FIGURE 1-4
Use the Preferences dialog
box to customize most parts
of Dreamweaver.

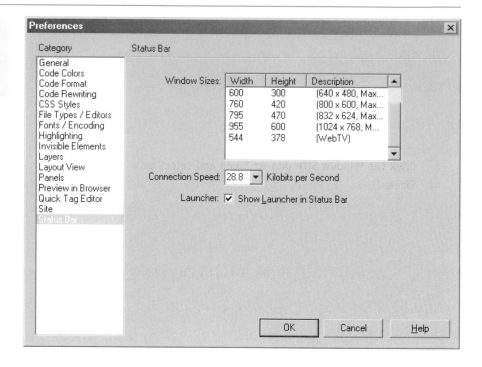

To Modify THE WINDOW SIZE POP-UP MENU:

1 Click any of the width or height values in the Window Sizes list and type in a
new value.

2 Click in the Description field to enter a description about the size you've made.

3 Click OK to save your changes and close the dialog box.

To add entirely new sizes to the pop-up menu, just click in the blank spaces below
the last values in the Width, Height, or Description column.

THE DOWNLOAD INDICATOR

The window to the right of the Window Size pop-up menu, the Download
Indicator, indicates the file size of the HTML document being created and the
estimated time it will take a user to load that page and any associated images or
media files it has using a given connection speed.

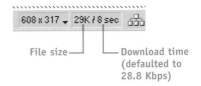

File size — └─ Download time
(defaulted to
28.8 Kbps)

If you want to change the connection speed used to calculate the estimated download time, you can do so in the same dialog box used to change the values for the Window Size pop-up menu.

To Change THE WINDOW SIZE POP-UP MENU VALUES:

1 Click the Window Size pop-up menu and select Edit Sizes.

2 Below the Window Sizes entry fields is the Connection Speed drop-down menu. Use the menu to select the connection speed you want to gauge your pages download speed against.

THE LAUNCH BAR

The Launch bar is a small version of the Launcher, which you saw in Figure 1-1. The Launcher is covered later in this chapter. If you find that having the floating Launcher palette takes up more of your desktop than you're willing to give, this mini version is a convenient alternative. If you find the reverse is true for you, you can always hide the Launch bar.

> **TIP** It has been estimated that the average user won't wait longer than about eight seconds for a page to load. Keeping this in mind when you build your pages and checking your page statistics in the Download Indicator window will help you make Web sites that don't get overlooked due to user frustration. There are a variety of techniques other than simple brevity of content that can help you keep your files small, particularly where graphic images are concerned. See Chapter 4 to learn more.

To Hide THE LAUNCH BAR:

1 Select Edit | Preferences from the Menu bar.

2 Select Status Bar at the bottom of the Category field.

3 Locate the checkbox titled Show Launcher In Status Bar in the center of the dialog box and click to deselect it.

THE TOOLBAR

The Toolbar (shown in Figure 1-5) takes a number of the more frequently used commands from across the various menus and puts them up front for easy access. The first three buttons of the Toolbar allow you to quickly switch between the different view styles of the Document window. You have a choice of the Design view (the default view you see when you first open Dreamweaver); the Code view, which displays only the HTML; and a third view that melds Design and Code view into one, splitting the screen in half. Other commands accessible on the toolbar, particularly the Option menus at the far right, change depending on which view you're in and the status of your document while you're editing it.

> TIP The Design, Code, and Design And Code views are also available through the View menu. If you've selected the Design And Code view, you can move the Design window above the Code window by selecting Design View On Top from the View menu. You can toggle the Toolbar on or off by choosing View | Toolbar.

The Toolbar button sure to get the most use is the Preview/Debug In Browser button represented by the small globe icon. This button allows you to launch a temporary version of the document you are working on in the browser of your choice. You want to continually test a page in various browsers during your development cycle to be sure it displays as you intend it to, and Dreamweaver allows you to define a total of 20 different browsers to perform the task.

To Define A BROWSER:

Press the Preview/Debug in Browser button, and select Edit Browser List from the menu. This opens the Preferences dialog box (Figure 1-6) displaying the Preview in Browser category.

FIGURE 1-5

Use the Toolbar to access the HTML code, add document titles, and preview your page in a Web browser.

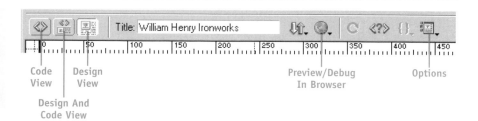

Title: William Henry Ironworks

Code View   Design View   Preview/Debug In Browser   Options

Design And Code View

FIGURE 1-6

The Preferences dialog box

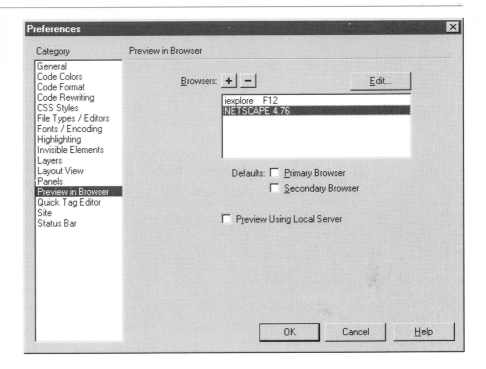

2 Click the Add(+) button next to Browsers and enter the browser name in the Add Browser dialog box. Use the Browse button to find the application on your hard drive (Figure 1-7).

3 Indicate if the browser will be the primary or secondary browser using the Defaults checkboxes. This gives you the ability to access the browser via keyboard shortcuts; F12 for primary and CTRL+F12 for secondary.

4 Click OK to finish.

FIGURE 1-7

The Add Browser dialog box

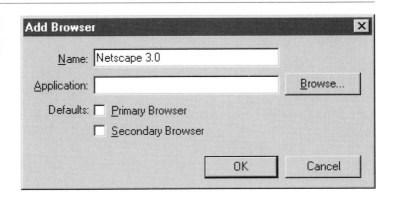

CUSTOMIZING THE DOCUMENT WINDOW

Dreamweaver's strength is its modifiable interface. The Document window has a number of tools you can employ to make it conform to your personal design needs, including rulers, a customizable grid, and a variety of visual aids that provide references for page elements that aren't visible in the browser window, like comments and scripting elements.

RULERS

Many layout and graphics tools take advantage of rulers to gauge spacing and dimension. Dreamweaver provides the same functionality for the Web designer. Rulers run across the top and down the left side of the Document window. The default unit of measure for the ruler is pixels, as shown in Figure 1-8. To view the Document window rulers, select View | Rulers | Show from the Menu bar.

> **TIP** You can never have too many browsers to preview your work in, hence the ability to define 20 different kinds of them. Try to have a number of versions of each major browser, for example Internet Explorer 5.*x* and 4.0, and Netscape 4.*x* and 3.0.

> **TIP** You can change the unit of measure for the ruler from pixels to inches or centimeters by selecting View | Rulers, and selecting the unit of your choice from the menu provided.

FIGURE 1-8

Document window rulers use pixels as a default unit of measure, but they can be easily customized to use inches or centimeters.

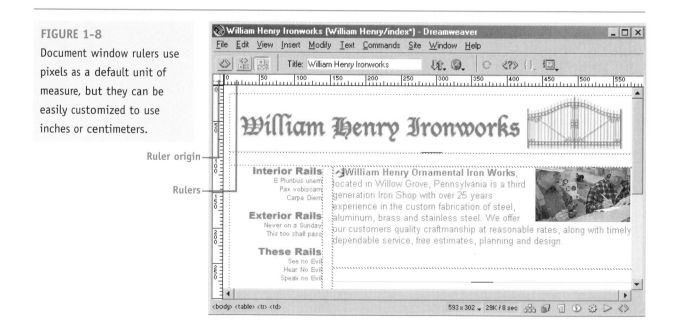

TO MODIFY RULER ORIGIN

You may need to move the ruler origin, or zero point, to make measuring easier. To do this, simply move your cursor to the upper-left corner where the ruler begins and click and drag the crosshairs to your desired location. The crosshairs will appear in the Document window and follow the cursor wherever you move them until you release the mouse. You can relocate the zero point as many times as you want while working on a document without affecting your page content in any way. To reset the ruler origin, right-click in the upper-left corner of the ruler and select Reset Origin.

THE GRID

Having a grid can be helpful when placing and resizing page elements visually. To bring up Dreamweaver's grid, as shown in Figure 1-9, select View | Grid from the Menu bar. Grid spacing can be as big or as small as you want. To change the grid spacing, select View | Grid | Edit Grid to call up the Grid Settings dialog box (see Figure 1-10). From here you can also set the grid's color and choose whether it appears as a solid or dotted line.

FIGURE 1-9

Use the grid to get an even higher level of control as you create and position items such as tables and layers.

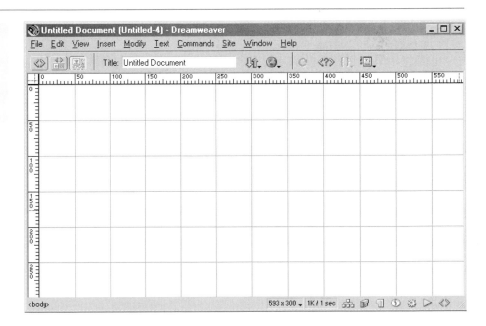

FIGURE 1-10
The Grid Settings dialog box

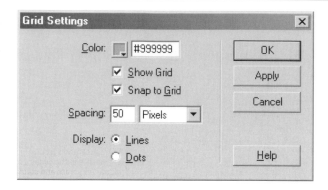

THE SNAP TO GRID OPTION

You can make certain Dreamweaver elements, such as layers or tables you construct with the Objects Panel's layout view, stick to grid points by toggling the Snap To Grid option on. This function works whether the grid is visible or not. To turn Snap To Grid on, select View | Grid | Snap To Grid from the Menu bar. To learn more about tables and layers, and how to use them, see Chapters 6 and 9.

WORKING WITH VISUAL AIDS

Using visual aids in Dreamweaver allows you to see things in your Document window that wouldn't ordinarily be visible when the page is displayed in a Web browser. For example, you might decide to use a large table to lay out your page, putting your site navigation links in one column, and your text and images in another and then set the border width of this table to zero so it's invisible to visitors.

Invisible tables are the cornerstones to many sites on the Web, but when you're working on such a page in Dreamweaver you will probably want to see just where that table is and where its cells begin and end. This is where visual aids come in. By turning various visual aids on or off, you can see ghost outlines of invisible table borders, view and edit the hotspots on image maps, or see icons that represent invisible elements, such as *comments*—lines in the HTML code that explain to people viewing the code what the designer was trying to do (see Figure 1-11).

FIGURE 1-11

Examples of visual aids in the Document window

Comment icon

Image map hotspots

Table borders

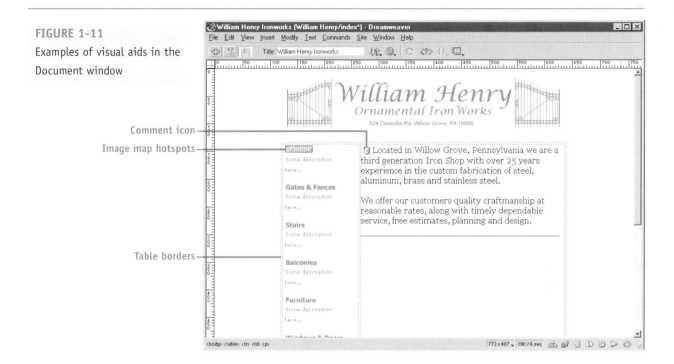

VIEWING VISUAL AIDS

You can toggle the various visual aids on and off via the View menu. Select View | Visual Aids from the Menu bar and select the aids you want.

CHANGING INVISIBLE ELEMENT PREFERENCES

Certain visual aids are referred to as invisible elements. These are parts of the HTML code that don't correspond to anything visual on the screen. This would include things like line breaks or JavaScript code (a programming language used to add dynamic content to Web pages), which exist and impact the page but aren't actually visual elements like text or images. Being able to see these elements is especially important to new users who may be editing a Web page created by someone else.

> **TIP** You can also get quick access to the Visual Aids menu via the Options menu at the far right of the toolbar if you are using Design view or Code and Design view.

> **TIP** To turn different invisible elements on or off, select Edit | Preferences from the Menu bar to open the Preferences dialog box. From there, select Invisible Elements from the Category list on the left and check the elements you want to display as icons in the Document window while working in Design view.

THE OBJECTS PANEL

The Objects Panel is the key to quick and easy page creation in Dreamweaver. Each button on the Objects Panel (shown here) allows you to insert different kinds of content into your document. If the Objects Panel is not displayed when you open Dreamweaver, select Window | Objects from the Menu bar or press CTRL-F2 (Windows) or ⌘-F2 (Macintosh). If you want to resize the Objects Panel, simply grab a corner and drag it to the desired dimensions.

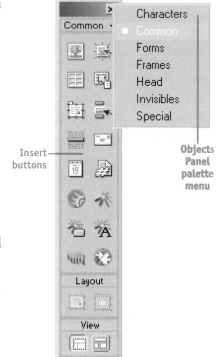

Insert buttons

Objects Panel palette menu

There are seven button palettes in the Objects Panel:

▶ **Characters** Uncommon characters, such as copyright and trademark symbols, that aren't represented on the keyboard (see Chapter 3).

▶ **Common** Primary elements such as images, tables, and multimedia objects. You can learn more about these topics in Chapters 4, 6, and 12, respectively.

▶ **Forms** Form objects such as text fields, checkboxes, and radio buttons (see Chapter 7).

▶ **Frames** Frameset layouts (see Chapter 8).

▶ **Head** Head section objects such as meta tags.

▶ **Invisibles** Things like scripts and comment tags; see "Working with Visual Aids" earlier in this chapter.

▶ **Special** Things like ActiveX controls and Java applets (see Chapter 14).

To switch among these seven palettes, simply click on the small drop arrow at the top of the Objects Panel and select the palette you want from the menu that appears. When you want to insert a particular element, simply click the appropriate button. In most cases, this will bring up a dialog box asking for more information about the object you want to insert, such as the location of the image on your hard drive, or how many rows and columns you want in a table. Once you've responded to the dialog box, your content will

> **TIP** Anything you can insert from the Objects Panel can also be added using the Insert menu on the Menu bar.

appear in the Document window and be available for any further formatting you want to apply.

THE PROPERTIES INSPECTOR

The Properties Inspector, shown in Figure 1-12, is the tool you'll use to modify any content you've placed in the Document window. It will change its appearance in response to whatever item you have selected, always providing the right tool for the job. If the Properties Inspector is not visible when you open Dreamweaver, select Window | Properties from the Menu bar, or press CTRL-F3 (Windows) or ⌘-F3 (Macintosh). You can make the Properties Inspector expand or contract by clicking the arrow in its lower-right corner.

THE LAUNCHER

The Launcher is used to open, or "launch," the seven other windows, palettes, and inspectors that make up the rest of the Dreamweaver interface. Click a button to open the corresponding window. Clicking it a second time will close it. If one of the windows is already open and is sitting behind another part of the interface, clicking its Launcher button brings the window to the front. As mentioned previously, the Launcher and the Document window Launch bar mimic each other, providing you with choices about how you want to set up your workspace.

FIGURE 1-12

The Properties Inspector changes its tools to accommodate whatever you select in the Document window.

Text Properties Inspector

Table Properties Inspector

Image Properties Inspector

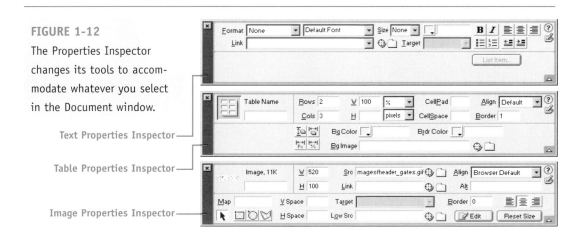

The seven buttons on the Launcher are

▶ **Site** This button opens the Site window, which is used for maintaining your site's file structure and publishing your sites to the Internet (see Chapter 2).

▶ **Assets** The Assets panel acts like a holding pen for all the elements you've associated with a particular site, such as images, colors, or links to other Web sites. This keeps track of all the items you've added to a site so you can quickly apply them again throughout your site's documents (see Chapter 11).

▶ **HTML Styles** HTML styles are Dreamweaver's way of letting you save frequently used text formatting so you can access them quickly and reuse them again and again (see Chapter 4).

▶ **CSS Styles** Similar to HTML styles, CSS styles are a more advanced method of applying formatting to text. This palette helps you to create and manage cascading style sheets (see Chapter 4).

▶ **Behaviors** The Behaviors Inspector allows you to apply predefined JavaScript actions to elements of your Web site.

▶ **History** The History palette lets you see all the actions you've taken while you've had Dreamweaver open. It allows you to undo or repeat things you've done, or copy and paste actions to other spots in the history. Actions you've taken can also be saved and reused.

▶ **Code Inspector** This inspector is similar to the Document window Code view, except it opens an entirely separate window to display the HTML code in. You may edit code in this window just as easily as in Code view and see it reflected in the Document window after the Code Inspector window is closed.

CUSTOMIZING THE LAUNCHER

You can customize the Launcher to hold a total of 13 buttons. For example, you might decide to insert a button to launch the Objects Panel, or you may want to remove the button that launches the Code Inspector.

To Add or Remove BUTTONS ON THE LAUNCHER:

TIP You can make the Launcher display either horizontally or vertically by clicking the orientation icon in the lower-right corner of the panel.

1 Select Edit | Preferences from the Menu bar, and click on Panels in the category list. The buttons currently displayed in the Launcher and Launch bar are listed to the right, in the box titled Show In Launcher.

2 To add a new button to the Launcher and Launch bar, click the Plus (+) button and select an item from the context menu that appears.

3 To delete a button from the Launcher and Launch bar, select the button name you want to remove from the Show In Launcher text box and click the Minus (-) button.

4 You can change the order in which buttons appear on the Launcher or Launch bar by selecting the button name and clicking either the up or down arrow to the right of the Plus (+) and Minus (-) buttons.

 ON THE VIRTUAL CLASSROOM CD-ROM Follow along with the instructor in Lesson 1, "The Dreamweaver Interface," as he guides you through a tour of the interface.

First Things First: Creating the Site

A Web site is more than a jumble of individual pages all linked together. In order to create a site that really works, you need to think about what you want the site to do and why you want to build it. Believe it or not, if you have a good idea as to why you're doing something, it's easier to determine what it is you have to do to make it happen.

There are a number of steps every good Web designer takes in order to ensure success. Granted, no two people are alike and working styles will vary, but the steps outlined below are a good starting point.

PLANNING YOUR WEB SITE

Before beginning to physically build a site, you'll want to ask yourself:

▶ What do you hope to accomplish with this Web site?

▶ Who do you expect the site's audience to be?

▶ How do you want your visitors to experience the site and get around in it?

▶ What hardware and software will these expected visitors use to view your site?

▶ How will the actual files of the site be laid out on the computer that hosts the site?

▶ What will the visual look of the site be?

Regardless of the size of your Web site or your level of skill, you'll want to have these questions answered so you can lay out your plan of attack before you start building individual pages. By having a strategy in place you'll save a lot of time and anguish over the life of any project. By keeping a written list of your answers you can help yourself stay focused throughout the development process. As luck would have it, Dreamweaver provides an excellent set of site management and development tools that when harnessed together help you address many of these questions, turning your written thoughts and plans into reality.

WHAT IS MY OBJECTIVE?

Whether you build a site for yourself or for someone else you'll want to ask what the site is being created for. This is not an exercise in existentialism, but in understanding the site's purpose. Is it going to be used as an information resource? To entertain? To sell a product? Determining the site's primary objective will help in answering the questions that follow. You'll make very different design choices in creating a site for a client that sells handmade button-down shirts than you would for a site that promotes an alternative rock band.

WHO'S MY AUDIENCE?

As I said before, answering the previous question will certainly help in answering the rest. If you know what your site is meant to do, it isn't too hard to figure out who your audience will be or who you'd like it to be. A site geared toward skate-boarding will have a pretty specific audience, whereas a site that sells sportswear will probably aim at a wider group of prospective visitors.

When considering your audience, there's a lot more to think about than just who you would like to visit your site. You also want to know *how* they're coming to your site. Are they mostly Windows users? Mac users? Maybe Linux users? Are they likely to have very big monitors, say 19" or larger, or 17" or smaller? Are they more likely to be using Internet Explorer or Netscape Navigator? Or are you specifically targeting users of the Operabrowser? What is their average modem speed? Are you looking to attract big business users who are probably connecting from work on super-fast T1 lines or home users who might have modem speeds as slow as 28.8 kps? All these issues will play a role in your design decisions. Ultimately, you'll want a site that looks good to a user of any of these hardware and software configurations. But knowing these things about your audience can help you make choices about design and what, if any, sacrifices you may have to make in order to deliver a site that looks good to a variety of users.

THINKING ABOUT BROWSERS

The two most popular browsers on the market are Internet Explorer and Netscape Navigator, each of which has had more than five different releases, or versions, and for each version new functionality has been introduced. What this means is that something Internet Explorer 5.5 can do may not be possible in Internet Explorer 2.0. And you can be assured that something Netscape can do may not be possible with Internet Explorer! These inconsistencies are the bane of the Web designer. This illustration shows the same two pages displayed in Netscape Navigator (right) and Internet Explorer (left). Observe the differences in dimensions of the form fields. Optimally, you want a site that behaves much the same way across both browsers

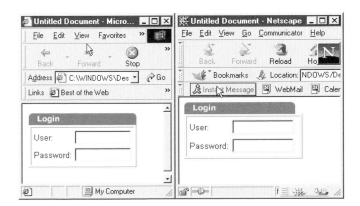

and across multiple versions of the same browser. As neither browser supports each new Internet technology exactly the same way, you will end up making compromises.

If you design a site that relies heavily upon new technologies, such as Dynamic HTML, certain kinds of animation, multimedia content, or complex interactivity, chances are you'll have trouble making your site work the way you want it to across a number of browsers. You will want to find a middle ground that provides greater accessibility to your target audience. Fortunately, Dreamweaver has taken this into account and provides many tools to let you create cross-browser compatible content. For more information on creating dynamic content, see Chapter 9.

STRUCTURING YOUR SITE

This chapter addresses this particular topic in detail. You want to avoid creating a number of separate Web page documents and then having to perform the arduous task of tying them all together before you upload them to your Web server. Instead, it is better to have a strategy prepared in advance. The best approach, particularly when using Dreamweaver as your primary development tool, is to create one main folder in which all your associated files will be stored, as shown in Figure 2-1. Dreamweaver calls this the Local Root folder. Inside this folder, you

FIGURE 2-1

A good preliminary step in organizing your Web site is to create a folder for your site's content before you even open Dreamweaver.

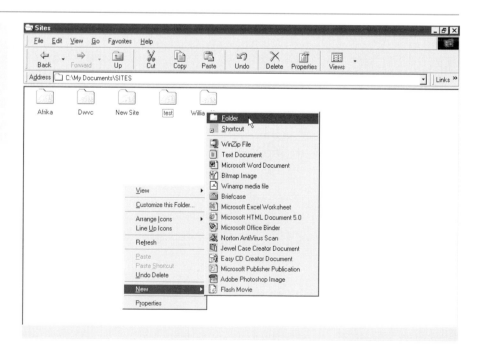

might have a folder that contains all your images, another that holds all the HTML documents, and others for things like sound files and multimedia clips. In this way, you create a fully functioning version of your Web site right on your own PC that you can then copy whole onto your Web server.

DESIGN LAYOUT

Okay, you've figured out what this site is meant to do, you've got a handle on who your potential audience is, what hardware and browser considerations you'll have to take into account, and you've set aside a little real estate on your PC for a local site folder and possibly even made a few folders inside it to better organize your content. Now comes the fun part, designing what the site will look like.

This is usually referred to as creating *mock-up* pages, and these mock-ups don't have to be anything more elaborate than a drawing of what you want the various pages of your site to look like before you go and start building things. You can lay something out on paper or you could use your favorite graphics software to create your mock-up. The choice is yours. The object is to have a visual representation of your layout so you have something to refer to as you move through the development process. The main reason for doing this is to help you in maintaining a level of consistency throughout your site. Users will tend to get confused if the look and feel of your site changes radically page by page, or if key elements such as navigation links are in different locations in every page.

NAVIGATING YOUR SITE

You also want to think about how your visitors will experience your site—how they will flow through it and go from one area to the next. First, visitors should always have a clear indication of where they are in your site and how to get back to the main, or home, page. Second, you want to make the process of finding information within your site as painless as possible. Lastly, it's a good idea to provide some way for visitors to contact you if they can't find what they're looking for or if they just want to give feedback about the site.

Later in the chapter, as we discuss working with Dreamweaver's Site window, you'll see how easy it can be to lay out the basic navigational structure for a site by simply dragging links visually from one page to another. This will insert simple text links in the various documents of your site, which you can then format any way you choose.

GATHERING YOUR ASSETS

A good strategy when developing any Web site, and the method best supported by Dreamweaver, is to gather into one location all the things you're going to need to build your site. For example, after you've mocked-up your basic design and know where you're going to need artwork or graphic buttons, it's a good idea to create or find these elements and have them ready to go before you start building your pages.

Dreamweaver refers to the individual components of your site—images, sound files, multimedia clips, and so on—as *assets* and provides an Assets panel (shown here) from which you can easily drag a particular item right into the Document window to add to your page.

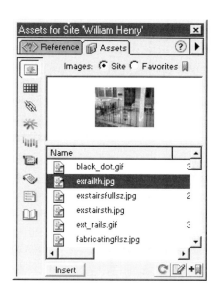

Two other great Dreamweaver features you can access from the Assets panel are templates and library items. Say you had a number of pages that relied on the same basic layout with minor modifications. You could use Dreamweaver to create a template that contained that basic layout and then apply it across any number of pages you wanted. What's more, you'd only need to edit the template to apply a change to all the pages that used it, instead of changing each individual page.

Library items work very much the same way. Instead of being a whole page layout, library items are little pieces of a page that you can save and insert where you need them. For example, imagine you've created a table that holds a group of navigation buttons that you plan to use in a number of places. You could select that table and its contents and save them as a library item that you can use again and again, inserting it just as easily as you would any Dreamweaver element. For more information on assets, templates, and library items, see Chapter 13.

CREATING THE LOCAL SITE

As mentioned above, before you even open Dreamweaver you should create a folder somewhere on your hard drive that will act as the main storage area for the files in your site. Dreamweaver refers to this as creating a Local Root folder. We use the term *root* when talking about file structure to define the base location from which everything else will originate. If you build everything from within your root folder and then copy its contents into the root folder of your Web server, all your links and file references will remain consistent. This means if a link works on the local copy of your site, it will work just fine when you upload it to your server, too.

To Set Up A NEW SITE:

1 Create a new folder somewhere on your hard drive, giving it a name of your choice.

2 From the Document window Menu bar, select Site | New Site to open the Site Definition dialog box, shown in Figure 2-2. The Local Info category is already selected.

3 Enter a name for your site in the Site Name field at the top of the dialog box.

4 Click the folder icon to the right of the Local Root Folder field to activate the Choose Local Folder dialog box.

FIGURE 2-2

The Site Definition dialog box is used to configure all of Dreamweaver's site management tools.

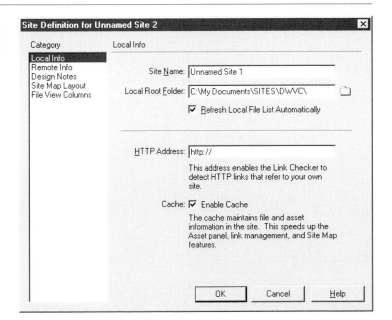

5 Browse your hard drive and select the folder you created in step 1.

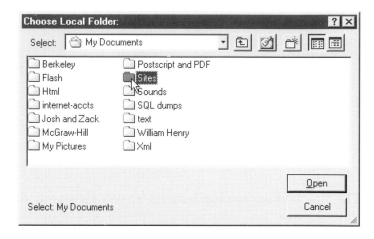

6 Select the Refresh Local File List Automatically checkbox if you want the local file list to automatically refresh every time files are copied into your folder. If you choose not to select it, files will copy faster, but you will have to manually refresh the Site window using the Refresh button to see the presence of new files.

7 If you know what the Internet address for your site will be, enter it in the HTTP Address field. Dreamweaver uses this to check links within your site that use absolute URLs. (For more information about URLs, links, and pathnames, see Chapter 5.)

8 Select the Enable Cache checkbox to create a local cache to maintain file and asset information about your site. This will speed Dreamweaver in checking links, maintaining a Site Map, and working with the Assets panel. If you do not select this option, the Assets panel will not be accessible.

9 Click the OK button to display the Site window.

Congratulations! You have successfully defined your first Dreamweaver site. When it's time to upload your site to your Web server, you will return to this dialog box to add more information about your site. For information about uploading your site to the Internet, see Chapter 14.

THE SITE WINDOW

Like most of the Dreamweaver windows and panels, the Site window pulls double duty, allowing you to perform a number of different tasks all from one spot. Just like Windows Explorer or Macintosh Finder, you can scout the file structure of your site using the Site window to move and delete items, or make new files and folders. You can also use its Site Map feature to view your site like an organization chart and create links between files by clicking the point-to-file icon and dragging to the file of your choice.

You can employ three different methods to open the Site window from the Document window (shown in Figure 2-3):

▶ Select Site | Site Files or Site Map.

▶ Select Window | Site Files or Site Map.

▶ Press F5 to display site files or CTRL-F5 to display the Site Map.

WORKING WITH SITE WINDOW VIEWS

The Site window toolbar buttons let you view your site files in a number of ways.

▶ **Site Files view** The Site Files view will show you the file structure of the local site you created in the left panel and the remote site in the right. This is the default view for the Site window whenever you access it. We'll cover setting up the remote site in Chapter 14, so for right now don't worry that there's nothing visible there yet.

▶ **Site Map view** The Site Map is a visual representation of your site. Looking like an organization chart, it shows you how the individual pages of your site relate to each other, what links they each contain, and how they are linked together. When you click the Site Map View button, a drop-down menu gives

FIGURE 2-3

The Site window is a file management tool, as well as a visual layout of your site's structure.

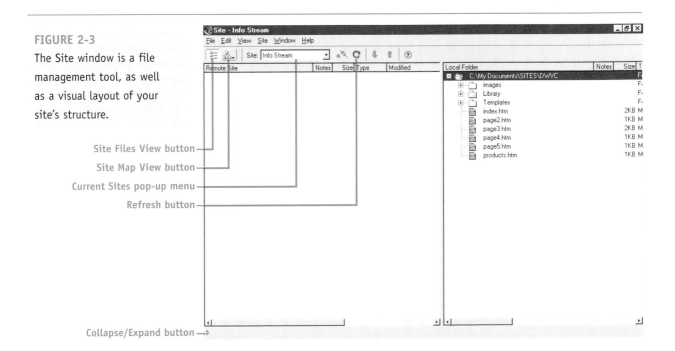

you a choice of viewing either the Site Map alone, or the Site Map in one panel and the local site files in the other (see Figure 2-4).

▶ **Current Sites pop-up menu** The Current Sites pop-up menu (shown here) lists all the sites you define in Dreamweaver. To switch to a different site, simply select its name from the menu.

If you want to create a new site or change the information in one of your preexisting sites, select Define Sites at the bottom of the menu list. This launches the Define Sites dialog box, shown to the right. From here, you duplicate, remove, create, or edit a site.

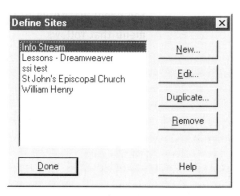

▶ **Refresh** The Refresh button updates the list of files in the Site window. If you create a site and choose not to select the Refresh Local File List Automatically checkbox, you can use the Refresh button to manually update the Site window view.

▶ **Collapse/Expand** Located in the lower-left corner of the Site window, this button allows you to toggle the Site window between viewing one or both panels.

FIGURE 2-4

Use the Site Map to view the structure of your site, print the map for documentation, and create links.

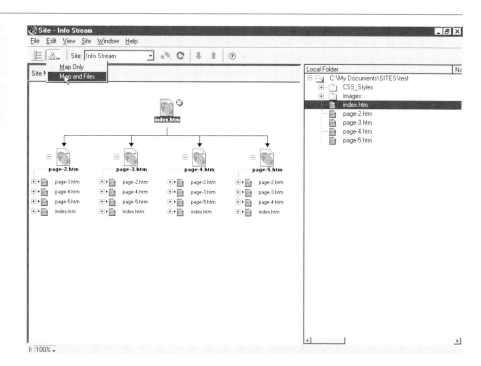

CHANGING THE SITE WINDOW LAYOUT

To Change THE PANES IN WHICH SITE FILES AND SITE MAPS APPEAR:

1 Select Edit | Preferences from either the Site window or Document window and choose the Site category (see Figure 2-5).

2 From the Always Show menu, select either Local Files or Remote Files and then choose the panel you'd like to see them displayed in from the Right Side/Left Side pop-up menu that follows.

3 Click the OK button to implement your changes.

If you set the location of either the local or remote site, you do not need to set the other location as well. The thing to remember is that whichever site file list you choose to modify, that list becomes the one displayed by default when you open the Site window. For example, if I were to modify the Preferences dialog box so that the top sentence read, "Always Show: Remote Files on the Right/Left," whenever I opened the Site window, the Remote Site files for my selected site would always be the ones displayed, even if I collapsed the window down to one pane.

FIGURE 2-5

The Preferences dialog box sets preferences for the entire application.

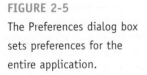

Preferences

| Category | Site |

General
Code Colors
Code Format
Code Rewriting
CSS Styles
File Types / Editors
Fonts / Encoding
Highlighting
Invisible Elements
Layers
Layout View
Panels
Preview in Browser
Quick Tag Editor
Site
Status Bar

Always Show: [Local Files ▾] on the [Right ▾]

Dependent Files: ☑ Prompt on Get/Check Out
☑ Prompt on Put/Check In

FTP Connection: ☑ Disconnect After [30] Minutes Idle

FTP Time Out: [60] Seconds

Firewall Host: [ ]

Firewall Port: [21]

Put Options: ☐ Save Files Before Putting

[Define Sites...]

[OK] [Cancel] [Help]

MODIFYING THE SITE WINDOW VIEWING AREA

To Increase Or Decrease THE VIEWING AREA OF THE INDIVIDUAL PANELS:

1 Position your mouse over the middle border separating the right and left window panes. When positioned correctly, it becomes a two-headed arrow, as seen in Figure 2-6.

2 Click and drag your mouse in either direction to change the panel sizes.

3 Use the bottom scrollbars to view contents of the panes beyond the displayed area.

WORKING IN THE LOCAL SITE FILES PANEL

The Site window is the file viewer for your Web site, just like Windows Explorer and the Macintosh Finder are file viewers for your operating system. You can use the Site window in much the same way to create or delete new files and folders and open documents. You can also select site files and then preview them in your Web browser.

FIGURE 2-6

Increase or decrease the viewing area of an individual panel to adjust your workspace.

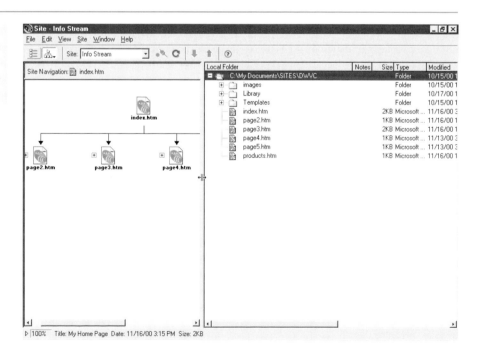

CREATING NEW FILES AND FOLDERS

In the Site window, select where you want the new file to be placed. You can then insert a new file using any of the following methods:

▶ From the Site window menu bar, select File | New File.

▶ With your mouse, right-click in the Local Site Files panel and select New File from the context menu.

▶ Press CTRL-SHIFT-N.

You can follow the same procedures to create new folders, selecting New Folder instead of New File, or pressing CTRL-ALT-SHIFT-N.

OPENING FILES

Once a new file or folder is created, you can open it or any existing file in the Site window using any one of three methods:

▶ Double-click the file's icon.

▶ Select the file and choose File | Open Selection from the Site window menu bar.

▶ Right-click on the file icon and select Open from the context menu.

Use one of these methods to select multiple documents:

▶ To select a range of documents, hold down shift, click the first document icon in the series, and then click the last document icon.

▶ To select files that aren't immediately next to one another, hold down ctrl while clicking each of the document icons in turn, as shown here.

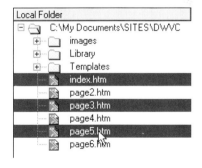

RENAMING FILES

To rename a file in the Site window, use one of the following methods:

▶ Click the file you want to rename and select File | Rename from the Site window menu bar.

▶ With your mouse, click once on the file to select it, and then click once on the file name. A box will surround the highlighted file name, shown next,

and a blinking cursor will appear at the end of the file extension awaiting input from you.

▶ Select the file you want to rename and press F2.

If there are any links to the file you have renamed, the Update
Links dialog box will appear asking you if you want to update
the links affected. Select Update to change the links to this document throughout the site and close the dialog box.

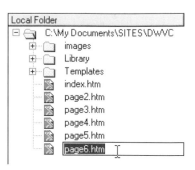

THE SITE MAP

The Site Map is a graphic depiction of your site's
link structure, displaying your linked documents
as a series of connected icons (see Figure 2-7).
By using the Site Map tools, you can lay out
your site's entire navigational structure before

SEE ALSO **To learn more about linking and navigation, see Chapter 5.**

FIGURE 2-7

The Site Map displays files as
icons—each link within a
document is listed in the
order it appears in the file.

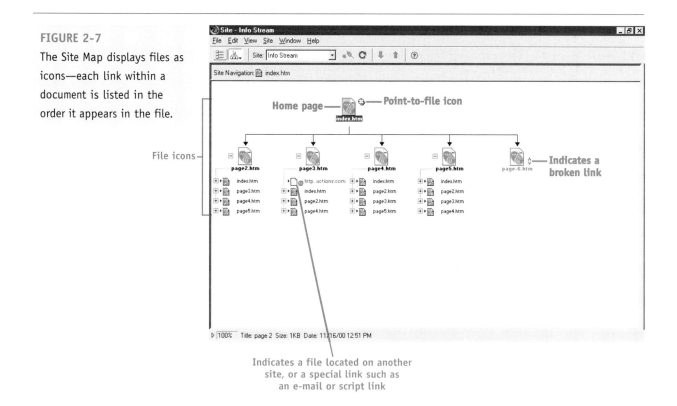

Indicates a file located on another
site, or a special link such as
an e-mail or script link

you've even created the first page. The Site Map can also be saved as a graphic to be used as a reference or demonstration aid during the development process. You can only apply the Site Map view to your local site files.

SETTING THE HOME PAGE

In order to access the Site Map, a home page must first be selected. If the site you've defined doesn't have any files inside it yet, follow the steps described earlier in the "Creating New Files and Folders" section of this chapter, and add a file to your site.

To Assign A HOME PAGE TO YOUR SITE:

1 From the Site window menu bar, select Sites | Define Sites, or select Define Sites from the Current Sites pop-up menu. This will launch the Define Sites dialog box, shown here.

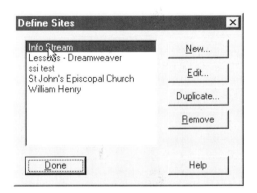

2 From the Define Sites dialog box, select the site you want to edit, and click the Edit button to launch the Site Definition dialog box.

3 Select Site Map Layout in the Category box on the left (see Figure 2-8).

4 Enter the path of the file you want to set as your site's home page in the Home Page text box, or click the folder icon on the right to open the Choose Home Page dialog box (see Figure 2-9).

5 Select the file you want as your home page and click Open to return to the Site Definition dialog box.

TIP A quick way to assign a home page to your site is to right-click a file in the Site Files view and select Set As Home Page from the context menu. By default, Dreamweaver will assign any file named index.html or index.htm as the home page.

6 Click OK in the Site Definition dialog box to close it and return to the Site window.

7 Click the Site Map View button to view the Site Map.

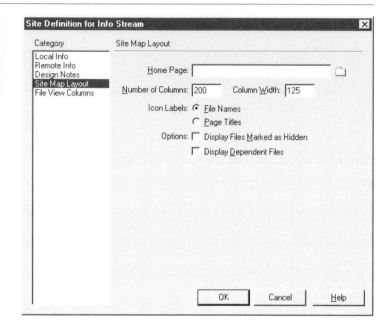

FIGURE 2-8

Define the home page in the Site Map Layout category of the Site Definition dialog box.

FIGURE 2-9

Select the file you want to use as your home page in the Choose Home Page dialog box.

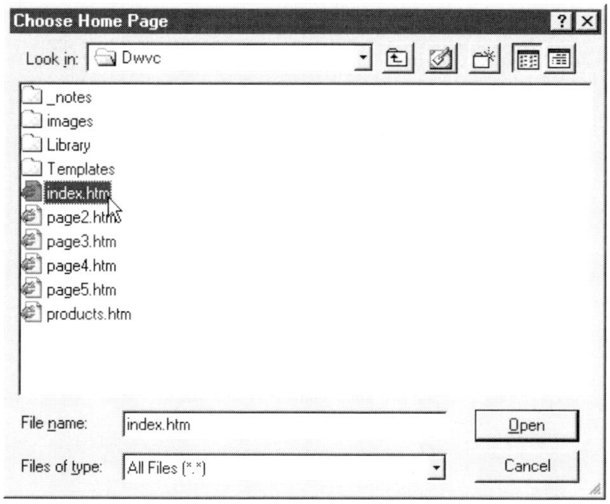

If at any time you want to change the home page of your site, perform any of the following actions:

▶ Select the file you want to set as your new home page and choose Site | Set As Home Page from the Site window menu bar.

▶ Select the file you want to set as your new home page and right-click, then choose Set As Home Page from the context menu.

▶ From the Site window menu bar, choose Site | New Home Page to create a new home page.

By default, the Site Map will display the home page as the top page in the hierarchy, but you can make any page display as the root page by right-clicking its file icon and selecting View As Root from the context menu, or by selecting a file icon and choosing View | View As Root from the Site window menu bar.

WORKING IN THE SITE MAP PANEL

All the methods for opening and renaming files in the Site Files panel are also applicable to the Site Map. The primary purpose of the Site Map is to establish links between your site documents and view the relationships these links create.

LINKING TO EXISTING FILES

Dreamweaver uses a really great visual metaphor for establishing links within the Site Map. This handy-dandy little tool is called the point-to-file icon and appears as a little crosshair scope in places where links can be created. If you click on a file in the Site Map, these crosshairs will appear to the right of the file icon (see Figure 2-10).

To Establish A LINK BETWEEN TWO DOCUMENTS:

1 Select a file in the Site Map to bring up the point-to-file icon.

2 Click and drag the icon onto the file you want to link to. This can be a file in either the Site Map or Site File panel, or any Dreamweaver document you have open in the Document Window. An arrow will follow your cursor while you drag the icon.

FIGURE 2-10

Create links by clicking and dragging the point-to-file icon onto files in either the Site Map or Site Files panel.

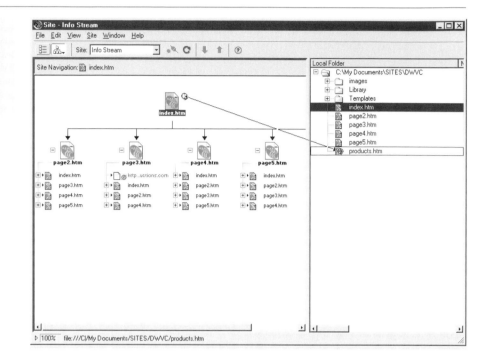

CREATING A NEW LINKED FILE

To Create A NEW BLANK FILE WITHIN YOUR SITE MAP AND HAVE IT LINKED TO A PARTICULAR FILE:

1 Select a file by clicking its icon in the Site Map.

2 From the Site window menu bar, choose Site | Link To New File. This launches the Link To New File dialog box.

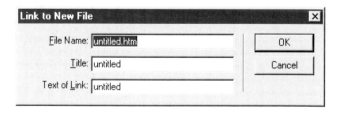

3 Enter a file name in the File Name field.

4 In the Title field, enter a page title.

5 Enter the text for your link in the Text Of Link field.

6 Click OK.

If you're simply building the link structure of your site at this point, don't be overly concerned with the text you enter in the Text Of Link field of the Link To New File dialog box. You will be editing this page in much greater detail later on, and may be assigning this link to an image file, or you may change your mind radically about what you initially wrote in this dialog box. It's okay—nothing you enter here is written in stone.

MODIFYING HTML PAGE TITLES

An HTML document's file name and its page title are two separate things. The file name of an HTML document is the name you give to it when you save it and what you are reading when you look at it in Windows Explorer or Macintosh Finder. The page title, on the other hand, is a value associated with a specific set of HTML tags called, as luck would have it, the Title tags. They look like this in your HTML source code: `<title>` *Your page title would go here* `</title>`. Anything placed between those tags will appear in the title bar at the top of a browser window (as shown in Figure 2-11).

FIGURE 2-11

The contents of the `<title>` tag appear in the title bar of the Web browser.

Browser window title bar

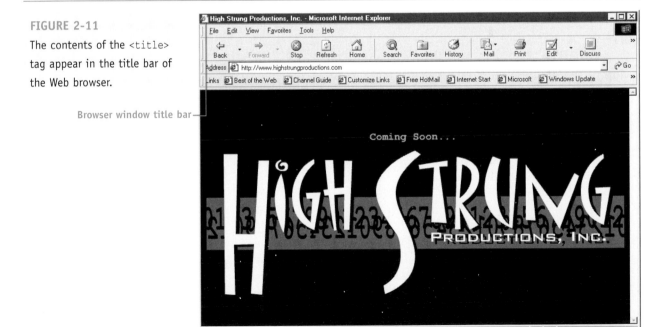

In Dreamweaver's Site Map window, you can choose to view files by either their file name or their page title. To view their page titles, select View | Show Page Titles from the Site window menu bar.

To Modify THE TITLE OF A PAGE:

1 Be sure the Show Page Titles option is selected.

2 Select View | Show Page Titles from the Site window menu bar.

3 With your mouse, click once on the file to select it, and then click once on the title name. A box will surround the highlighted title name and a blinking cursor will appear at the end of the title name, awaiting input from you.

> **TIP** You can title a document any time you like by simply typing a name into the Title field of the Document window menu bar.

UPDATING THE SITE MAP

To Update THE SITE MAP AFTER YOU'VE MADE CHANGES:

1 Click anywhere in the Site Map window to deselect any files.

2 Select View | Refresh Local from the Site window menu bar.

SAVING THE SITE MAP

As mentioned before, you can save your Site Map as a graphic to be used as a reference or demonstration aid.

To Save THE SITE MAP AS A .BMP OR .PNG FILE:

1 Select File | Save Site Map As from the Site window menu bar. This launches the Save Site Map dialog box (see Figure 2-12).

2 Select .bmp or .png from the pop-up menu in the Save As Type field.

3 Choose the location to which you want to save your file, and enter a file name.

4 Click Save.

FIGURE 2-12

You can use a printed site map to work out changes to your site navigation on paper before committing any real changes to the site.

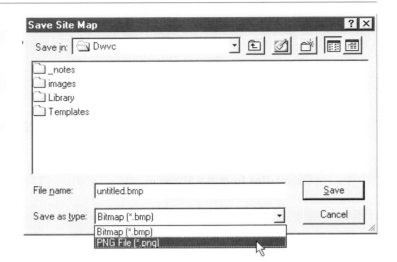

 ON THE VIRTUAL CLASSROOM CD-ROM In Lesson 2, "Using the Site Window," the instructor will demonstrate how to create a local site and how to use the Site window to create a preliminary site structure.

3

In a Word: Working with Text

Using a graphic Web design tool like Dreamweaver increases your work speed and allows you to observe your final product while you're working on it, instead of having to manually hand-code your documents and then test them in a browser. If you use a word processor, you've been working in an environment similar to that of Dreamweaver's without even knowing it. You don't write your letters in the code your printer understands; rather, you let your word processor do the translating for you. You make choices about formatting and implement those choices by clicking buttons and making menu selections from the word processor toolbars. Dreamweaver formats text in much the same way—it provides menu commands and toolbar buttons with which to format your document, converting your formatting instructions into code a Web browser understands.

As this chapter demonstrates, you don't have quite the same level of control over text in Web pages that you do when working with a word processor. HTML is limited in this respect; however, as HTML and Web browsers advance, this gap continues to narrow. There is still a long way to go and new advancements are often not compatible with older browsers. Dreamweaver appreciates the compromises that are made in creating Web pages and offers multiple solutions to help the designer deliver cross-browser, backward-compatible Web content.

INSERTING TEXT

This may be the shortest set of instructions in this book:

▶ To insert text in a document, open Dreamweaver and start typing (see Figure 3-1).

FIGURE 3-1

When you open Dreamweaver, an empty Document window appears with the cursor blinking in the upper-left corner. Simply begin typing.

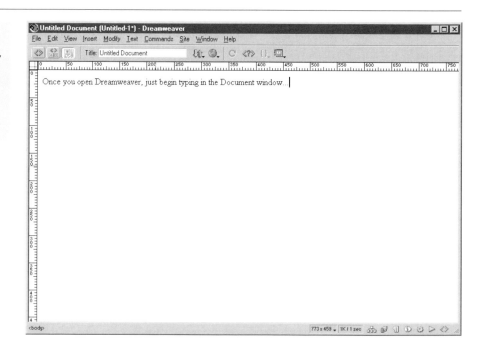

It's that easy. When entering text in this fashion, Dreamweaver behaves in much the same way your word processor does. Text is entered and appears in a default font, size, and style. You're free to select text in other applications as well, and copy and paste those selections into Dreamweaver documents via your computer's clipboard.

Once you have text in your Document window, Dreamweaver allows you to manipulate it the same way you would in a word processor or text editor. You can select text in Dreamweaver several different ways:

▶ Click at the point you want to begin your selection and drag the cursor across the text you want to select.

▶ To select an entire line of text, move the cursor to the left margin. When the cursor becomes a right-pointing arrow, click once. To select multiple lines, click and drag down the page, keeping the cursor in the left margin as you drag.

▶ Click at the point you want to begin your selection, then press and hold down SHIFT and click at the end of your selection.

▶ To select text using the keyboard, press and hold down SHIFT and move the cursor using your keyboard's arrow keys, moving left and right to select characters, up and down to select entire lines.

You can cut, copy, and paste selected text with the following combinations of menu commands or keyboard shortcuts:

▶ To cut text, select Edit | Cut or press CTRL-X.

▶ To copy text, select Edit | Copy or press CTRL-C.

▶ To paste text, select Edit | Paste or press CTRL-V.

> TIP Because you're using a graphic layout tool and an operating system that sports a graphical user interface or GUI (pronounced "gooey"), you might want to take advantage of the one thing the GUI is most noted for: drag-and-drop. You can select text using the mouse or keyboard and then click and drag the highlighted text to a new location.

When you copy and paste text from another application, it won't maintain any of its original formatting information—the text will automatically adhere to Dreamweaver's formatting for the location where the text is pasted.

As with almost everything in Dreamweaver, you can also access the cut, copy, and paste commands via Dreamweaver's context menus by right-clicking selected text and choosing Cut, Copy, or Paste (see Figure 3-2).

FIGURE 3-2

Access a context menu by right-clicking the highlighted text you've selected.

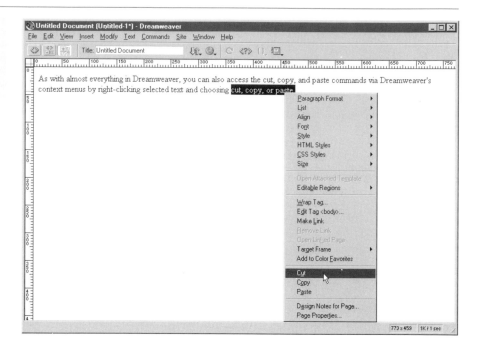

FORMATTING TEXT

When you have a chunk of text selected in the Document window, the Properties Inspector puts on its appropriate text-formatting face (shown next). Each drop-down list and button on the Properties Inspector affects a specific aspect of your text's appearance. There are drop-down menus to select paragraph or heading styles, fonts, and font sizes. There is a color well for text color, and there are buttons for applying physical styles (bold and italic), aligning text, formatting lists, and indenting your text.

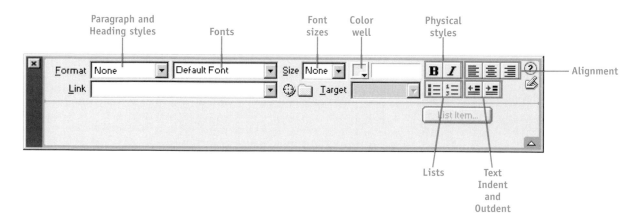

PARAGRAPHS AND HEADINGS

A browser doesn't know anything about English, so what it recognizes as paragraphs has little to do with what is taught in school about their proper structure or contents. To you and me, a paragraph is a group of sentences that pertain to a specific topic, has rules about how that topic is elaborated upon, and also has a format style—usually indenting the first sentence. To HTML and Dreamweaver, a paragraph is purely a formatting technique that affects how a block of text is displayed by a browser, without any concern for grammar.

In the simplest terms, a block of text formatted as a paragraph will force a blank line above and below it. The HTML tags that are used to define a paragraph are `<p>` and `</p>`, and any text that falls between them is recognized as a paragraph by the browser and displayed accordingly. To learn more about HTML, read Appendix A.

When you start typing in a blank document, no tag is associated with your text (see Figure 3-3) until you press ENTER for the first time. After you do that, these opening and closing paragraph tags are placed around your first paragraph, and a second set of paragraph tags are inserted for the next block of text, as shown in

FIGURE 3-3

At first, text entered into the Document window has no tags.

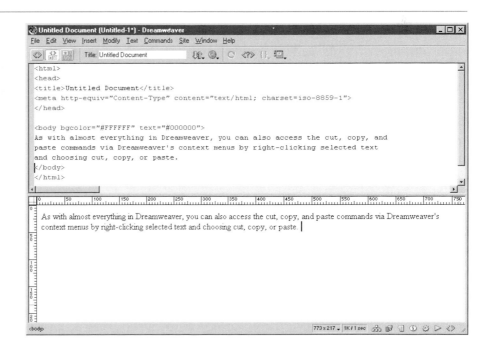

FIGURE 3-4

Once you press ENTER, Dreamweaver places paragraph tags in the appropriate places.

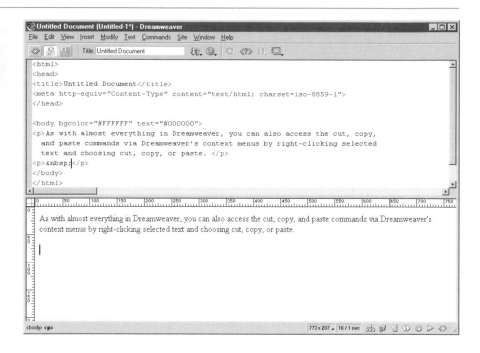

Figure 3-4. You could continue entering text like this just as if you were typing in your word processor.

If you've brought text in from another application, its formatting won't carry over into Dreamweaver. To format blocks of text into paragraphs, choose one of these methods:

▶ Select the text you want to format and choose Paragraph from the first Format drop-down menu in the Properties Inspector:

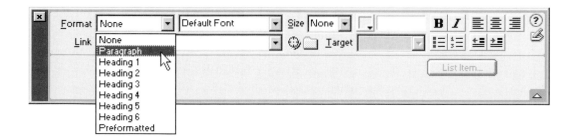

▶ Select a block of text and choose Text | Paragraph Formatting | Paragraph from the submenu.

Headings are just like headlines in the newspaper—they're used to introduce topics and separate one section of a document from another. There are six heading styles, which range, largest to smallest, from Heading 1 to Heading 6 (`<h1></h1>` to `<h6></h6>`). Just like in paragraphs, blank lines are forced above and below headings.

> **TIP** Obviously, there are times when you don't want an empty line between two text elements. Not a problem. Instead of pressing ENTER, use SHIFT-ENTER, and a line break will be inserted without applying the paragraph formatting associated with pressing ENTER.

To convert text to a heading, select a string of text and use one of these methods:

▶ Choose a Heading style from the first Format drop-down menu in the Properties Inspector.

▶ Choose Text | Paragraph Formatting and then select a Heading style from the submenu.

INDENTING TEXT

To indent text, simply select the text you want to indent and click the Text Indent button in the Properties Inspector (shown next), or select Text | Indent from the menu. To remove indentation, use the Text Outdent button, or select Text Outdent from the menu bar.

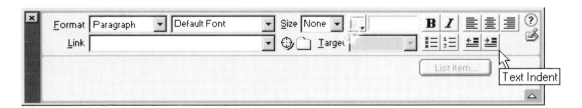

WORKING WITH FONTS

As we discussed in the previous chapter, how visitors experience your site has as much to do with their hardware and software as it does with the design you create. Unfortunately, Web design isn't like creating something for the print world, where you have complete control over how the audience will experience the finished product. As a Web designer, you have to make choices that ensure each visitor's experience is as true to what you intended as possible. This principle extends to your choice of fonts, because the fonts visitors actually have on their computers dictate which fonts they can view on a given Web site.

When assigning font values to text the standard practice is to use *font families*, a series of fonts with similar characteristics, in an attempt to guarantee the highest level of fidelity to your original design. Doing this defines a short list of three or four possible fonts for visitors' browsers to pick from, so if they don't have your first choice, they might have one of the others that is very similar (see Figure 3-5). At the very worst (and most unlikely), they won't have *any* of the fonts you chose and then the text will be rendered in the default font set in their browser preferences.

SELECTING A FONT FACE

You can assign a font to selected text, or you can choose a font before you begin typing. To select a font, use one of two methods:

▶ From the Properties Inspector, select a font family from the second Format drop-down list:

▶ From the menu, select Text | Font, and then choose the font family of your choice from the submenu.

FONT SIZE

When setting font sizes, the size you select will always be relative to the base font size your visitors have set in their browser. It has been my experience that few users even know they can change the base font setting, and I have found it safe to assume that the average user's browser is still set at the default size it started with when it was first installed on the computer. This default size is usually 12 points.

FIGURE 3-5

Notice how the HTML tags in the lower part of the figure list the font names separated by commas (font face="Arial, Helvetica, sans-serif").

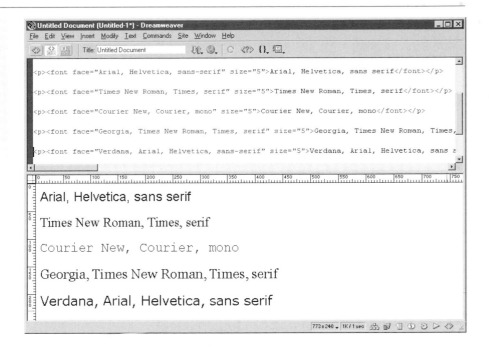

Unlike word processors, HTML uses numbered scales instead of point sizes. There are two scales you can use to format your font sizes: absolute and relative.

▶ **Absolute** The absolute scale is numbered 1 through 7, with a size of 3 being equal to the base font size of a user's browser. Consequently, this scale isn't exactly "absolute," because any font size you set with this scale will still be relative to whatever base font size the visitor's browser is set to.

▶ **Relative** The relative scale is numbered −7 through +7, and will set the font size in relation to the base font of the visitor's browser. So, if the visitor's browser is set to a base font of 12 points, setting the font size to +1 would make the text appear one size larger, or 13 points.

The relative scale will not permit you to display a font size that would fall outside of the absolute scale of 1 through 7. Remember that the base font size is always considered to be a size 3 in the absolute scale. Using a relative scale value, you couldn't apply a +7 and get a size of 10. It would only be able to display the equivalent of an absolute value of 7, in other words +4. Anything higher would be ignored, defaulting to the +4 value.

To format the font size of selected text, use either of these methods:

▶ Select a value from the Size drop-down list in the Properties Inspector:

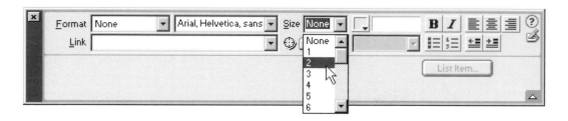

▶ From the menu, select Text | Size to apply an absolute scale value, or select Text | Change Size to apply a relative scale value.

MODIFYING TEXT COLOR

There are two basic ways of formatting the color of your text. You can apply color to specific pieces of text throughout your document, or you can set the default color for all your text document-wide. In most cases, you will probably wind up doing both. To format the color of individual pieces of text, click the color well of the Properties Inspector (see Figure 3-6).

To choose a color, use either of these techniques:

▶ Select a color from the palette using the eyedropper.

▶ Hold down the left mouse button and drag the eyedropper to any location on your screen, inside or outside of Dreamweaver, then release the mouse button over the color you want to select (see Figure 3-7).

You have access to multiple color palettes in Dreamweaver: Color Cubes, Continuous Tone, Windows OS, Mac OS, and Grayscale. To select a different palette, click the

FIGURE 3-6
Click the Properties Inspector color well to display a color palette.

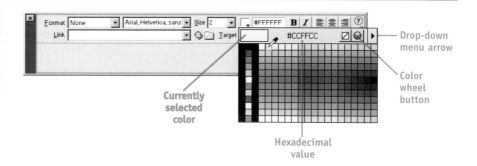

Currently selected color

Drop-down menu arrow

Color wheel button

Hexadecimal value

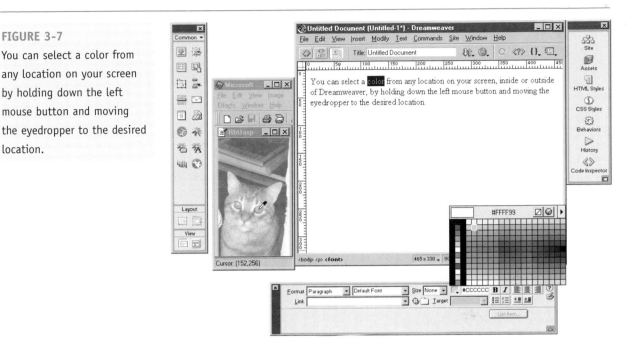

FIGURE 3-7

You can select a color from any location on your screen by holding down the left mouse button and moving the eyedropper to the desired location.

drop-down menu arrow located in the upper-right corner of the palette display (see Figure 3-8).

The Color Cubes and Continuous Tone palettes contain Web-safe colors; the other palettes do not. By selecting Snap To Web Safe from the drop-down menu, any color selected from the other palettes that is not Web-safe will be switched to the closest Web-safe color. Consequently, the resulting color may not be the exact color you originally selected. To learn more about Web-safe colors, see the sidebar of the same name.

> **TIP** To remove the current color of selected text without replacing it with another value, click the red and white Strikethrough button located next to the hexadecimal display on the color palette.

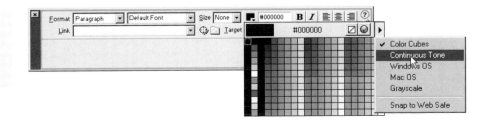

FIGURE 3-8

Click the drop-down menu arrow to display the list of available color palettes.

To Assign A DEFAULT COLOR VALUE FOR ALL THE TEXT IN A DOCUMENT:

1 From the menu, select Modify | Page Properties, which opens the Page Properties dialog box (shown in Figure 3-9).

2 In the Page Properties dialog box, locate the Text color well and click to access the color palette.

3 Select a color from the palette with the eyedropper, or hold down the left mouse button and use the eyedropper to select a color from anywhere on your screen.

WEB-SAFE COLORS *Web-safe* refers to the 216 colors that will be displayed consistently in both Netscape Navigator and Internet Explorer (both Mac and PC) when that computer is running in 256-color mode. Any color that falls outside the 216 range would be pushed to its closest Web-safe neighbor on any machine not capable of displaying more than 256 colors. The reason designers try to conform to the Web-safe palette, even though many newer computers are capable of displaying millions of colors, is to make sure their sites look the same across the greatest number of computers.

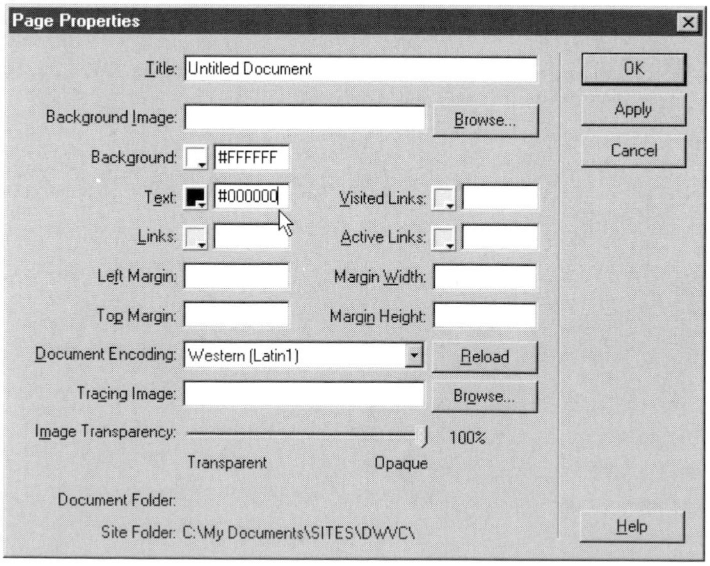

FIGURE 3-9

The Page Properties dialog box allows you to set colors for text, links, and documents backgrounds.

By setting the default text color in this way, you have told the visitor's Web browser to make all text appear in this color, unless otherwise specified. You could choose not to specify any default text color, in which case the text would be displayed in the default color set in the user's browser preferences.

ALIGNING TEXT

As you've probably noticed, when text is placed in the Document window it will align naturally to the left margin. Of course, you can align selected text to the right or center as well, using either of these methods:

▶ Using the Properties Inspector, click the Left, Right, or Center alignment button:

▶ From the menu, select Text | Alignment and then Left, Right, or Center from the submenu.

CREATING LISTS

There are three kinds of lists you can create in Dreamweaver: bulleted, numbered, and definition. In "Web-speak," a numbered list is referred to as an *ordered list*, while a bulleted list is an *unordered list*.

You can apply list formatting to text already in your document, or you can set your list formatting preferences and then type your list items directly into the Document window. You can also combine lists inside other lists, in a manner referred to as nesting. Creating an outline with lettered and numbered levels is a good example of how to use nested lists.

BULLETED AND NUMBERED LISTS

To Create A NEW LIST:

1   In the Document window, place your cursor where you want your list to begin.

2   In the Properties Inspector, click the Unordered or Ordered List button, or from the menu, select Text | List and then from the submenu choose the kind of list you want to insert.

3   Enter your list items, pressing ENTER to begin each new list item.

4   Press ENTER twice to end your list.

Lists can be made from text already in your document, but each item in the list must already be formatted as a paragraph.

To Turn PREEXISTING TEXT INTO A LIST:

1   Make sure each item is formatted as a paragraph (see "Paragraphs and Headings" earlier in this chapter).

2   Select the series of text entries you want to format as a list.

3   In the Properties Inspector, click the Unordered or Ordered List button, or from the menu, select Text | List and then choose either Unordered or Ordered List from the submenu.

MODIFYING LIST PROPERTIES

Dreamweaver lets you modify a list's overall appearance, as well as individual list items. For example, you may want your numbered list to use letters or Roman numerals rather than the default values of 1, 2, 3. In a bulleted list, you have the option of using either circular or square bullets.

To Access the List Properties dialog box:

1 Select a list item or series of items in the Document window.

2 In the Properties Inspector, click the List Item button. If this button is not visible in the Properties Inspector, click the expander arrow in the lower-right corner of the Properties Inspector to view its entire set of tools and options. Or select Text | List | List Properties from the menu:

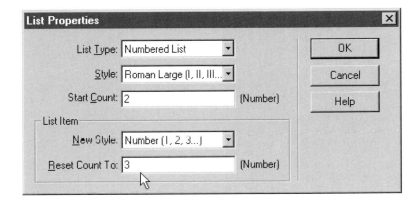

Depending upon the type of list selected in the List Type field, the following fields are available to you:

▶ **List Type** Indicates whether the list is bulleted, numbered, menu, or directory

▶ **Style** Formats the overall style of bullets or numbers used in a list

▶ **Start Count** Sets the value for the first item in a numbered list

▶ **New Style** Allows you to select a different style for an item in the list

▶ **Reset Count To** Allows you to modify the number or letter sequence of items in the list

NOTE The Menu and Directory list options in the List Properties dialog box reveal the shifting state of the HTML standard. In the early days of HTML, it had been planned to have two other list types: one that had no bullets (Menu) and another that supported multiple columns (Directory). Unfortunately, browser manufacturers never got around to supporting these list types and treat both as bulleted lists. Dreamweaver takes an optimistic stance and keeps these options available to designers.

DEFINITION LISTS

A definition list formats your text in the same fashion as terms in a glossary. The term to be defined is left-justified, with its associated definition sitting indented directly beneath it, as shown in Figure 3-10.

Of course, you aren't limited to using this list format simply to define terms.

To Create A DEFINITION LIST:

1 In the Document window, place your cursor where you want your list to begin.

2 From the menu, select Text | List | Definition List.

3 Begin entering your first list term. Pressing ENTER will advance you to the next line, indented beneath the first, where you can enter the definition for the term above. Pressing ENTER again will return you to the left margin to begin the next term in your list.

4 Press ENTER twice to finish the list.

FIGURE 3-10

Definition lists are sometimes used for indenting instead of simply for terms and their meanings.

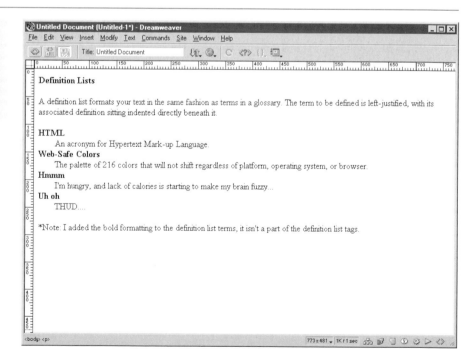

NESTING LISTS

Nesting is a term that gets used a lot in Web design, but it's just a fancy (and considerably shorter) way of saying you're putting something inside something else. Therefore, a nested list is simply a list inside a list. The simplest example of this would be a formal outline, as shown in Figure 3-11.

To Create A NESTED LIST:

1 Select the list items you want to nest.

2 Click the Text Indent button in the Property Inspector, or select Text | Indent from the menu. The list item indents but is in fact a new list inheriting the properties of the list it is nested in.

3 With the cursor on the indented list item, click the List Item button in the Properties Inspector, or select Text | List | Properties from the menu.

4 Select a new list type or style for the indented list item.

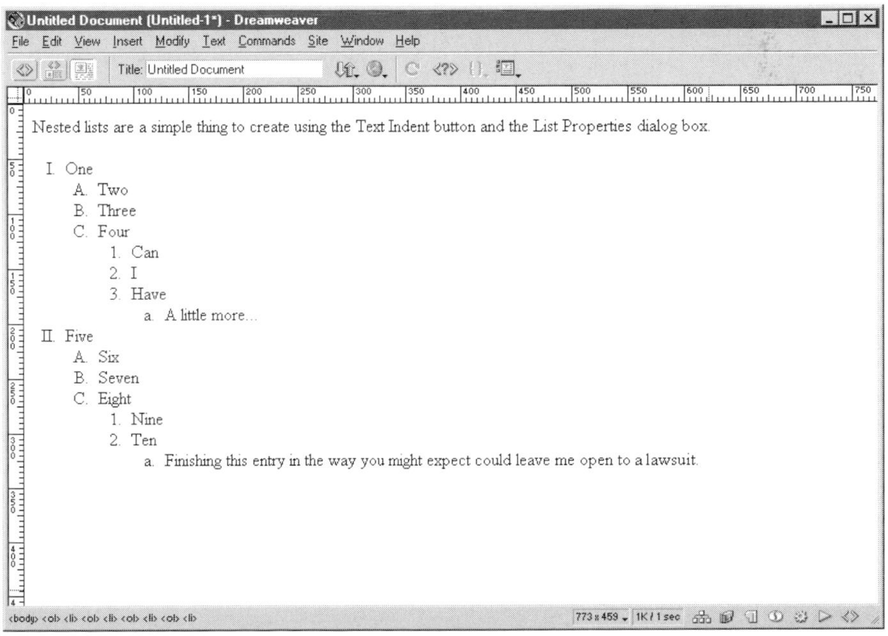

FIGURE 3-11

Use the Text Indent button and the List Properties dialog box to easily create nested lists.

WORKING WITH TEXT STYLES

Any time you bold, italicize, or underline text you're applying a style. HTML recognizes two kinds of styles: physical and logical. In many cases, physical and logical styles are identical in how they are actually displayed by a browser. This is a similar situation to the Menu and Directory list types; the original plans of HTML's creators are waiting to come to fruition.

PHYSICAL STYLES

Physical styles (see Figure 3-12) are the ones you're already familiar with from using word processing software. They literally tell the browser how text should look when displayed.

▶ **Bold** Click the Bold button in the Properties Inspector (shown next), or choose Text | Style | Bold from the menu.

FIGURE 3-12

Physical styles directly supported by Dreamweaver

▶ **Italic** Click the Italic button in the Properties Inspector, or choose Text | Style | Italic from the menu.

Some styles can only be applied from the menu, using the Text | Styles submenu:

▶ **Underline** Choose Text | Style | Underline.

▶ **Strike through** Choose Text | Style | Strikethrough.

▶ **Teletype or typewriter style** Choose Text | Style | Teletype.

LOGICAL STYLES

Logical styles are descriptive terms applied to text that leave their interpretation and display up to the browser (see Figure 3-13). To date, these styles are rendered identically to physical styles. However, with the increasing sophistication of text-to-speech technology, browsers may begin to read logical styles and alter the way words that have these styles are pronounced.

Each of these styles can be applied from the menu by selecting Text | Style and then the style name.

FIGURE 3-13

Supported logical styles and their corresponding physical styles

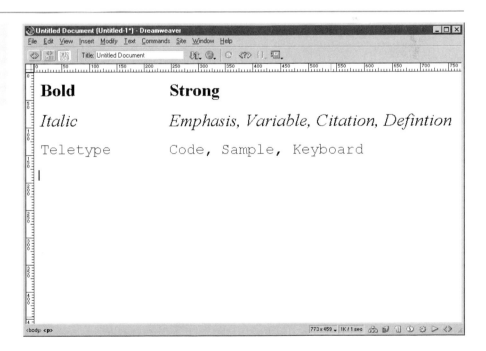

SPECIAL CHARACTERS IN HTML

Special characters are symbols and certain types of punctuation that don't have their own corresponding key on your keyboard, such as the copyright and trademark symbols or the em dash. These symbols are also referred to as *character entities*. When they are viewed inside the code of an HTML document, they appear as names or numbers bracketed between an ampersand and a semicolon. For example, the character entity used to display the currency symbol for the Japanese yen is written `&#165;` or `&yen;`.

To Place SPECIAL CHARACTERS IN A DOCUMENT:

1 Place your cursor where you want to insert the character.

2 Select Characters from the Objects Panel palette menu (shown to the right), and press the button for the character you want to insert. Alternatively, you can choose Insert | Special Characters and then select the character of your choice from the submenu.

3 If the character you want to insert is not one of the Objects Panel presets, click the Insert Other Character button located in the lower-right corner of the Characters palette, or choose Insert | Special Characters | Other from the menu. This opens the Insert Other Character dialog box:

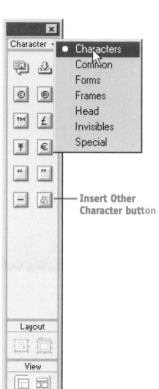

Insert Other Character button

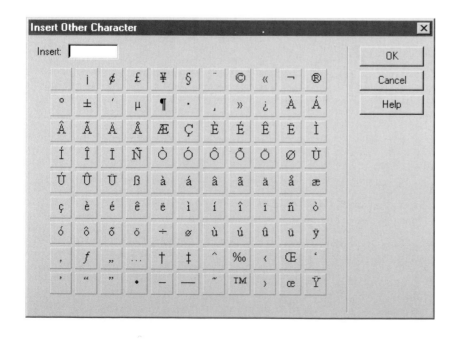

From here, you can select from the full range of preset Dreamweaver character entities, or if you know the code for an entity not represented in the dialog box, you can enter it directly in the Insert field in the upper-left corner.

The number of character entities is enormous, including foreign alphabets and mathematical symbols. For more information about character entities go to http://www.w3.org/TR/WD-html40-970708/sgml/entities.html and view the World Wide Web Consortium's documentation on the subject.

Spell Checking

Dreamweaver, like any good tool that works with text, also provides spell checking. To launch the spell checker, simply select Text | Check Spelling from the menu. The Check Spelling dialog box will appear:

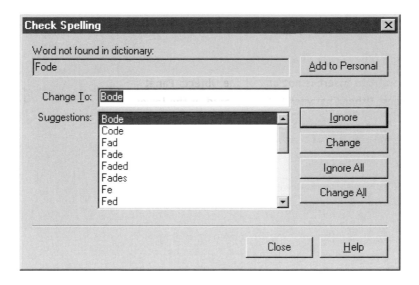

Dreamweaver will begin at the top of the document, working down, and display misspelled words in the Word Not Found In Dictionary field. The Check Spelling dialog box will offer suggested spellings in the Suggestions field, allowing you to click the one you want to be placed in the Change To field. You have the choice of ignoring the instance of the misspelled word, ignoring all instances of the misspelled word, or changing one or all instances. You can also add the word in question to Dreamweaver's personal dictionary so it will not be singled out as a misspelling in the future.

USING FIND AND REPLACE

You can use Find And Replace to locate specific text in your current document, specific files, a whole folder, or your entire local site. If you're HTML savvy, you can use Find And Replace to search through the source code of your documents as well.

To Locate TEXT IN DOCUMENTS:

1 Choose Edit | Find And Replace from the menu. This opens the Find And Replace dialog box.

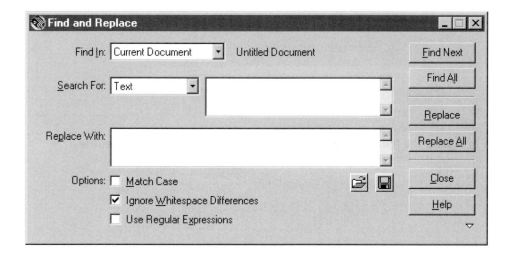

2 In the Find In field, select the file or files to search. Your options:

- Current Document **Searches your present document**
- Selected Files in Site **Searches only files and folders currently selected in the Site window; you must choose Find And Replace from the Site window menu bar for this option to work.**
- Entire Local Site **Searches every file in the site you have open**
- Folder **Searches a specific directory folder; click the folder icon to browse and select the folder you want to search.**

3 In the Search For field, select the kind of search to perform and enter the text you want to find in the text box to the right. Your options for search type include:

- Text   Searches the Document window for the specific text you enter

- Text (Advanced)   Allows you to search for text based on the HTML tags applied to it. For example, if you needed to find all the occurrences of "Enter" that are formatted in bold (<b></b>), you would select Inside Tag from the drop-down list and then select "b" from the list to the right. To find all the occurrences of "Enter" not associated with a particular tag, select Outside Tag from the drop-down list.

- Source Code   Searches through the HTML code of your document for the specific piece of text you've entered

- Specific Tag   Searches for exact HTML tags and their associated attributes and values. See Appendix A for more information on HTML tags.

4 Click the Find Next button to highlight the first occurrence of your text, or Find All to highlight all occurrences.

5 If you want to replace the found text with something else, enter your replacement text in the Replace With text box. Use the Replace button in conjunction with Find Next to replace text on a case-by-case basis or Replace All to replace all occurrences of the text you specified.

IMPORTING WORD HTML

Dreamweaver offers a very convenient tool to import text from the most widely used word processing program on the market, Microsoft Word. Word offers a Save As Web Page function to allow users to quickly format text documents for the Web. By using Dreamweaver's Import Word HTML command, you can quickly bring text from a Word document into the Document window and maintain much of its original formatting.

To Import TEXT FROM A WORD DOCUMENT:

1 Save the Word document using the Save As Web Page command from Word's File menu.

2 In Dreamweaver, select File | Import | Import Word HTML from the menu. This opens the Clean Up Word HTML dialog box (shown here). Dreamweaver automatically selects the version of Word the imported document was written in.

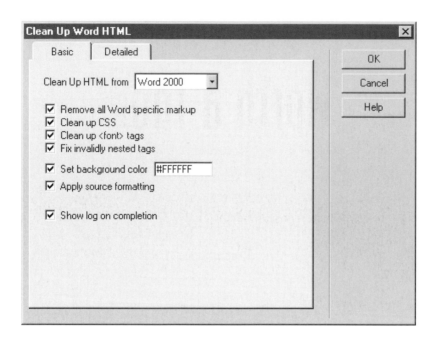

3 Click OK. Dreamweaver will display exactly what corrections have been made to the HTML code.

Dreamweaver goes through this process because Word creates HTML documents that include formatting specific only to Internet Explorer. While HTML documents created in this fashion will display almost exactly in a Microsoft browser as they did in Microsoft's word processor, they won't display with the same fidelity in other browsers. In some cases, the document won't display at all.

Worth a Thousand
Words: Using Images

The Internet, as most people know it, has been with

us a relatively short time. Yet in that time, the technology that

feeds the Internet has increased exponentially. Initially, there

was no support for the display of images in a Web browser.

Looking at the average Web site today, it's hard to imagine

how we ever got along without it. You could even argue that

the concept of "Web design" would be nonexistent if Web

documents were still a purely text-driven medium.

Images can be used to add accents to a Web site, or they can be at the core of a site's design. Images can be basic photographs or elaborate graphic and text art. Transparent images are even used as devices to maintain spacing between other Web page elements. Whether they're used as pictures, graphic art, or tools, the limits of what can be accomplished with images will continue to shrink as the technology required to facilitate their usage expands.

WORKING WITH IMAGES

Just like anything else you put into your document, you can easily select and manipulate images directly in the Document window. Using the Properties Inspector, you can add links to an image, put borders around it, change its dimensions, increase the space that surrounds it, and set its alignment on the page. By using a combination of Dreamweaver tools, you can create complex graphic elements, such as image maps, mouse rollovers, and navigation bars.

Dreamweaver also enables you to define the image editing tool of your choice via the Preferences dialog box, where you can launch the editing program and edit an image while you're working in Dreamweaver.

INSERTING IMAGES

Before you can start manipulating images in Dreamweaver, you have to get them into your document. Dreamweaver allows you to insert images in a number of ways. To insert an image, place your cursor in the Document window where you'd like the image to appear, and use one of the following actions:

▶ From the Objects Panel (shown here), click the Insert Image button.

▶ From the Document window menu bar, select Insert | Image.

▶ From the keyboard, press CTRL-ALT-I.

Each of these methods displays the Select Image Source dialog box (see Figure 4-1). From here you can search your computer for an image. Click the icon of the image you want to insert, or type in the file path directly. Click the Select button to insert the image and close the dialog box.

FIGURE 4-1

Use the Select Image Source dialog box to search for images on your computer.

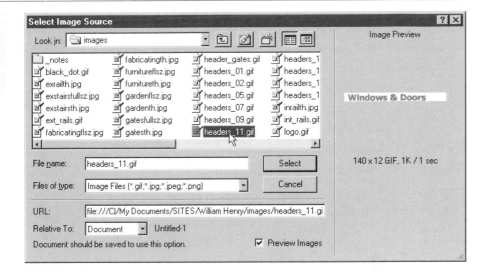

A WORD ON FILE FORMATS Creating high-quality Web graphics is a book unto itself (in fact, one of the coauthors has written a book on this very subject, *Web Design Virtual Classroom*, Osborne/McGraw-Hill, 2001). This shameless plug aside, there are a few basic concepts that don't require you to rush out and buy another book (not that we'd complain if you did).

The two primary file types supported by most Web browsers are GIF and JPEG. GIF (Graphic Interchange Format) was created by CompuServe. JPEG is the acronym for the group that came up with the format, the Joint Photographic Experts Group.

The simplest rule of thumb concerning usage of these two formats is to use JPEGs for photographs and GIFs for simple images like clip art, line art, and grayscale images (including black-and-white photos). Without going into too much technobabble, the reasons for this rule are as follows. GIFs can only support up to 256 individual colors; consequently, they are great for images that don't have a lot of detail or don't contain a lot of color variation. JPEGs, on the other hand, can support millions of colors, and they can handle more of the subtle shades of color that exist in a photograph, or the kinds of photo-realistic images you can create with tools like Adobe Photoshop.

If you have an image that isn't in either of these formats, you can open it in the image editor of your choice and either save or export the file as GIF or JPEG.

If you have not yet saved the document, an alert box will be displayed informing you that a relative path won't be created until you do. If the image you have selected resides outside your site's local root folder, Dreamweaver will ask if you want to copy the image into the site folder.

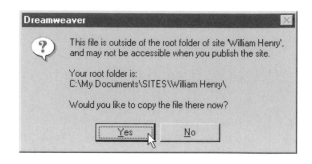

If you click Yes, the Copy File As dialog box will appear (see Figure 4-2), where you can save the image directly into the site root folder, or create a new folder inside the site root folder to save the image in. For more information about creating local sites and understanding relative and absolute pathnames, see Chapter 2.

Once you insert an image into a document, it will appear in its selected state, with an outline around the image and handles along the bottom and right sides as well as in the lower-right corner (see Figure 4-3). To deselect the image, click anywhere in the Document window. Clicking on any image in your document will select it. To select multiple images, simply hold down SHIFT while clicking on the images you want to select.

If you want to replace an image you've inserted in a document, you can double-click it to display the Select Image dialog box. Then choose a new image, or use the point-to-file icon next to the Src field of the Properties Inspector and drag it to another image file icon in your Site window. For more information about creating links in the Site window, see Chapter 2.

FIGURE 4-2

Save an image directly into the site root folder using the Copy File As dialog box.

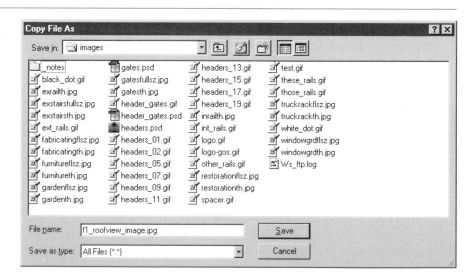

FIGURE 4-3

A selected image with handles

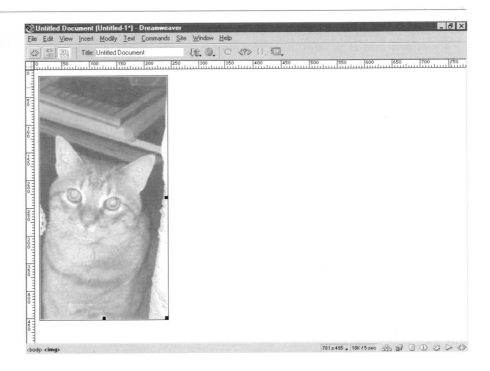

FORMATTING IMAGES

After you have inserted an image into your document, you can decide how you want to format it. For example, you can take a button image and assign a link to it. You might have an image that stands out better with a border around it. You may want to tweak the dimensions of a particular image or increase the amount of physical space that surrounds it. You'll more than likely have some thoughts about how you want that image aligned on your page. There are also image attributes you can define that help a page load faster. This illustration shows the Properties Inspector as it appears when an image is selected.

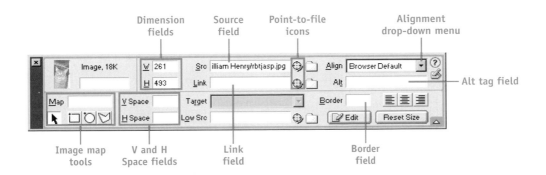

CREATING IMAGE LINKS

Assigning a link to an image is a simple process. To create an image link, select the image you want to assign a link to, and use one of the following methods:

▶ Drag the point-to-file icon next to the Link field in the Properties Inspector to a file icon in the Site window.

▶ Click on the folder icon beside the point-to-file icon to browse for a document in your site.

▶ Type the path to the file you want to link to directly into the Link field.

You'll find these methods are the standard way of creating links of any kind in Dreamweaver, regardless of whether the element you're making a link out of is an image or text. To learn more about creating links, see Chapter 5.

ADDING A BORDER

If you want to place a border around your image, simply enter a pixel width value in the Border field of the Properties Inspector.

If you add a border to an image, the border color is identical to the text color of the paragraph the image is inserted in. If the image you add a border to has a link assigned to it, the border color will reflect whatever color value you have set for links in the Page Properties dialog box. If no link color value has been set for the particular document, the border color will reflect the default link color of the Web browser viewing the page.

RESIZING

To resize a selected image in the Document window, use either of the following methods:

▶ Click and drag any of the handles around the image. If you want to resize the image proportionally, hold down SHIFT while dragging the corner handle.

▶ Enter pixel values into the W (width) and H (height) fields of the Properties Inspector.

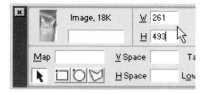

When you insert an image into the Document window, Dreamweaver will automatically enter the original width and height values for the image. By having these values defined, a Web browser will reserve that space for the image while it loads the rest of the document.

If you resize the image, the values displayed in the Properties Inspector will become bold, indicating they are not the original values for the image.

To return the image's dimensions to their original values, use either of these actions:

▶ Click on the field labels, W and H.

▶ Click the Reset Size button in the lower-right corner of the Properties Inspector.

Be careful how much you resize an image. Drastic changes in an image's height or width can cause it to appear distorted in a Web browser. If you want to radically change the scale of an image, use external editing software before you insert your image into Dreamweaver.

IMAGE ALIGNMENT

Use the Align drop-down menu on the Properties Inspector to modify the alignment of an image:

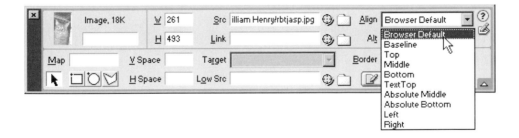

When you use this menu, you are setting the image alignment relative to other page content in the same line or paragraph.

The Align menu provides you with ten possible values for an image's alignment attribute:

▶ **Browser Default** Sets no alignment attribute for the image, but gives the same result as Baseline

▶ **Baseline** Aligns the bottom of any content on the line with the bottom of the selected image

▶ **Top** Aligns the image with the top of the tallest element on the line

▶ **Middle** Aligns the baseline of elements on the line with the middle of the selected image

▶ **Bottom** Equivalent to Baseline

▶ **TextTop** Aligns the image with the top of the tallest text character in the line

▶ **Absolute Middle** Aligns the image to the absolute middle of the line

▶ **Absolute Bottom** Aligns the absolute bottom of the elements in the line with the bottom of the selected image; see sidebar "What's a Baseline?"

▶ **Left** Anchors the image to the left of the document, table cell, or layer and wraps text to the right of the image

▶ **Right** Sets the image to the right of the document, table cell, or layer and wraps text to the left of the image

---

WHAT'S A BASELINE? **Having trouble with all this talk of baselines? Not to worry. Remember penmanship and writing out your letters along all those lines? The baseline is the line the text sits on. Some lowercase letters—g, j, p, q, and y—have descenders that drop below the baseline. This is where absolute bottom comes in. Absolute bottom would align an image with the bottom of the descenders on a line instead of the text's baseline.**

VERTICAL AND HORIZONTAL SPACE

There may be times when you want to modify the amount of physical space around an image, particularly if the image is set in a paragraph with text wrapped around it. The image attributes that control the space around an image are called V Space (vertical) and H Space (horizontal). Together, these two attributes create a margin of empty or "white" space above and below (V Space) and to the left and right (H Space) of the image.

To modify the V Space and H Space of an image, simply enter values into the corresponding fields in the Properties Inspector.

ALTERNATIVE TEXT

In general, it is considered good form to provide alternative text content for all images you include on your site. By entering text into the Alt field, you provide a text reference for users who may choose to turn off the images in their browsers. Although this sounds like an odd thing to do, some users do so if they have a slow Web connection, and this also benefits visually impaired visitors to your site who use text-to-speech software. The text should be concise and either describe the image or what it does.

> **TIP** When you first insert an image, the V Space and H Space fields are empty, and these two attributes are as yet undefined. You would probably assume that if no values have been defined, the browser default would be the same as setting the values to 0. Actually an H Space setting of 3 produces the same effect as not defining the attribute at all. The V Space attribute's browser default is, in fact, the same as setting it to 0.

ASSIGNING AN EXTERNAL IMAGE EDITOR

By assigning an external image editor, such as Fireworks or Photoshop, Dreamweaver allows you to access that program and make changes to a selected image by simply clicking the Edit button in the Properties Inspector. You can make your changes and see them updated in Dreamweaver without the hassle of opening and closing applications and hunting for the file you want to edit. You can even assign different programs to edit different types of images. For example, you could set one program to edit GIFs and another to edit JPEGs.

To Assign AN EXTERNAL IMAGE EDITOR:

1 From the Document window menu bar, select Edit | Edit With External Editor to open the Preferences dialog box with File Types/Editors preselected in the Category field (see Figure 4-4).

2 Select the file type to which you want to assign an editor by clicking on a file extension in the Extensions list.

3 Click the Add button over the Editors list to open the Select External Editor dialog box (see Figure 4-5). Browse for the program with which you want to edit that file type.

FIGURE 4-4

The Preferences dialog box, with File Types/Editors selected

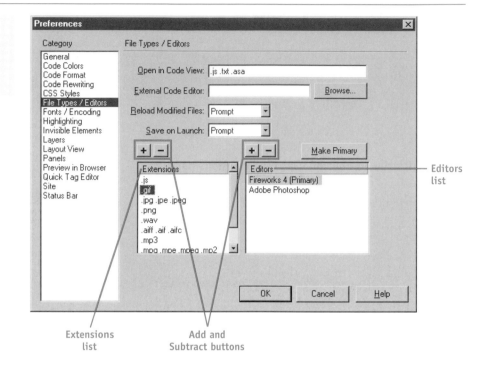

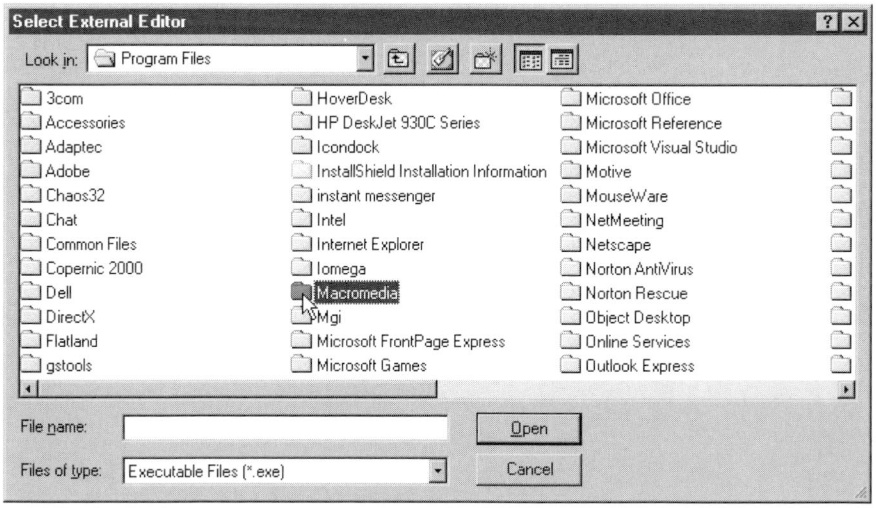

Editors list

Extensions list

Add and Subtract buttons

FIGURE 4-5

Use the Select External Editor dialog box to select the program with which to edit your image.

If this is the first editor assigned for a particular file type, Dreamweaver automatically makes it the primary editor. To add multiple editors for a particular file type, repeat steps 2 and 3. To change the primary editor for that file type, select the editor you want from the Editors list and click the Make Primary button.

To Add A NEW FILE TYPE TO THE EXTENSIONS LIST:

1 Click the Add button over the Extensions list.

2 Enter the file type extension, for example .gif, in the field provided, as shown here.

Depending on the software you already have installed on your computer, editors may already be in place. If these are your editing tools of choice, by all means keep them. If you already have Macromedia Fireworks installed on your machine, Dreamweaver will automatically set it as your primary editor. You can, of course, change it at any time.

CREATING AN IMAGE MAP

When you create an image map (see Figure 4-6), you designate areas of an image, called *hotspots*, to act as links to other files in your site or other sites. The image map tools found on the Properties Inspector allow you to create and modify what are referred to as *client-side image maps*.

Client-side image maps maintain all the link information inside the HTML document you create and are processed by the client's (visitor's) PC. There are also server-side image maps that keep all the information on the server and must be processed there each time a visitor clicks a link on the image map. It's faster to have each of your visitors process the map information individually than to have a number of visitors asking one computer to do the processing for them as a server-side map does. Consequently, client-side image maps have become the map of choice and are supported by all versions of Internet Explorer and every version of Netscape Navigator since version 2.0.

FIGURE 4-6

Use the Image Map tools in the Properties Inspector to create hotspots.

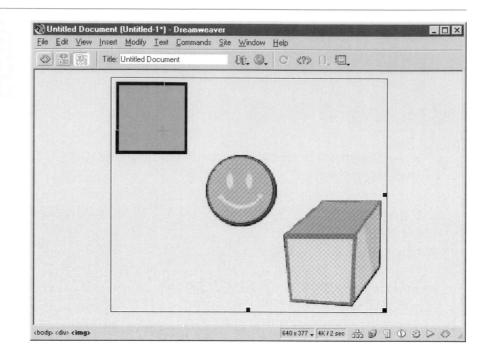

To Create AN IMAGE MAP:

1 In the Document window, select the image you want to use as an image map.

2 In the Properties Inspector, type a name for your image map in the Map field. If you're creating more than one image map in the same document, make sure each map has a unique name.

3 Use one of the following methods to create a hotspot:

- For a rectangular hotspot, choose the rectangle tool and drag the cursor over an area of the image. Holding down SHIFT while dragging will produce a square hotspot.

- For a circular hotspot, choose the circle tool and drag the cursor over an area of the image.

- For a polygon, choose the polygon tool and click once on the image for each corner you want to add.

When you finish creating a hotspot, the Properties Inspector changes so the hotspot can be modified.

FORMATTING HOTSPOTS

Once you create a hotspot, you'll need to assign links in order to make the map function.

To Format A HOTSPOT:

1 In the Properties Inspector, enter a name for your image map if you did not do so previously.

2 Enter a link in the Link field, or use the point-to-file icon and drag it to a file in your Site Map.

3 If you are working in a frameset, enter a target frame for the link in the Target field. (To learn about frames and framesets, see Chapter 8.)

4 If you haven't already done so, enter alternative text for the image in the Alt field.

RESIZING HOTSPOTS

To resize a hotspot, click the hotspot pointer tool in the Properties Inspector.

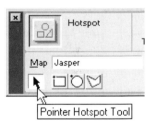

Select the hotspot you want to resize, then click and drag any of the hotspot's handles to modify the size or shape of the hotspot.

MOVING HOTSPOTS

If you want to move a hotspot, select the hotspot pointer tool, then click and drag the hotspot to the location of your choice. You can also select the hotspot and use the arrow keys on your keyboard to move it. Using the arrow keys moves the hotspot one pixel at a time. If you hold down SHIFT when using the arrow keys, the hotspot moves ten pixels at a time.

> **TIP** If you want to select multiple hotspots, hold down SHIFT while you select them. You can also press CTRL-A to select all the hotspots in a selected image map.

CREATING AN IMAGE ROLLOVER

An image rollover is like a light switch. When the page loads, one image is displayed, and when the mouse moves over it, another image takes its place—image on, image off (or off, then on, depending on your point of view). Such an effect requires JavaScript, which is where Dreamweaver shows its muscle. Dreamweaver inserts the JavaScript for you.

When creating rollover effects, make sure both images you plan to use are the same size. If they aren't, Dreamweaver will resize the second image to match the first, possibly distorting the second image.

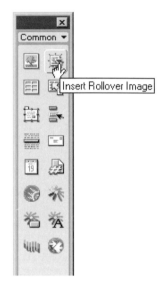

To Create AN IMAGE ROLLOVER:

1 Place your cursor in the Document window where you'd like the rollover image to be inserted. Use one of the following actions:

- From the Objects panel, click the Insert Rollover Image button, shown to the right.

- From the Document window menu bar, select Insert | Interactive Images | Rollover Image. The Insert Rollover Image dialog box is displayed:

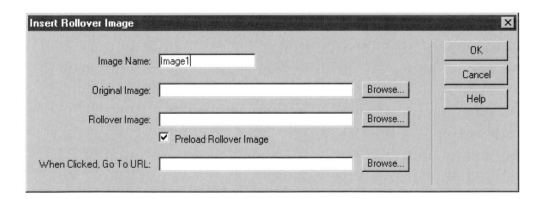

2 Enter a name for the rollover image in the Image Name field.

3 Use the Browse buttons beside the appropriate fields to locate the images you want to use for the original image and the rollover image.

4 In the When Clicked, Go To URL field, enter the file name or URL of the page you want the rollover image to link to, or click Browse to locate a file within your site.

5 Click OK.

TIP The Preload Rollover Image check-box in the Insert Rollover Image dialog box is checked by default. It's best to leave this checked so that both images are loaded by the browser. This way, a visitor won't have to wait for the second image to load when they mouse over the original image.

ON THE VIRTUAL CLASSROOM CD-ROM In Lesson 3, "Working with Images," the instructor demonstrates the process of inserting and modifying images, the creation of a rollover effect, and how image map hotspots are made, turning areas within a graphic into hyperlinks.

It's All Connected: Navigation and Linking

The beauty of a spider's web is found in the intersection of its lines, its myriad connections. This beauty wasn't lost on the creators of the Hypertext Transfer Protocol when envisioning the potential their new "web" would have for bringing people and information together, and again, it is the connections—hyperlinks—that make it all possible.

You can create a link to almost anything that can reside on a computer: the most obvious being other HTML documents, but also image files, multimedia files, and downloadable files like software and zip files. You can also make links to specific locations *within* an individual HTML document.

UNDERSTANDING PATHNAMES

A Web site is nothing more than a collection of files that resides on a computer. Computers used for this purpose are called Web servers. They "serve" files to your browser when you click on hyperlinks or type URLs (Uniform Resource Locators) in the browser's address line. The address metaphor comes in handy here because every file, whether it's an HTML document, image file, or multimedia clip, has an address on the Web server. That address is expressed using a *pathname*.

You see pathnames all the time when you use tools like Windows Explorer or Macintosh Finder. Chances are you've seen something like this before: C:\My Documents\Word Docs\. It's easier to understand a pathname if you read it backwards, so this path would mean you're in a folder called Word Docs, which is sitting inside a folder called My Documents, which is found on a hard drive called C. A Web server isn't radically different from your own PC. They're both computers, and all computers have something called a file structure. The pathname is simply an address to a file within that file structure.

Pathnames fall into two categories:

▶ **Absolute pathnames** These pathnames declare the full address to a file, such as http://www.your_site.com/index.html. These are best used when pointing to a location outside your own site.

▶ **Relative pathnames** These pathnames are abbreviated addresses and are best for referencing files within your own site. Relative pathnames fall into two categories:

  • **Document-relative pathnames** These use the document that the link or file reference is in as a starting point for looking to other files. For example, the pathname sports/soccer.html tells the browser to start in the same folder the present document is in and locate the folder called sports, then look inside that folder to find the document soccer.html.

- **Site root–relative pathnames** These use the Web server's file structure as a base, with the root folder of the site as the starting point. For example, /html_files/sports/soccer.html says to start at the very top of the file structure (/) and work down to the folder html_files, then find the folder called sports inside of it, and finally find the file soccer.html inside of that.

Dreamweaver will use relative pathnames when you create links and file references once you create a local site (see Chapter 2). If you don't create a local site, Dreamweaver uses absolute pathnames reflecting your own hard drive—for example, file:///C:/My Documents/sports/soccer.html. This would wreak havoc when you upload your pages to a Web server, because (a) it wouldn't have the same file structure as your PC and (b) Web servers are different enough from your PC to be confused by file:///C:.

By using relative pathnames, you can work on a site on any machine, transfer it to a Web server, and preserve the file relationships. This is the whole reason you want to begin by creating a site in Dreamweaver rather than just making pages ad hoc. Once you've done so, you give the otherwise arduous task of link maintenance to Dreamweaver so you can be free to deal with more creative concerns.

CREATING HYPERLINKS

Dreamweaver's graphic method of establishing links makes link building simple and intuitive. You can create a hyperlink to a local file three different ways. Select the text or image you want to assign a link to, and use one of the following methods:

▶ Drag the point-to-file icon next to the Link field in the Properties Inspector to a file icon in the Site window (see Figure 5-1).

▶ SHIFT-drag from the selected text or image to a file icon in the Site window.

▶ Click on the folder icon beside the point-to-file icon to browse for a document in your site.

To create a link to a location outside your site, select the text or image you want to assign a link to, and enter the URL into the Link field of the Properties Inspector.

> **TIP** If you want to make sure you don't make a typographical error when entering a link to a location outside your site, open the page you want to link to in your Web browser, select the URL from the browser's address bar, and copy and paste it into the Link field of the Properties Inspector.

FIGURE 5-1

Use the point-to-file icon to quickly create your links visually.

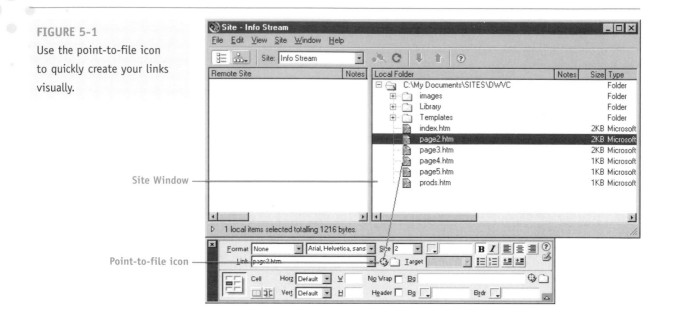

Site Window

Point-to-file icon

FORMATTING LINK COLORS

There are three text link colors you can define, each corresponding to the different states a text link possesses: an active link, a visited link, and a link the visitor has yet to click. By assigning a different color for each state, you provide visual cues for your visitors to determine where they are, where they've been, and where they've yet to go. Using the Page Properties dialog box, you can assign link colors using the same type of color picker seen throughout the many faces of the Properties Inspector.

To Assign LINK COLORS:

1 Select Modify | Page Properties from the Document window menu bar.

2 In the Page Properties dialog box (shown in Figure 5-2), click the individual link color wells to access a color palette.

3 Select a color from the palette with the eyedropper. Dreamweaver also allows you to select a color from anywhere on your screen by simply holding down the left mouse button and positioning the eyedropper over the color you want to select.

If you happen to know the hexadecimal values you want to use, you may enter them directly into the fields provided next to the color wells.

FIGURE 5-2

The Page Properties dialog box

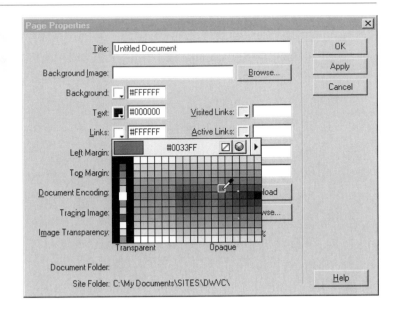

CREATING NAMED ANCHOR LINKS

Named anchors allow you to specify locations inside a document to which you can then create a link. This is a good strategy when you have a particularly long document you don't want your visitors to have to scroll through. You could make a table of contents at the top of the document and have the individual entries link to their corresponding sections further down the page.

Implementing named anchors is a two-part process: creating the named anchor and then assigning a link to that named anchor. The anchor effectively becomes a sub-address of the document it is in.

To Create A NAMED ANCHOR:

Place the cursor where you want to insert the named anchor, and:

- From the Objects panel (shown here), select the Invisibles category, and click the Insert Named Anchor button.

- From the menu bar, select Insert | Invisible Tags | Named Anchor.

- From the keyboard, press CTRL-ALT-A.

FIGURE 5-3

The Insert Named Anchor
dialog box

Each of these methods displays the Insert Named Anchor dialog box (shown in Figure 5-3).

2 Enter a name for the anchor in the Anchor Name field.

After going through this process, if you don't see an anchor marker in the Document window similar to the Insert Named Anchor button icon in the Objects panel, go to the Menu bar, choose Edit | Preferences, and click on Invisible Elements in the Category field of the Preferences dialog box. From here, make sure the Named Anchors checkbox is selected (see Figure 5-4).

FIGURE 5-4

The Preferences dialog box
displaying the Invisible
Elements category

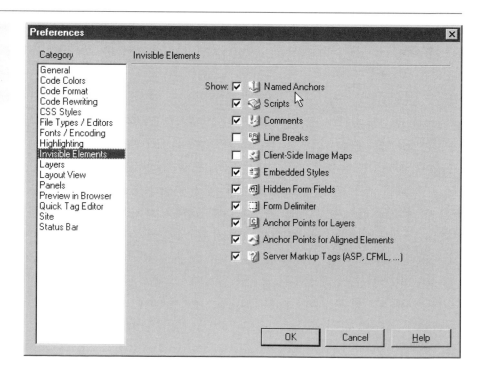

If you still don't see an anchor marker, go to the Menu bar and choose View |
Visual Aids | Invisible Elements to turn Invisible Elements on.

To create a link to a named anchor, select the text or image you want to assign a
link to, and use any of the following methods:

▶ Click the point-to-file icon next to the Link field in the Properties Inspector,
and drag it to the anchor you want to link to, either in the same document or
in another open document.

▶ In the Document window, SHIFT-drag from the
selected text or image to the anchor to which
you want to link.

▶ Enter a number sign (#) followed by the name
of the anchor in the Link field of the Properties
Inspector. If the anchor is not in the same document, the correct path to the
file must be entered, followed by the number sign and anchor name.

> **NOTE** Anchor names are case-sensitive
> and should not contain any spaces.

CREATING E-MAIL LINKS

An e-mail link assigns a particular e-mail address to an image or piece of
text so that when the link is clicked the visitor's e-mail software is
launched with that address already filled in. To create an e-mail link, use
any of the following methods:

▶ Select a piece of text or an image, and click the Insert Email Link
button on the Objects panel (shown here). In the resulting dialog
box, enter the e-mail address into the E-mail field (shown in
Figure 5-5).

▶ Select a piece of text or an image, and type **mailto:** followed
immediately by the e-mail address directly into the Link field of
the Properties Inspector (see Figure 5-6).

▶ Place your cursor where you want to insert a text e-mail link, and
select Insert | Email Link from the menu bar. Then enter the text
to which you want the e-mail link attached and its corresponding
e-mail address into the appropriate fields of the Insert Email Link
dialog box.

FIGURE 5-5

The Insert Email Link
dialog box

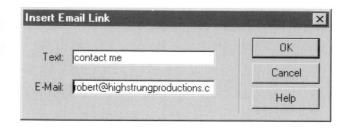

FIGURE 5-6

Make sure there are no spaces
between "mailto:" and the
address.

LINK MANAGEMENT

Dreamweaver has the ability to update your site's links any time you move or
rename a file. In order to take full advantage of these features you must, of
course, set up a local site on your machine.

To Ensure THAT LINK MANAGEMENT IS ACTIVE:

1 From the Document window menu bar, select Edit | Preferences to open the Preferences
   dialog box, then choose the General category (see Figure 5-7).

2 Select Always or Prompt from the Update Links When Moving Files drop-down menu.

3 Click OK.

To speed the updating process, Dreamweaver creates a cache file that maintains all the link information in your local site. The cache file is created
when you define your local site and select the
Enable Cache checkbox.

SEE ALSO **To learn more about creating a local site see Chapter 2.**

FIGURE 5-7

The Preferences dialog box

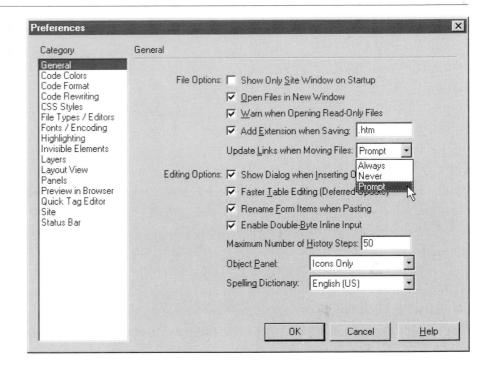

MODIFYING LINKS WITH THE SITE MAP

Chapter 2 demonstrated how to create links using the Site Map's point-to-file icon, which inserts text links into a document you can then format any way you like. The Site Map also provides a number of ways to edit the links within your site.

To Remove A LINK IN THE SITE MAP:

▶ Right-click the document whose link you want to remove, and select Remove Link from the context menu, or select Site | Remove Link from the Site window menu bar.

To Change A LINK:

1 Right-click the document whose link you want to modify, and select Change Link from the context menu, or select Site | Change Link from the Site window menu bar.

2 In the resulting dialog box, browse to locate the file to which you want the link to point.

To Open A DOCUMENT TO THE SOURCE OF A LINK:

▶ **Right-click a document in the Site Map, and select Open To Source Of Link from the context menu, or choose Site | Open Source Of Link from the menu bar.**

This opens the document containing the link to the selected file, with that link highlighted, in the Document window.

Each of these processes can seem a bit confusing, since you're selecting one document to effect a change in another. Just remember that you are visually selecting the document the link refers to in order to edit the individual link. The physical link itself is in the page above that document in the Site Map hierarchy.

MODIFYING A LINK SITEWIDE

Dreamweaver allows you to do more than just modify individual links one at a time. By selecting a local document in the Site window, you can then take all the links in your site that point to it and redirect them somewhere else.

To Modify A LINK SITEWIDE:

1 Select a local file in the Site window.

2 From the menu bar, select Site | Change Link Sitewide.

3 In the Change Link Sitewide dialog box, enter the new location to which you now want the affected links to point in the Into Links To field:

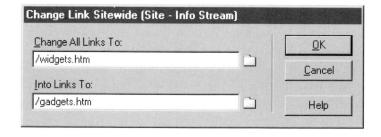

4 Click OK.

This is an extremely useful feature if you simply want to swap a new document into your site in place of another. For example, each page in your site might have a link to a document called widgets.html. At some point, the company you made this site for decides to stop making Widgets and needs a whole new page describing their new Gadget line of products. After you make this new gadget document, you can go into your local site and select the widgets.html file and change all the links in the site that point to it to point to the new gadgets document instead. Afterward, you are free to delete the widgets.html document or save it in case the widget business takes a sudden upturn.

CHECKING YOUR LINKS

Dreamweaver can scan your site for broken links, external links, and orphaned files on a file, folder, or sitewide basis. Orphaned files are documents within your site that have no links or references made to them that could be taking up valuable disk space. External links can't be validated by Dreamweaver, so it simply notes them for you to test directly in a browser.

To check the links in the currently open document, use either of these methods:

▶ Select Files | Check Links from the Document window menu bar.

▶ Press SHIFT-F8.

To check the links within a segment of the local site, use either of these methods:

▶ Right-click a file or folder in the Local site files panel and select Check Links | Selected Files/Folders from the context menu.

▶ Select a file or folder from the Local site files panel and choose File | Check files from the Site window menu bar.

> TIP **You can save the results of these link checks as a tab-delimited text file by clicking the Save button.**

To check all links sitewide, use either of these methods:

▶ Right-click anywhere in the Site window and select Check Links | Entire Site from the context menu.

▶ From the Site window menu bar, select Site | Check Links Sitewide.

FIGURE 5-8

The Link Checker dialog box

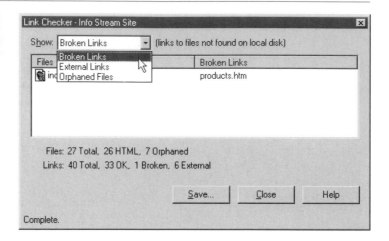

All of these methods display the Link Checker dialog box (see Figure 5-8). The Show drop-down menu allows you to view the information of your choice: Broken Links, External Links, and Orphaned Files.

FIXING BROKEN LINKS

Broken links and file references can be easily mended right in the Link Checker dialog box. Alternatively, you can double-click any file in the list to open it in the Document window with the broken link highlighted. You can then edit the link in the Properties Inspector.

To Mend A BROKEN LINK:

1 In the Link Checker dialog box, select Broken Links from the Show drop-down menu.

2 Select the broken link in the Broken Links column, and click the folder icon that appears to the right (see Figure 5-9) to browse for the file to which you want to link, or enter the pathname in the field provided.

3 Click the Select button.

FIGURE 5-9
The Link Checker dialog box
folder icon

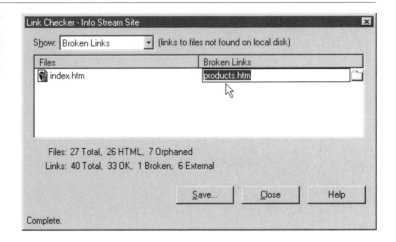

If there is more than one broken link to a specific file, Dreamweaver asks if you want to fix the remaining broken references to this file. Click Yes to fix all the links to this file. Click No to fix only the current link.

CREATING A NAVIGATION BAR

In Chapter 4, we discussed making a rollover image. The navigation bar takes the concept of the rollover image a step further. Using Dreamweaver's Insert Navigation Bar command, you can set up a series of rollover buttons that can respond to up to four different mouse events:

▶ **Up** Displays the initial image prior to any interaction from the visitor

▶ **Over** Displays a new image in response to the mouse moving over the image area

▶ **Down** Displays a third image in response to the visitor clicking the image

▶ **Over While Down** Displays a fourth image in response to the mouse remaining over the image area after it has been clicked

For each button in your navigation bar, you'll need to have the appropriate amount of images per button for the number of mouse events you want to use.

To Insert A NAVIGATION BAR:

1 Select the Insert Navigation Bar button from the Objects panel (shown here). The Insert Navigation Bar dialog box is displayed (see Figure 5-10).

2 In the Element Name field, enter a name for the first button of the navigation bar.

3 For each mouse state you want to use—Up, Over, Down, and Over While Down—enter the path and file name of the image in the appropriate field, or click Browse to locate the image.

4 In the When Clicked, Go To URL field, enter the path and file name of the document to which you want to link, or browse to locate the file.

5 Select Horizontally or Vertically from the Insert drop-down menu to determine the Navigation bar's orientation.

6 If you want the navigation bar created in a table, click the Use Tables checkbox.

7 Click the Add (+) button and repeat steps 2 through 4 to create the next button.

8 To finish, click OK.

If you decide you want to remove one of the button elements from the navigation bar, simply select its name in the Nav Bar Elements field and click the Subtract (–) button. Just like the rollover image, the Insert Navigation Bar dialog box checks the Preload Images checkbox by default. Since the navigation bar is a file-intensive element, it is best to keep this option selected so visitors won't have to wait for each image to load when they are requested by each mouse event.

If you want to edit your navigation bar, select Modify | Navigation Bar from the Document window menu bar. This will display the Modify Navigation Bar dialog box (shown in Figure 5-11), which is virtually identical to the Insert Navigation

FIGURE 5-10

The Insert Navigation Bar
dialog box

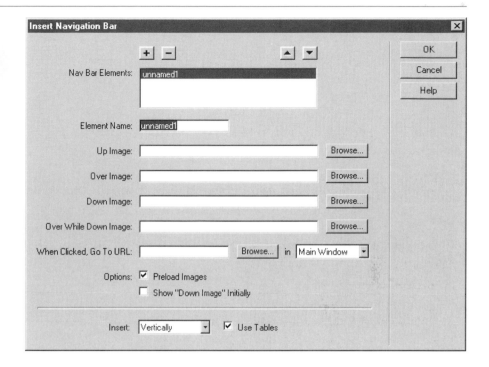

FIGURE 5-11

The Modify Navigation Bar
dialog box

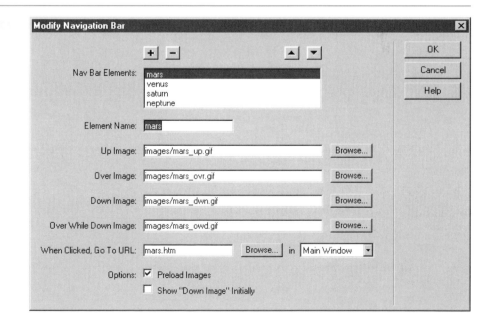

Bar dialog box, with the exception of the horizontal/vertical options and the Use Tables checkbox. From here you can remove elements or select different images just as you would when creating the navigation bar initially.

You can only insert one navigation bar in a document. Dreamweaver will assume you are trying to edit the existing navigation bar if you attempt to insert another one and will ask if you want to modify it.

TIP Consistency is the thing to remember when making a navigation bar. Each image for the various states of a button should be the same dimension so there is no image distortion from state to state. The overall effect of each button shouldn't be radically different—for example, if the first button in your navigation bar appears to recess when moused over, and then changes color when clicked, that effect should be reflected through the rest of the buttons on the bar. Granted, rules are there to be broken, but you should have a very good reason for doing so when you're dealing with how your visitors are going to move around your site.

6

Working with Tables

In the dark ages of HTML, tables were intended to do what tables have traditionally done: display data. Very boring. Columns and rows of numbers and words, with column headings and borders—it seems too much like spreadsheets and word processing, which was probably the intention. What you need to realize, however, was the original scholarly intent of the HTML specification. The folks at CERN, an international high-energy physics research center in Switzerland, were planning on posting research papers, thesis dissertations, and the like, which, in the hard sciences particularly, have a substantial amount of data to be displayed. Initially, no one was considering the public and commercial expansion of this new medium, and with that expansion, the birth of Web design.

Once that expansion began to happen, it didn't take long before people started to realize tables could be used as more than just "tables." Tables also worked wonders as layout tools in a medium that possessed no inherent positioning attributes of its own. As time went by and the HTML specification grew, attributes for tables expanded—the long and short of it being that today tables are one of the most common elements found in Web pages.

TABLE TALK Tables are made up of a series of container tags, meaning each type of tag has both an opening and closing version, and each set of these opening and closing tags defines a specific table element.

For example, the opening and closing table tags are `<table>` and `</table>`. Rows are defined using `<tr>` and `</tr>`, the *tr* signifying *table row*. Each cell is defined with `<td>` and `</td>` tags, which stands for *table data*.

There is a logic to how these tags are laid out in an HTML document. A table contains rows, and rows contain cells, so an HTML table is written like this:

```
<table border="1">
    <tr>
        <td> One </td>
        <td> Two </td>
    </tr>
    <tr>
        <td> Three </td>
        <td> Four </td>
    </tr>
</table>
```

This source code creates a table two rows high by two columns wide with the words One through Four as cell content, as shown here. Notice that columns are not specifically defined, but are more a by-product of the stacking of rows.

This table is as "vanilla" as they come. There are a number of attributes that can be defined in each type of the opening tag (border thickness, width, height, and color) using different parts of the Dreamweaver interface.

Continued

As you experiment with tables, try setting the Document window to Code and Design view. This way you can see the changing structure of the HTML tags involved as you make modifications to the various table elements.

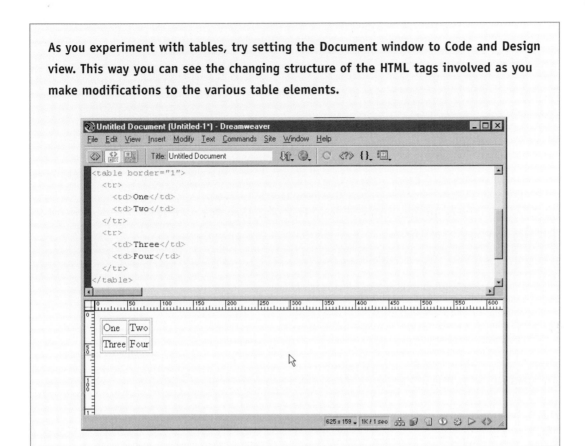

INSERTING TABLES

To insert a table, place your cursor in the Document window where you want your table to appear and use any of these methods:

► From the Objects Panel, click the Insert Table button.

► Select Insert | Table from the menu bar.

► Press CTRL-ALT-T.

Each of these methods displays the Insert Table dialog box (see Figure 6-1).

The Insert Table dialog box has six fields:

► **Rows** Defines the number of rows

► **Columns** Defines the number of columns

► **Cell Padding** Defines (in pixels) the amount of space between the content of the cell and its borders (see Figure 6-2)

FIGURE 6-1

The Insert Table dialog box

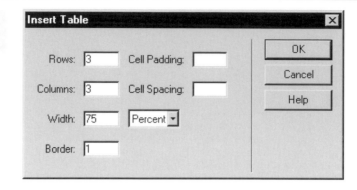

▶ **Cell Spacing** Defines (in pixels) the amount of space that separates each cell (Figure 6-3)

▶ **Width** Defines the width of the table as a fixed pixel amount or a percentage of available space within the element that contains it—the browser window, a layer, or another table cell (Figure 6-4)

▶ **Border** Defines the border width (in pixels) around the table

FIGURE 6-2

Cell padding set to 50 pixels

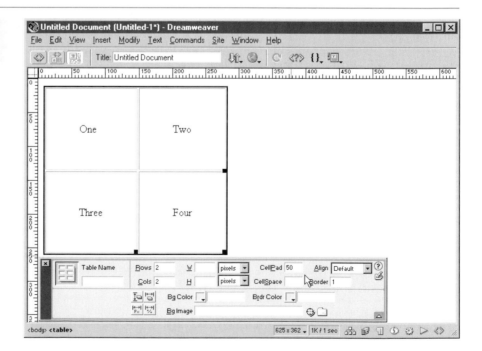

FIGURE 6-3

Cell spacing set to 50 pixels

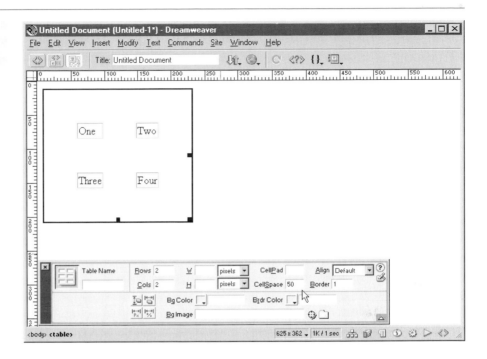

FIGURE 6-4

Percentage widths based on a
table's placement

100% of the window ——

100% of a table cell ——

100% of a layer ——

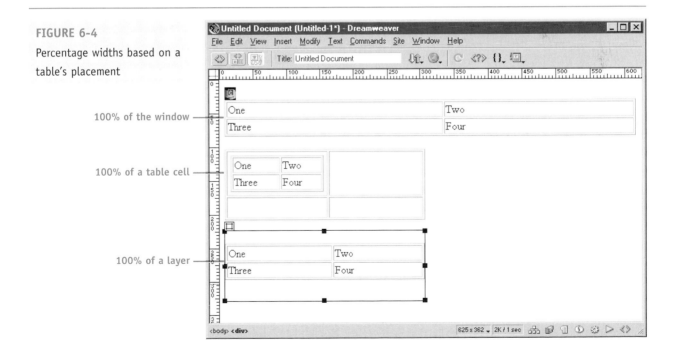

The first time you invoke the Insert Table dialog box after installing Dreamweaver, the default values are for a three-row by three-column table set to a width of 75 percent with a one pixel border. You can modify these values any way you like. From this point forward, Dreamweaver will display the values from the last table inserted. Don't be concerned if you don't have exact values set in your mind before inserting a table. As you'll see, modifying an existing table is a snap.

SELECTING TABLE ELEMENTS

You can select any part of a table, from an individual cell to the whole table itself, and just about any combination of table elements in between.

To select a table, use any of the following methods:

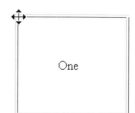

▶ Position the cursor in the upper-left corner of the table, or anywhere along the bottom edge until the cursor changes to a four-arrowed cross, and click.

▶ Right-click on the table and select Table | Select Table from the context menu.

▶ Click in the Document window to either the left or right side of the table and drag across it.

▶ Place the cursor inside any cell and choose Modify | Table | Select Table from the menu bar.

▶ Place the cursor inside any cell, and click the `<table>` tag in the Document window Tag Selector.

To select rows or columns, use either of the following methods:

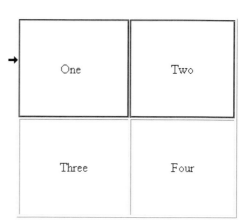

▶ Position the cursor to the left of a row or over a column until the cursor changes to a selection arrow, and click.

▶ Click inside a cell and drag across or down to select multiple rows and columns.

To select cells, use any of these methods:

▶ Click inside any individual cell to select it.

▶ Click inside a cell and drag across or down to select multiple cells.

▶ Click inside a cell, then SHIFT-click in another cell to select all cells between the two.

▶ CTRL-click to select noncontiguous cells.

ENTERING TABLE CONTENT

Entering content into a table is equally painless. Simply click in a table cell to insert the cursor and enter any type of content you want just as you would anywhere else in the Document window.

You can move the cursor forward, cell by cell, by pressing the TAB key. When you reach the last cell of the bottom row, pressing TAB will insert a new row into the table. Pressing SHIFT-TAB moves the cursor backward through the table cells.

IMPORTING TABULAR DATA

If you have a spreadsheet program that can save files in a *delimited format* (text separated by commas, tabs, or some other character), you can then import that data into a table in Dreamweaver.

To Import TABULAR DATA:

1 In your spreadsheet program, save the file in a delimited format.

2 From the Document window menu bar, select File | Import | Tabular Data, or Insert | Tabular Data. This displays either the Import Tabular Data or Insert Table Data dialog box, which are the same in form and function (Figure 6-5).

3 Enter the name of the file you want to import in the Data File field, or click Browse to locate the file.

4 From the Delimiter drop-down menu, select the type of delimiter you used when saving the file in your spreadsheet program. If the delimiter you used doesn't appear in the list, choose Other and enter the delimiter you used in the field provided.

FIGURE 6-5

The Import Table Data dialog box

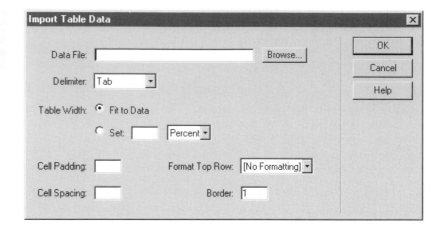

5 Define a width for your table by selecting either Fit To Data or Set and entering a pixel or percentage value.

6 Enter any formatting you want into the fields provided for cell padding, spacing, and border. You can select text formatting for data in the top row from the Format Top Row drop-down menu—for example, if your original spreadsheet had table headings you wanted formatted differently from the rest of the data.

7 Click OK. The imported data will appear in a new table in the Document window.

FORMATTING TABLES

Dreamweaver's array of formatting tools lets you quickly modify very specific properties of each table element: cells, columns, rows, or the table itself. With this level of control, it is possible to assign a number of values that effectively apply to the same table region. For example, you could set the background color of a cell to red, the row the cell is in to white, and the background color of the entire table to blue. Which element's properties win out?

The hierarchy for table elements goes from cell to row to table, so the cell formatting supercedes the row, and the row supercedes the table. Columns lose out simply because HTML defines tables as a collection of rows that hold a number of cells, effectively creating columns by stacking rows on top of each other. Columns just become an inevitable result of that stacking, not something independently defined in the HTML code. This can be a bit of a conceptual hurdle for people familiar with spreadsheets, where columns are a distinct entity.

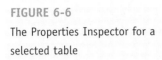

FIGURE 6-6

The Properties Inspector for a
selected table

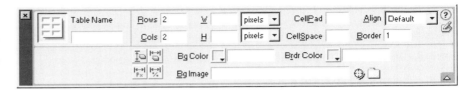

MODIFYING TABLE PROPERTIES

When you select a table, the Properties Inspector displays the properties you initially
defined in the Insert Table dialog box (see Figure 6-6). Using the Properties Inspector,
menu bar, or context menus you can modify every aspect of the overall table.

ALIGNING A TABLE

Using the Properties Inspector, you can align a table in much the same fashion you
align an image, forcing text to wrap around it to one side or the other. Using the
Text menu on the Document window menu bar, you can also treat a table like text
and apply the traditional left, right, or center style alignment to it if you prefer
your text not wrapped.

To Align A TABLE WITH THE PROPERTIES INSPECTOR:

1 Select the table you want to modify.

2 In the Properties Inspector, select a value from the Align drop-down menu:

- Default **Sets no alignment attribute for the table. This table stays to the left of the document, but text will not wrap around it.**

- Left **Keeps the table to the left, wrapping text around it to the right.**

- Center **Places the table in the center of the page.**

- Right **Sets the table to the right, wrapping text around it to the left.**

To Align A TABLE WITH THE TEXT MENU:

1 Select the table you want to modify.

2 From the Document window menu bar, select Text | Alignment, and choose Left, Right, or Center.

Be sure the alignment value in the Properties Inspector is set to Default; otherwise, the two alignment values will compete with each other, creating unwanted effects.

RESIZING TABLES

Just like an inserted image, when you select a table, a border forms around it with handles in the same locations, as shown in Figure 6-7.

To resize a selected table, use either of the following methods:

▶ Click and drag any of the handles around the table. If you want to resize the image and maintain its proportions, hold down the SHIFT key while dragging the corner handle.

▶ Enter pixel values into the W (width) and H (height) fields of the Properties Inspector (refer to Figure 6-6).

CELL PADDING AND SPACING

Adjusting the cell padding and cell spacing of a selected table is so easy and intuitive, you may wonder why I waste ink on it. All you need do is insert pixel values into the CellPad and CellSpace fields in the Properties Inspector (refer to Figure 6-6).

FIGURE 6-7

A selected table

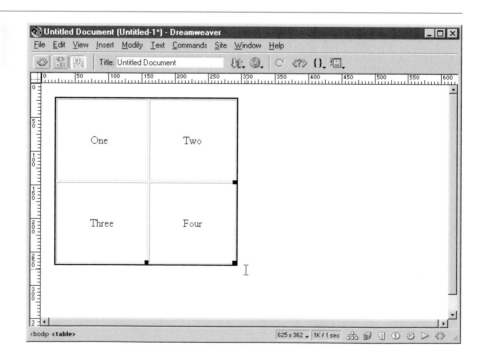

As with many other attributes in HTML, leaving the cell padding and cell spacing undefined is *not* the same as setting them to zero. Not defining a table's cell padding produces the same effect as setting it to 1. An undefined cell spacing produces the same result as setting it to 2.

INSERTING ROWS AND COLUMNS

There are a number of ways you can add new rows and columns to a table, using whichever part of the Dreamweaver interface you're most comfortable with.

To insert one row or column, use any of the following methods:

▶ Right-click in a cell where you'd like to insert a new row or column, and select Table | Insert Row or Insert Column from the context menu.

▶ Click in a cell and select Modify | Table | Insert Row or Insert Column from the menu bar.

▶ Click in a cell and press CTRL-M to add a row, or CTRL-SHIFT-A to add a column. (If you are in the last cell of a table, pressing TAB will also add a row to the bottom of the table.)

Each of these methods inserts a row directly above the cell in which you clicked. If you insert a column, it is placed directly to the left of the selected cell.

To insert multiple rows and columns, use one of these methods:

▶ Right-click in a cell where you'd like to insert new rows or columns, and select Table | Insert Rows or Columns from the context menu.

▶ Click in a cell and select Modify | Table | Insert Rows or Columns from the Document window menu bar.

Each of these methods displays the Insert Rows or Columns dialog box (Figure 6-8). From here, click either the Rows or Columns radio button, enter the number you want to add, and then select where you want them inserted relative to the cell you clicked.

DELETING ROWS AND COLUMNS

Deleting rows and columns is much the same as adding them. To delete a row or column, use any of the following methods:

FIGURE 6-8

The Insert Rows or Columns
dialog box

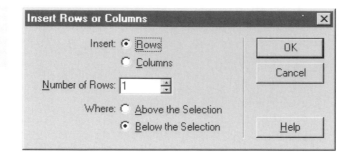

- ▶ Select a row or column and press the DELETE key.

- ▶ Right-click in a cell and select Table | Delete Row or Delete Column from the context menu.

- ▶ Click in a cell and choose Modify | Table | Delete Row or Delete Column from the menu bar.

- ▶ Click in a cell and press CTRL-SHIFT-A to delete a row, or CTRL-SHIFT -- (hyphen) to delete a column.

> **TIP** If you simply need to add or remove columns or rows and their exact location is not a concern, just change the number of rows or columns in the Properties Inspector. Rows are added or removed along the bottom of a table, while columns are added and removed along a table's right side.

FORMATTING TABLE BORDERS AND BACKGROUNDS

There are four fields in the Properties Inspector, shown in Figure 6-9, that allow you to modify the border and background attributes of a selected table:

- ▶ **Border** When you set a border value, you increase or decrease the thickness of the solid outline around your table. Setting a border value will also place outlines around each cell, which remain the same regardless of the border width you define. The space between each cell is controlled by modifying the CellSpace value in the Properties Inspector. Browsers usually display a border using a highlight color to create a three-dimensional effect. If you want your table borders to be invisible to your visitors, set the border width to 0.

FIGURE 6-9
Table border and background formatting tools in the Properties Inspector

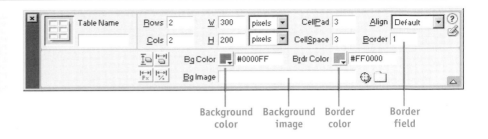

Background color · Background image · Border color · Border field

▶ **Brdr Color** Most browser's default border color is a neutral gray. You can set a color of your choice by using the border color well, or by entering a hexadecimal value into the field beside it. Browser support for defined border colors varies. Internet Explorer will display a solid colored border, losing the three-dimensional effect describe above, while Netscape uses a percentage of the color you defined to maintain that effect.

▶ **Bg Color** You can use the background color well to apply a color to a table's background. Again, browser support for this attribute varies. Internet Explorer will show the color behind the interior cell borders, while Netscape does not.

▶ **Bg Image** You can assign an image as a table background, by either entering the path and filename into the field provided, using the point-to-file icon and dragging it to a file icon in the Site window, or clicking the folder icon to browse for the file. Again, Internet Explorer and Netscape display the table borders the same way they do when using a background color.

MODIFYING ROW, COLUMN, AND CELL PROPERTIES

You can modify the properties of any individual cell, column, or row. In fact, you can modify any grouping of cells you choose to select. The tools in the Properties Inspector (Figure 6-10) don't vary a great deal between these elements, other than to signify what you've selected, since their attributes are virtually the same.

MODIFYING ALIGNMENT

Vertical and horizontal alignment of rows, columns, and cells is formatted using the Horz and Vert drop-down menus in the Properties Inspector:

FIGURE 6-10

The Properties Inspector displays the same tools for cells, rows, and columns.

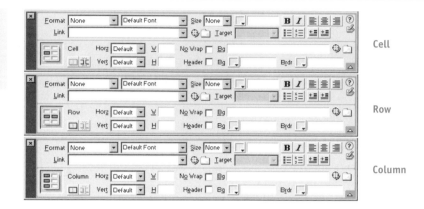

▶ **Horizontal Alignment** This can be set to the usual Left, Right, Center, or remain in the Default setting. Default defines no specific alignment attribute in the HTML code, leaving it to the browser, which usually aligns cell content to the left.

▶ **Vertical Alignment** This can be set to Top, Middle, Bottom, Baseline, or remain in the Default setting. The Default setting usually results in a middle browser alignment.

There is a difference between setting the alignment attribute of cells, rows, and columns and formatting the alignment of the specific content within them.

Imagine you set a row's alignment to the right. This is like hanging a sign that says, "Anything that falls into these cells lines up on the right side." However, you could also enter some text into one of those cells, select it, and then use the text alignment tools and align it to the left. Here we are with another dilemma about formatting precedence.

In HTML, the specific element always beats the more general one, so though cells beat rows, and rows beat tables, formatting applied to specific content inside the table cells trumps them all.

SETTING WIDTH AND HEIGHT

You can modify the width and height of selected table elements in a number of ways. You can enter pixel or percentage values directly into the W (width) and H (height) fields of the Properties Inspector, or you can position the cursor over a row or column border until the cursor changes to a two-headed arrow, then click and drag the border to the desired position (Figure 6-11).

Resizing columns and rows with the cursor displays the selected table's Properties Inspector, not that of the individual column or row being modified. Consequently, you cannot see the height and width values change in the Properties Inspector as you do when resizing a table. Therefore, your level of accuracy is diminished when modifying heights and widths in this fashion.

If the initial width value you set for the table in the Insert Table dialog box was a percentage, width values created by dragging borders will remain in percentages. If at any time you want to convert

> **TIP** If you set cell heights and widths to specific values, those settings will be adhered to unless you place content inside them that is bigger than the allotted space. In most cases, a cell's height will always expand to fit content. Width values will force text to wrap, however, unless the text is a continuous string, in which case the cell and table will conform to fit the text. It is possible to turn the automatic wrapping of cells off by clicking the No Wrap checkbox in the Properties Inspector.

 width values between percentage and pixels, select the table you want to modify and use the Convert Table Widths buttons in the Properties Inspector.

CLEARING ROW HEIGHTS AND COLUMN WIDTHS

Because you can enter height and width values directly into the Properties Inspector, it is possible to set mathematically impossible combinations that Dreamweaver will not override. For example, you could set the width of a

FIGURE 6-11

Dragging borders in the Document window to adjust width

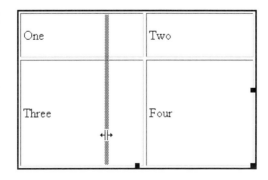

two-column table to 300 pixels and then go in and set the cells in each column to 50 pixels.

Though at first you may not notice any problems with the math or see an immediate malfunction in the Document window, you would be giving a browser fits, forcing it to decide what you intended, particularly in light of the widths of whatever content you may have placed in the offending cells. If you find yourself in such a predicament, or if for any other reason you wish to clear any height or width values you set, Dreamweaver provides a very handy tool for this purpose.

To Clear THE HEIGHT VALUES FROM A SELECTED TABLE:

▶ **Click the Clear Row Heights button to remove all height values from a table.**

To Clear THE WIDTH VALUES FROM A SELECTED TABLE:

▶ **Click the Clear Column Widths button to remove all width values from a table.**

MERGING AND SPLITTING CELLS

Making cells span multiple rows or columns is effortless in Dreamweaver, provided the selection of cells to be merged is contiguous and rectangular. Cells can just as easily be split into new rows and columns.

To merge any number of selected cells, use any of the following methods:

▶ Click the Merge Cells button in the Properties Inspector.

▶ Right-click the selected cells and choose Table | Merge Cells from the context menu.

▶ Select Modify | Table | Merge Cells from the Document window menu bar.

▶ Press CRTL-ALT-M.

To split a selected cell, use any of the following methods:

▶ Click the Split Cell button in the Properties Inspector.

▶ Right-click the cell you want to split and choose Table | Split Cell from the context menu.

▶ Select Modify | Table | Split Cell from the Document window menu bar.

▶ Press CTRL-ALT-S.

TABLE HEADERS

Table headers are a modified form of the cell tags `<td>` and `</td>`, written `<th>` and `</th>`. When they are used, any content placed in the cell is automatically aligned to the center, and any text in the cell is made bold.

To convert a selected cell to a table header, simply click the Header checkbox in the Properties Inspector.

FORMATTING CELL BORDERS AND BACKGROUNDS

Just like selected tables, you can also modify the backgrounds and borders of individual cells. The Properties Inspector for selected cells (shown in Figure 6-12) offers tools for these formatting choices similar to the Tables Properties Inspector.

▶ **Brdr color** A cell's border is a one-pixel-thick lining along the interior of a cell. Again, browser support for cell border colors varies. Internet Explorer supports this attribute, while the 4.*x* versions of Netscape do not.

▶ **Bg color** The background color attribute is also available for individual cells. Both Internet Explorer and Netscape support this attribute.

▶ **Bg image** As with the cell's big brother the table, you can also apply a background image to individual cells.

FIGURE 6-12

Cell border and background formatting tools in the Properties Inspector

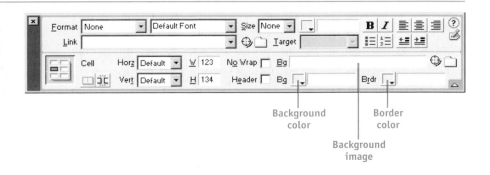

Background color   Background image   Border color

TABLE DESIGN SCHEMES

Dreamweaver offers a convenient interface for applying preset design schemes to data tables. Preset design schemes make it easy to quickly set colors and alignments across an entire table with one command.

To Apply A DESIGN SCHEME TO A SELECTED TABLE:

1 Select Commands | Format Table from the Document window menu bar to display the Format Table dialog box (Figure 6-13).

2 Select a design scheme from the scrolling list in the upper-left corner.

3 Use the Row Colors, Top Row, and Left Col options to make specific modifications to a design scheme.

4 Enter a border width value in the Border field.

5 Click OK.

FIGURE 6-13

The Format Table dialog box

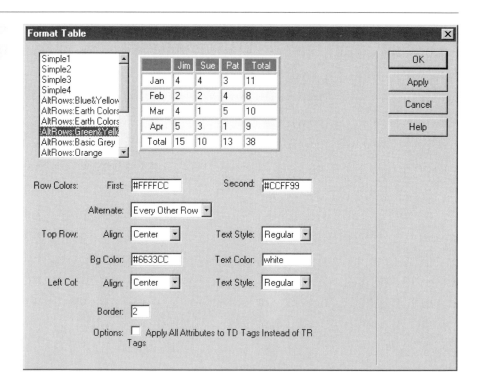

Since specific elements always take precedence over more general ones, you have the option of converting all your row formatting over to cell formatting using the Apply All Attributes To TD Tags Instead Of TR Tags checkbox. The table will still look the same; it will simply apply the formatting choices to each cell in the row instead of applying them once to the row itself. If you have a very large table, however, it is best to keep the formatting applied to the row since it will require less code, creating less work for the visitor's browser.

NESTING TABLES

Nesting simply means to put something inside something else. With HTML tables, you can easily nest an entire table inside the cell of another, as shown here. To nest a table, you need only place the cursor inside the cell of an existing table and use any of the table insertion methods discussed earlier in this chapter.

> **NOTE** In the example of table tags at the start of this chapter, I showed how cell tags sat inside row tags, which in turn sat inside table tags. This too is an example of nesting, only here you can't pull the individual row or cell tags out of a table and have them stand on their own. They can only exist in relation to one another. In a sense, because most HTML tags are container tags, you could say an entire HTML document is a series of nests—the opening and closing `<html></html>` tags holding the `<body></body>` tags, and these body tags in turn holding the other container tags that make up the visible document. Objects inside objects inside objects. To learn more about HTML, see Appendix A.

One	Two		
Three	Four		
		One	Two
		Three	Four

Nested tables are the prevalent strategy used to position elements on a page. Each table is an entity unto itself, modified as much or as little as the design requires. These tables in turn are placed within a larger table that defines regions and perimeters of the page itself. Figure 6-14 shows a browser's view of a page that was laid out using a number of nested tables, each with its border set to zero. Figure 6-15 shows the same page with the borders visible and the cell padding and spacing increased so you can see how the page is constructed.

FIGURE 6-14

Can you guess the number of tables?

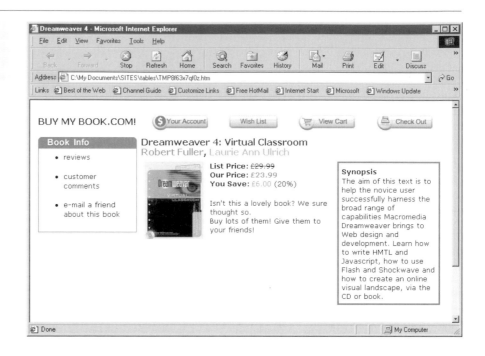

FIGURE 6-15

Here they are...

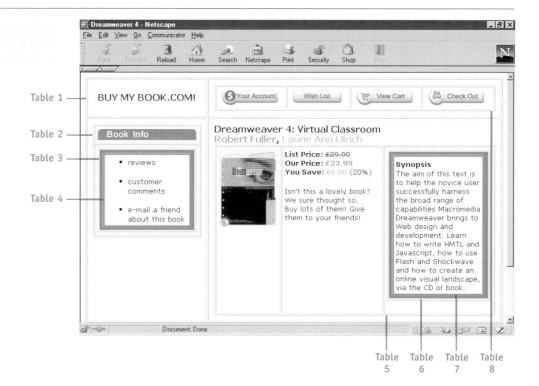

USING DREAMWEAVER LAYOUT VIEW

In this version of Dreamweaver, Macromedia introduces an innovative approach to table construction, called Layout view. It is a visually intuitive process that takes its cue from traditional print layout programs like Quark Xpress and Adobe PageMaker. For the first time in a visual Web design tool, you can now draw table cells directly into your document instead of defining them through a dialog box or other static interface component. Once you've drawn your cells, you can easily modify them and move them wherever you want.

Draw Layout Cell button

Draw Layout Table button

Layout view is accessed using the lower buttons of the Objects Panel (shown here). You can shift back and forth between Standard view and Layout view at will, and nothing created in either view will be lost. It simply changes how your table is represented in the workspace and the toolset at your disposal.

DRAWING CELLS AND TABLES

In Layout view, you can start by drawing the initial table perimeter and then populating the table with cells, or you can begin drawing cells straight away.

To Draw A TABLE:

1 Click the Layout View button of the Objects Panel. This displays the Getting Started In Layout View dialog box (Figure 6-16), which gives a brief explanation of the related Objects Panel buttons.

2 Click the Draw Layout Table button in the Objects Panel. The cursor will change to a crosshair.

3 Move the cursor to the desired location in the Document window, then click and drag to draw the table perimeter. Hold down the CTRL key to draw several tables in a row.

A tab appears at the top of each table created, which is used for selection purposes. The width of each table is displayed in the Column Header (Figure 6-17) at the top of the table.

FIGURE 6-16

The Getting Started In Layout
View dialog box

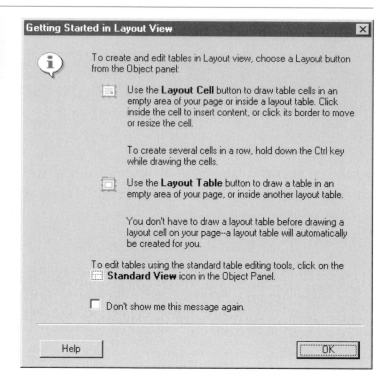

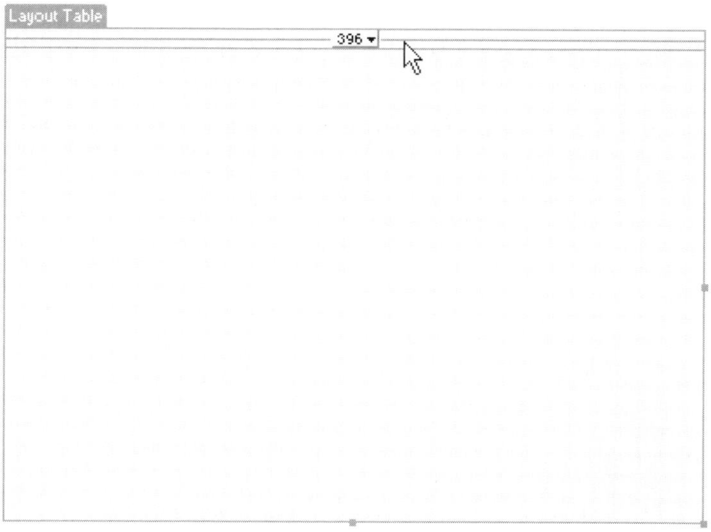

FIGURE 6-17

A layout table with column
header

To Draw A CELL:

1 Click the Draw Layout Cell button on the Objects Panel.

2 Move the cursor to the desired location in the Document window, then click and drag to draw the cell. Like drawing tables, holding down the CTRL key allows you to draw multiple cells without repeatedly clicking the Draw Layout Cell button.

If you insert a cell first, a table is automatically created to hold the cell, since it obviously can't exist outside of one. The table Dreamweaver creates will expand to fit the entire Document window, but can easily be modified to a fixed pixel width or a percentage value.

When cells are drawn close enough to each other, they will snap together. They will also snap to the edge of the Document window if drawn close enough to it. If you want to disable this snapping effect, press and hold the ALT key while drawing your cells.

NESTING TABLES IN LAYOUT VIEW

Nesting tables in Layout view is no different than drawing cells. Once you've created a layout table using any of the methods described earlier, simply click the Draw Layout Table button and draw another table inside its confines. You can even draw a nested table around cells in the existing layout table, making those cells part of the new nested table instead. If you change your mind, you can quickly remove a nested table by clicking the Remove Nesting button in the Properties Inspector (shown here), or by selecting the nested table and pressing DELETE.

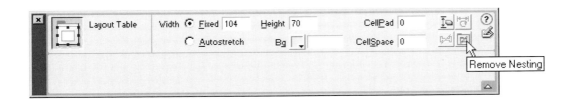

FIGURE 6-18

Mousing over a cell border

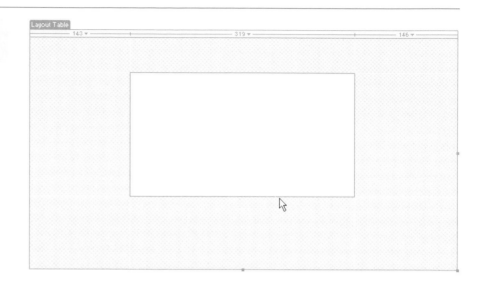

SELECTING LAYOUT CELLS AND TABLES

Selecting cells and tables is a bit more intuitive in Layout view than it is in Standard view. To select a table, simply click the tab in the table's upper-left corner. To select a layout cell, position the mouse over the cell's edge until the outline changes to red and click it (Figure 6-18). You can also select a cell by holding down the CTRL key and clicking anywhere inside it.

MOVING AND RESIZING CELLS AND TABLES

Layout view gives you the ability to visually adjust the size and location of cells and nested tables inside a layout table, and makes fine-tuning your page layout a fast and easy process.

To resize an individual table or cell, use either of the following methods:

▶ Select the table or cell to display its handles, and drag any of these to the desired size.

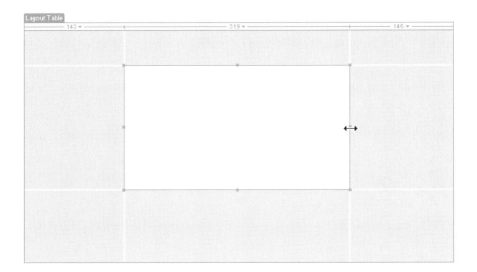

▶ Select the table or cell and enter width and height values directly into the Properties Inspector.

To move a cell or nested table, use either of these methods:

▶ Click the cell border or table tab and drag the element to the desired location.

▶ Select the cell or table and use the arrow keys to nudge the element one pixel at a time. Holding down the SHIFT key while using the arrow keys allows the cell or table to be moved ten pixels at a time.

FORMATTING CELLS AND TABLES

Most of the formatting options in Layout view relate to dimension and alignment, forsaking attributes that deal with visual properties. This is simply because the purpose of layout cells and tables is to provide invisible spacing elements for other page content, such as text and images.

Virtually all formatting of cells and tables in Layout view is accomplished with the Properties Inspector. Here you have control over height, width, cell alignment, cell padding and spacing, and background color. As you can see in Figure 6-19, the Properties Inspectors for each element are very similar.

FIGURE 6-19

The Properties Inspectors for
both selected cells and tables

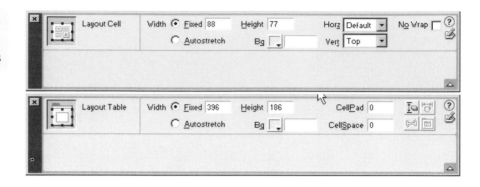

FIGURE 6-19

The Properties Inspectors for
both selected cells and tables

SETTING WIDTH AND HEIGHT

Setting the dimensional properties of both cells
and tables is a no-nonsense operation. Simply
select the element you want to modify and enter
pixel width or height values into the corresponding fields of the Properties Inspector. You'll
notice that in order to enter width values, the
Fixed radio button must be selected.

> TIP Just as in Standard view, you can
> set a cell's content to not wrap by
> clicking the No Wrap checkbox in the
> Properties Inspector.

If you need to remove the defined cell height values from a table to
make it better conform to the content you've placed inside it, select the
table and click the Clear Row Heights button.

If you have content that is forcing a cell to stretch beyond the originally defined
width, the new value will be displayed in parentheses in the table column header

(Figure 6-20). So as not to create conflicts for the browser, you can convert the column width to the value forced by the cell contents by clicking the Make Widths Consistent button.

SETTING CELL PADDING AND SPACING

To modify a table's cell padding or spacing, select the table and enter the desired
values directly into the Properties Inspector using the CellPad and CellSpace fields,
respectively (refer to Figure 6-19).

FIGURE 6-20

The Column Header displays both the original width and the forced width

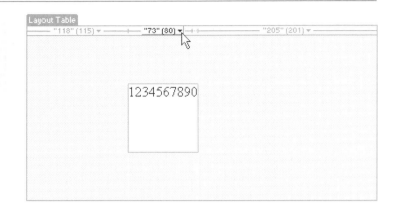

SETTING CELL ALIGNMENT

The alignment options for layout cells are identical to those in Standard view. To set a cell's horizontal and vertical alignment, select the desired cell and use the Horz and Vert drop-down menus in the Properties Inspector (refer to Figure 6-19).

BACKGROUND COLOR

Layout view also allows you to define background colors for tables and individual cells. Setting color attributes for either element employs virtually the same process used in Standard view. Simply select the element for which you want to define a background color, and use the Bg color well as you would with any other element that accepts a color value. You can also enter a hexadecimal value directly into the field provided (see Figure 6-21).

FIGURE 6-21

The Bg color well and value field in the Properties Inspector

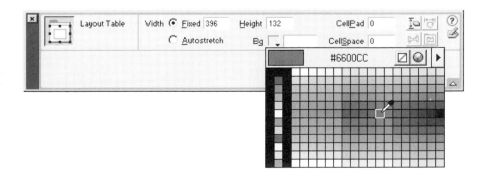

UNDERSTANDING LAYOUT WIDTH AND SPACER IMAGES

Up to this point, when discussing the widths of cells and tables, we've dealt with either pixels or percentages. Layout view refers to any width specified in pixels as being fixed width, because it's absolute, it can't vary, it's "fixed" in place.

To set a column width to fixed width, use either of the following methods:

► From the Column Header menu, select Make Column Fixed Width. This will set the column width equal to the width of the content already inside that column.

► Select a column cell and click the Fixed radio button, then enter a width in the field provided.

Where Standard view allowed you to enter percentage values for widths, Layout view offers *autostretch*, which effectively means setting a value of 100%. How can you set something to a value of 100% and still fit anything else on the screen, you ask? The answer is spacer images.

A spacer image is a 1 pixel × 1 pixel transparent GIF used by Dreamweaver to play a little trick on the browser. Instead of defining certain fixed widths directly in the HTML code, Layout view places an appropriately sized transparent GIF into an otherwise empty column cell of your layout table. When you define another column as autostretch, it attempts to fill the width of the screen, but runs up against the other column—the width of which is being maintained by the transparent GIF. The transparent GIF prevents the column from being collapsed.

To Set A COLUMN TO AUTOSTRETCH:

▌ Click the small arrow at the top of a column header to display the Column Header menu (Figure 6-22), and select Make Column Autostretch, or select a column cell and click the Autostretch radio button in the Properties Inspector. This displays the Choose Spacer Image dialog box, shown here.

FIGURE 6-22

The Column Header menu

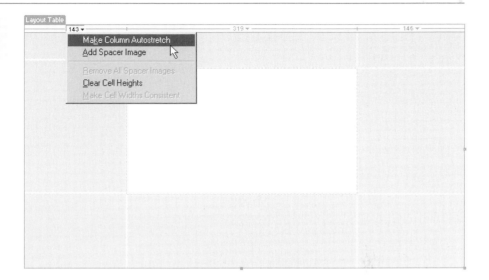

2 Select Create A Spacer Image File, and click OK. Then save the new spacer image to an appropriate location within your local site, as prompted by the Save Spacer Image File As dialog box.

If you have created a spacer image in another site and want to copy it to your present site, you can opt to use an existing spacer image file and then locate and save it to your present site. If you choose to turn off spacer images for autostretch columns, you will be warned that to do so may adversely affect your layout cells. If you do intend to use this option, be aware that all columns will shrink to the width of their cell's content. If there is no content in a column, it will collapse entirely. Though there may be times when you want to take advantage of this "shrink-wrapping" quality, it is best to still maintain the ability to use spacer images by setting one up, and simply choosing to remove any that are automatically inserted in the autostretch process.

To remove a column spacer image, simply select Remove Spacer Image from the Column Header menu. If you want to remove all spacer images from a layout table, select this option from the Column Header menu, or click the Remove All Spacers button in the Properties Inspector, shown next.

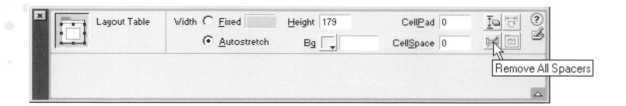

If at any time you need to insert an image spacer, that option is also available from the Column Header menu.

 ON THE VIRTUAL CLASSROOM CD-ROM Follow along with the instructor in Lesson 4, "Tables as Layout Tools," as he demonstrates how to use tables for more than just displaying data.

Building User Forms

A search engine uses a form to take a query from a visitor and return corresponding contents from its database. E-commerce sites use forms to fulfill orders and gather payment information. Guestbooks use a form to record visitor comments and post them back to the Web site. Forms, then, are used to structure and process information. They supply a level of interactivity, providing for the passage of information between Web sites and their visitors.

There is more to forms, however, than just the interface you create in a Web page. The form itself is just the point at which the information gets entered. In order for anything to become of that data, something needs to be done with it.

Enter the CGI script. CGI stands for the Common Gateway Interface. It is a standard for an external application (a script or program) to communicate with the Web server. The form sends information to the Web server, which passes it to the script. The script processes the information and either has the Web server pass something back to the visitor or holds and maintains the data for a future purpose. CGI scripts are written in languages such as Perl, C++, JavaScript, and VBScript. Unfortunately, Dreamweaver does not write CGI scripts for you. What it does do is allow you to quickly and effortlessly lay out a proper form, format its elements, and direct its input to a script on your Web server.

CREATING FORMS

There is more to creating a form than inserting form objects and formatting them to accept specific pieces of information. A visitor must understand what the form is meant to do and what is expected when filling it out. At the very least, the form must be functional. Any effort on your part to make it aesthetically pleasing won't be lost on your visitor either.

Even though this is a chapter on forms, realize that every aspect of Web design is touched on when making a good form. You could insert every possible form object discussed in this chapter and create a useful form (see Figure 7-1). If form objects are just dropped on the page with no thought to their placement and relationship to each other, however, and there are no words to describe their function, the form is useless to the visitor (see Figure 7-2). There is no other aspect of Web design that emphasizes the relationship between art and utility more clearly than creating forms does.

Form objects don't lay out cleanly when simply placed on a line next to text and images. For the most part, they are rectangular interface components that tend to stand out jarringly if not lined up evenly. Being that they are rectangular, they work quite well with another rectangular HTML element, tables. Figure 7-3 shows the form from Figure 7-1 as displayed in the Document window.

> **TIP** You are not limited to tables when laying out forms. Any HTML element can be used inside a form to affect its layout, the only restriction being that forms cannot be nested.

FIGURE 7-1

This form is laid out using a table, with the information required of the visitor clearly defined.

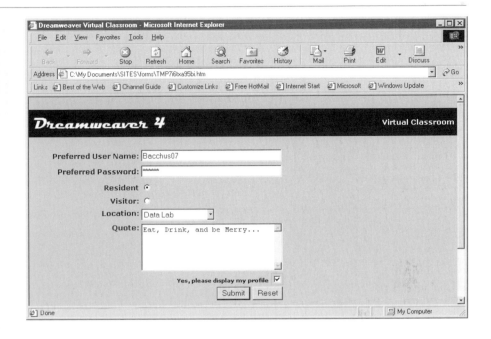

FIGURE 7-2

This form, however, has no form to it at all. The fields aren't labeled and there is no structure to the layout.

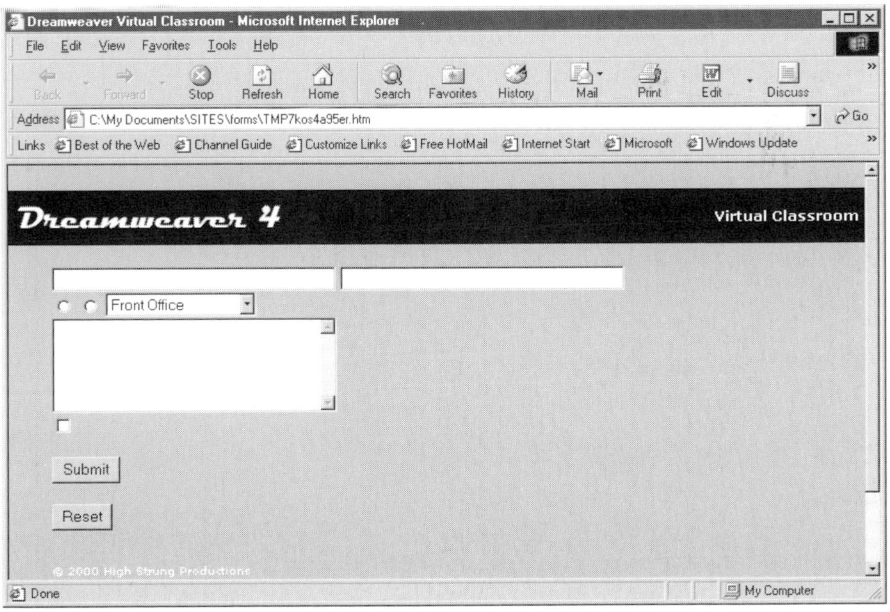

FIGURE 7-3

Forms and tables

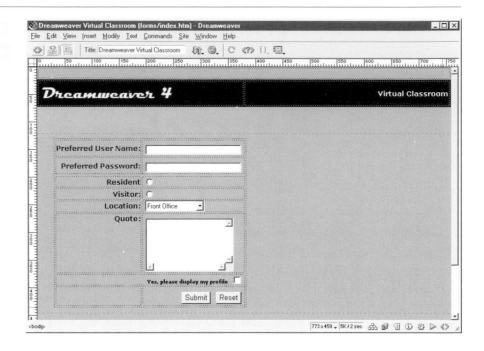

INSERTING FORMS

The Objects Panel provides a palette for inserting form objects. To access that palette, choose Forms from the Objects Panel menu (shown here).

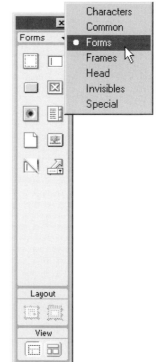

To insert a form, use either of the following methods:

▶ On the Objects Panel, click the Insert Form button.

▶ Select Insert | Form from the Document window menu bar.

You can also begin a form simply by inserting any of the form objects. Dreamweaver will ask you immediately if you want form tags inserted. Form objects occurring outside of, or without, form tags cannot submit data to a script, and in some cases will not be displayed by browsers.

Forms are delineated in the Document window with a broken orange line. Though this outline runs the width of the page, it is not a physical layout element and cannot be formatted. It is only a visual reference for you to see where forms begin and end.

If you do not see the form outline, make sure that Invisible Elements is turned on by selecting View | Visual Aids | Invisible Elements from the

FIGURE 7-4

The Form Delimiter checkbox

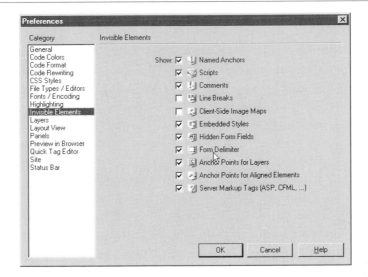

menu bar. If the outline still does not appear, select Edit | Preferences from the menu bar to open the Preferences dialog box. Choose Invisible Elements and click the Form Delimiter checkbox (see Figure 7-4).

There are three attributes for the overall form you will define in the Properties Inspector (see Figure 7-5):

▶ **Form Name** Used to identify the form, permitting it to be directly referenced by a script.

▶ **Action** Defines what is to be done with the form data. It is usually the URL to the script that will process the form.

▶ **Method** Defines how the information is sent to the Web server. POST sends the information to the server in the body of a message. GET sends the information to the server appended to the URL. Default leaves the method up to the browser, which is usually the same as GET. In most circumstances you will use the POST method, and this is the value Dreamweaver defaults to.

FIGURE 7-5

The Properties Inspector for a selected form

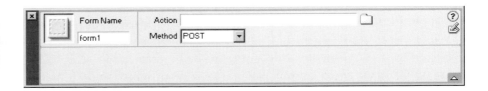

Once this initial form element is in place, the remainder of the process is adding the physical form objects that will receive the data from visitors. If at any time you want to select the form element, move the cursor over the form outline and click. When you go to insert form objects into the form, make sure the cursor is placed inside the form outline.

> **TIP** Every form object has a name attribute. When naming your form objects, avoid using spaces or uppercase characters. If you must have some type of separator, use underscores. For example, enter my_form for a form name, or first_name for a text field.

ADDING TEXT BOXES

A text box is just what the name implies. It is a field that allows the visitor to enter text-based information into the form (see Figure 7-6). There are three kinds of text boxes:

▶ **Text fields** Most commonly used for single-line, short responses, such as names, addresses, phone numbers, and so on.

▶ **Password fields** Text fields formatted so that text entered in them is hidden, appearing as asterisks.

▶ **Text areas** Used for multiple-line responses, such as user comments.

The method of inserting each type of text box is the same. You will define the type you want to create by selecting the appropriate radio button in the Properties Inspector (see Figure 7-7). Dreamweaver's default text box type is the text field.

To add a text field, place the cursor inside the form outline and use either of these methods:

FIGURE 7-6

Text boxes in action

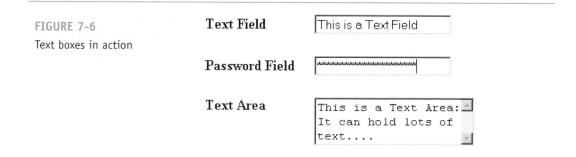

FIGURE 7-7

The Text Field Properties
Inspector

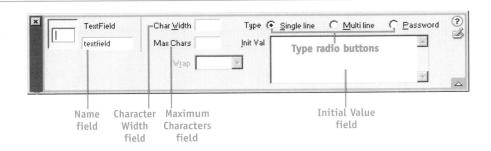

Name field   Character Width field   Maximum Characters field   Initial Value field

▶ Click the Insert Text Field button on the Objects Panel.

▶ Select Insert | Form Objects | Text Field from the menu bar.

TIP To quickly insert repeated form objects, select a form object and CTRL-drag it to a new location within the form. This instantly creates a new copy of the object which you can then format appropriately.

FORMATTING TEXT FIELDS

Once you have the text field inserted, you can format the following attributes:

▶ **Name** Use the field next to the Text Field icon on the left of the Properties Inspector to define a name for the object. Remember that fields must have unique names.

▶ **Character Width** Defines how many letters or numbers can be displayed in the text field at one time. The browser default for an undefined character width is approximately 20 characters.

▶ **Maximum Characters** Defines the total number of characters that can be entered into the text field. This is useful for preventing visitors from entering too much information into a field—for example, making an area code field only accept three digits.

▶ **Initial Value** Defines what, if anything, will be displayed in the field when the page initially loads.

▶ **Type** Use these radio buttons to select which type of text box you want to create: single-line text field, multi-line text area, or password field.

FORMATTING PASSWORD FIELDS

To Create A PASSWORD FIELD:

1 Insert a text field using either of the methods mentioned earlier.

2 Click the Password radio button in the Properties Inspector.

You can format the other attributes as you would an ordinary text field, only now when data is entered in the field, the contents will appear as asterisks or bullets.

FORMATTING TEXT AREAS

To Insert A MULTI-LINE TEXT AREA:

1 Insert a text field using either of the methods mentioned earlier.

2 Click the Multi-line radio button in the Properties Inspector.

Unlike a text field where you can limit the amount of text entered with the Maximum Characters attribute, text area input cannot be constrained. In the Properties Inspector, the Initial Value field expands to accommodate more text, and the Maximum Characters field changes to Number Of Lines. You can define the dimensions of your text area using the Character Width and Number Of Lines fields. The previously dimmed Wrap drop-down menu also becomes available (as shown here).

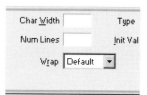

The Wrap drop-down menu allows you to control how a visitor's text is displayed when input goes beyond the original dimensions of the text area, as well as how that data gets submitted to the script. The following wrap options are available:

▶ Default Leaves the wrap attribute undefined. Internet Explorer will automatically wrap the text area input in the browser window. Netscape will not, causing text to scroll to the left when it exceeds the text area's original dimensions. The visitor must press the RETURN key to move to the next line. In either case, the information is submitted in a single line of text.

▶ Off Prevents Internet Explorer from wrapping text in the browser window. Data is still submitted in a single line of text.

▶ **Virtual** Wraps the displayed text in the browser window for both Netscape and Internet Explorer, but still submits the text in a single line.

▶ **Physical** Wraps the displayed text in the browser window for both Netscape and Internet Explorer. Data is now submitted with line break codes included, indicating the end of each displayed line in the text area.

ADDING RADIO BUTTONS AND CHECKBOXES

Radio buttons are used to have a visitor make a single selection from a list of choices. Any number of radio buttons can be inserted, but only one radio button can be selected at a time (see Figure 7-8). Checkboxes, by contrast, are used when multiple selections are desired of the visitor. For example, asking them to select a number of interests from a list of choices (see Figure 7-9).

FORMATTING RADIO BUTTONS

To insert a radio button, place the cursor inside the form outline, and use either of these methods:

▶ Click the Insert Radio Button icon on the Objects Panel.
▶ Select Insert | Form Objects | Radio Button from the menu bar.

Radio buttons and checkboxes have three attributes to be defined in the Properties Inspector (see Figure 7-10):

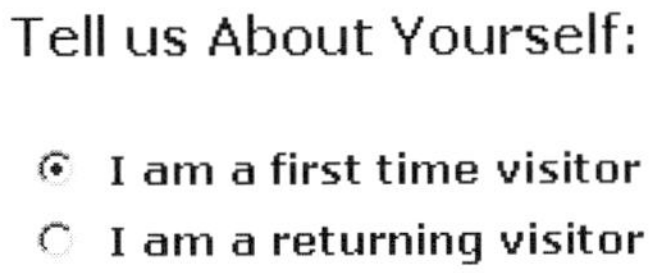

FIGURE 7-8
Radio buttons are for questions with only one valid answer.

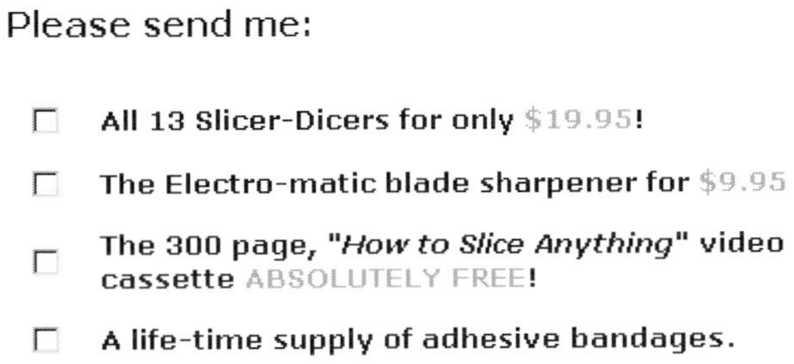

Tell us About Yourself:

⦿ I am a first time visitor
○ I am a returning visitor

FIGURE 7-9
Checkboxes are for multiple selections.

Please send me:

☐ All 13 Slicer-Dicers for only $19.95!

☐ The Electro-matic blade sharpener for $9.95

☐ The 300 page, "*How to Slice Anything*" video cassette ABSOLUTELY FREE!

☐ A life-time supply of adhesive bandages.

FIGURE 7-10

The Radio Button and Checkbox Properties Inspectors

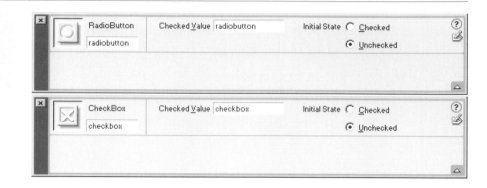

► **Name** Use the field next to the Radio Button icon on the left of the Properties Inspector to define a name for the object.

► **Checked Value** Defines the value to be sent to the processing script when the radio button is selected.

► **Initial State** Defines whether the radio button is checked or unchecked when the page loads.

Because radio buttons are used where only one valid selection is possible, they are normally added in groups of two or more. Where most form objects should receive their own unique name, a group of radio buttons should share an identifying name. The checked value will be what tells them apart. For example, if you have a required field that can only have one response, such as "Gender," you would insert two radio buttons and name them both something like **gender**, then set the checked values to "male" and "female". The data sent would then appear like this: "gender = male" or "gender = female."

> **TIP** By grouping radio buttons with identical names, you give them the ability to turn off when another in their group is selected. If you are able to select two radio buttons that are supposed to be in the same group, check to see that you've named them properly.

FORMATTING CHECKBOXES

To insert a checkbox, place the cursor inside the form outline, and use either of these methods:

► Click the Insert Checkbox button on the Objects Panel.

► Select Insert | Form Objects | Checkbox from the menu bar.

Unlike radio buttons, more than one checkbox can be selected at a time. Use them like you would an ordinary checklist, for example, to supply a list of options. Give each a unique name and a logical checked value, such as **pay_raise** and **yes**. When a checkbox is selected, its name and checked value are submitted. If the checkbox is left unchecked, it is not submitted.

ADDING MENUS AND LISTS

Menus and lists make excellent use of screen real estate. A drop-down menu, as shown to the right, lets you offer as many choices as you like while only taking up a single line.

To turn a menu into a list (as shown to the left), you simply change a formatting attribute, telling the list to display more lines. More options on the list than lines defined in it? That's okay—it sprouts scrollbars. This way you can control how many options are visible at one time. You can also let visitors make multiple selections from a list.

FORMATTING DROP-DOWN MENUS

To Insert A DROP-DOWN MENU:

1 Place the cursor inside the form outline.

2 Click the Insert List/Menu button on the Objects Panel, or select Insert | Form Objects | List/Menu from the menu bar.

3 Enter a unique name for the menu in the Name field of the Properties Inspector.

4 Select the Menu radio button.

5 To populate the menu with items, click the List Values button. This opens the List Values dialog box.

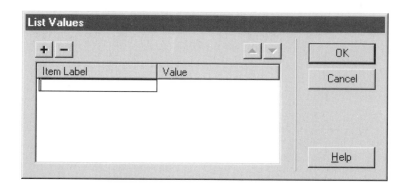

6 In the Item Label column, enter the menu item text you want displayed.

7 Press TAB to move to the Value field, and enter the data you want sent to the server when a visitor selects the menu item.

You can continue to press TAB to move through the dialog box, adding item labels and values until you are finished (see Figure 7-11), or you can use the Add (+) and Remove (–) buttons to add or remove items and values. If you want to change the order of items, select an item label and use the arrow buttons to the upper-right of the dialog box to move them up or down in the list.

When you've finished adding items, click OK to close the List Values dialog box. You will see the item labels displayed in the Initially Selected field of the Properties Inspector (see Figure 7-12). If you want one of the menu items to be displayed when the page loads, simply click one of them in the Initially Selected field, and you will see the selection reflected in the Document window.

FORMATTING SCROLLING LISTS

To insert a scrolling list, follow the same procedure involved in inserting a drop-down menu, but select the List radio button in the Properties Inspector.

> TIP If you want to conserve even more screen space when using a drop-down menu, make the first item label an instruction, instead of devoting a portion of the page to saying what the drop-down menu is for. Leave the value blank, and select that first item label in the Initially Selected field. To make a visual break between the prompt and the other list items, make the second item label a line by entering dashes. An example of this technique is visible in the drop-down menu and list examples on the previous page.

FIGURE 7-11

Press TAB to move through the dialog box fields, adding item labels and values.

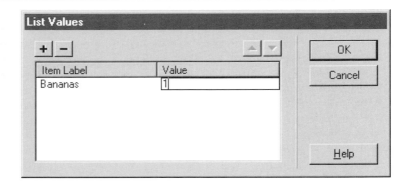

FIGURE 7-12

The Initially Selected field

The previously dimmed Height field and Allow Multiple Selections checkbox are now available.

Use the Height field to enter a line height value. If you select a line height that is lower than the actual number of list items, a scrollbar will appear in the right of the list. You can format the list to accept multiple selections by clicking the Allow Multiple Selections checkbox.

> **TIP** Your visitors have no way of knowing that multiple selections are possible unless you tell them. It is also a good idea to let them know *how* to make multiple selections, which varies based on your operating system. In Windows, visitors must hold down the CTRL key. In Macintosh, they use the COMMAND key.

WORKING WITH HIDDEN FIELDS

Hidden fields allow you to pass information to the server that you don't want the visitor to see. For example, you might use one script to process forms from a number of Web sites. You can use a hidden field to identify which site the form is sending data from.

To insert a hidden field, place the cursor inside the form outline, and use either of these methods:

▶ Click the Insert Hidden Field button on the Objects Panel.
▶ Select Insert | Form Objects | Hidden Field from the menu bar.

FIGURE 7-13

The Hidden Field Properties

Inspector

The Hidden Field icon will appear selected in the Document window. You can then enter a unique name and the value you want submitted in the appropriate fields of the Properties Inspector (see Figure 7-13).

The Hidden Field icon is one of Dreamweaver's invisible elements, so you must have them enabled in order to view, select, and modify them. If you do not see the small Hidden Field icon in the Document window, check to see that invisible elements are enabled by selecting View | Visual Aids | Invisible Elements from the menu bar. If the Hidden Field icon still does not appear, select Edit | Preferences from the menu bar to open the Preferences dialog box. Choose Invisible Elements and click the Hidden Form Fields checkbox.

ADDING FORM BUTTONS

Your visitors use form buttons to send the completed form to the server, clear the form if they make a mistake, or, if you have a knack for programming, execute a defined function. With these three basic possibilities come the three form button types:

▶ **Submit** Does pretty much what it says. It sends the form data on to the server, or technically, it invokes the ACTION using the specified METHOD.

▶ **Reset** Clears the form if the visitor made a mistake and wants to start over.

▶ **Button** This kind of blank button allows you to perform some desired task you can assign with JavaScript or other programming language.

FORMATTING BUTTONS

To insert a button, place the cursor inside the form outline, and use either of these methods:

▶ Click the Insert Button icon on the Objects Panel.

FIGURE 7-14

The Form Button Properties
Inspector

▶ Select Insert | Form Objects | Button from the menu bar. A default Submit
button is placed in the Document window.

Form buttons have three attributes you can define in the Properties Inspector
(see Figure 7-14).

▶ **Name** Enter a name for the button in the Button Name field.

▶ **Label** Enter the text you want to appear on the button's face in the Label
field.

▶ **Action** Use the Action radio buttons to control what happens when the visitor
clicks the button. Select None if you plan to assign an action with JavaScript
or other language.

USING GRAPHIC BUTTONS

If the typical buttons defined in HTML wreak havoc with your page design, you
can create graphic buttons with your favorite image editor and use them instead
by taking advantage of the image field form object. This method can only be used
to make Submit buttons.

To Insert AN IMAGE FIELD:

1 Place the cursor inside the form outline.

2 Click the Insert Image Field button on the Objects Panel, or select
Insert | Form Objects | Image Field from the menu bar.

3 From the Select Image Source dialog box (shown next), select your image from your
hard drive as you would when inserting any image, or enter the path to the image in
the field provided.

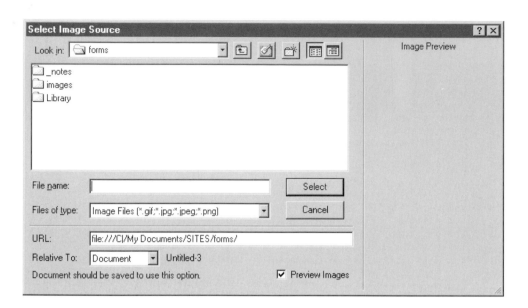

4   Click OK to close the dialog box and insert the image field into the Document window.

5   In the Properties Inspector, type submit in the Image Field field and enter alternative text in the field provided.

You have many of the same formatting options for an image field as you do with a regularly inserted image, with some exceptions. You can modify the dimensions of the image using the width and height fields in the Properties Inspector. You can also modify the image's alignment, but the formatting will be visible when the page is tested in a browser.

WORKING WITH FILE FIELDS

By inserting the File Field form object, you give your visitors a form-based method for uploading a file from their computer to your server. This method has largely been replaced by the use of e-mail file attachments.

To insert a file field, place the cursor inside the form outline, and use either of these methods:

▶ Click the Insert File Field button on the Objects Panel.

▶ Select Insert | Form Objects | File Field from the menu bar.

This inserts a text field and a Browse button (see Figure 7-15). You can format the text field's character width and maximum character length in the Properties Inspector (see Figure 7-16). You cannot modify the button's text or size. In a browser window, clicking the Browse button will open a Choose File dialog box, through which the visitor can select a file to submit with the form.

CREATING A JUMP MENU

A jump menu is a JavaScript-enabled drop-down menu that provides a space-saving method of navigating your site. With a jump menu, a visitor clicks the down arrow, makes a selection from the choices you provide, and is sent (or "jumps") to the appropriate location.

To avoid any unnecessary frustration, there are a few things you need to know about jump menus. With a plain-vanilla jump menu, visitors can't navigate back to the jump menu page and reselect a menu item they've already used. Essentially, each menu item becomes a one-shot deal. Believe it or not, there are times when this type of functionality is useful, particularly when you are building a form where you actually want to limit a visitor's options; but when creating your navigation strategy, this is not a good idea.

FIGURE 7-15

The File Field form object

FIGURE 7-16

The File Field Properties Inspector

There are two ways around this small obstacle:

▶ Instruct Dreamweaver to insert a blank menu item as the first choice in the list, and insert code that makes the browser reset to this item each time the page is loaded.

▶ Instruct Dreamweaver to insert a Go button so that the jump to the next location is activated by the button click instead of the item selection.

Implementing either of these methods is simply a matter of selecting the one you want to use in Dreamweaver's Insert Jump Menu dialog box and then making a few modifications, as described below.

To Insert A JUMP MENU:

1 Click the Insert Jump Menu button on the Objects Panel, or chose Insert | Form Objects | Jump Menu from the menu bar. This displays the Insert Jump Menu dialog box (shown in Figure 7-17).

2 Enter the text for the first list item in the Text field.

3 Click the Browse button next to the When Selected, Go To URL field to select the file you want to jump to when the list item is selected, or enter the pathname or URL

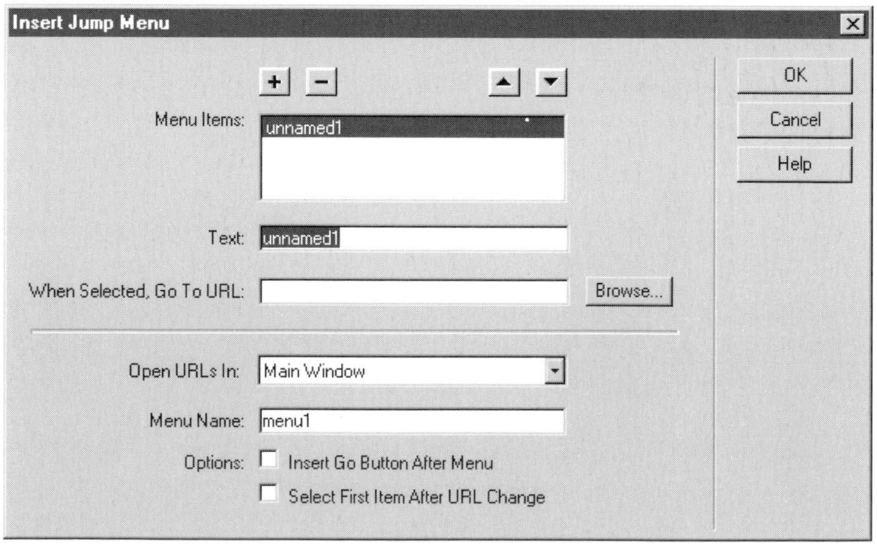

FIGURE 7-17

The Insert Jump Menu dialog box

Insert Jump Menu		
Menu Items:	unnamed1	OK / Cancel / Help
Text:	unnamed1	
When Selected, Go To URL:		Browse...
Open URLs In:	Main Window	
Menu Name:	menu1	
Options:	☐ Insert Go Button After Menu	
	☐ Select First Item After URL Change	

directly. If you are planning on using the blank menu item approach described above, don't enter a URL for the first list item.

4 Click the Add (+) button and repeat steps 2 and 3 to add list items.

5 Enter a unique name in the Menu Name field.

6 Under Options:

● Check Insert Go Button After Menu to insert a Go button to initiate each page jump.

● Check Select First Item After URL Change to have the menu reset to the first blank menu item after each jump.

7 Click OK to finish.

FORMATTING JUMP MENUS

There are two ways to format jump menus. You can select the jump menu and click the List Values button in the Properties Inspector, editing the menu through the List Items dialog box as you would an ordinary form menu. Alternatively, because a jump menu's functionality is predicated on the JavaScript behaviors Dreamweaver has inserted, you can access a dialog box very much like the one you used to build the jump menu by using the Behaviors panel (see Figure 7-18).

To access the Behaviors panel, use any of these methods:

▶ Click the Behaviors button on the Launcher (shown here).

▶ Click the Show Behaviors button in the Document window launch bar.

▶ Select Windows | Behaviors from the menu bar.

▶ Press SHIFT-F3.

Select the jump menu in the Document window, and double-click the highlighted Jump Menu event in the Behaviors panel to display the Jump Menu dialog box (see Figure 7-19). This dialog box mirrors the Insert Jump menu dialog box except the Go button option is not available.

FORMATTING GO BUTTONS

When you first insert a jump menu with a Go button, the button only activates a jump for the item presently displayed in the menu. If you select another item, the

FIGURE 7-18

The Behaviors panel

FIGURE 7-19

The Jump Menu dialog box

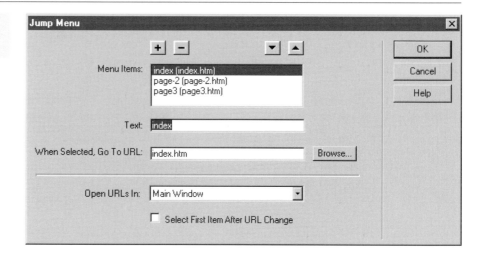

menu jumps without the use of the button. When you navigate back to the jump menu page, the last menu item selected is still displayed and you'd have to use the Go button to get to that page a second time. You can easily go into the Behaviors panel and make a small adjustment to make the Go button the only method for initiating a jump.

To Modify THE GO BUTTON:

1 Select the jump menu object.

2 Open the Behaviors panel using any of the methods described earlier.

3 Select and delete the Jump Menu event.

You can also use a graphic instead of the generic gray buttons.

To Insert A GRAPHIC BUTTON FOR A JUMP MENU:

1 Create a jump menu as described earlier. Do not select either of the checkboxes in the Options section.

2 Insert the image you want to use for your Go button beside the jump menu in the Document window.

3 Select the insert image and open the Behaviors panel.

4 Click the Add (+) button to display the available behaviors, and select Jump Menu Go from the event menu (shown to the right). This displays the Jump Menu Go dialog box (shown below).

5 Select the name of the jump menu from the drop-down menu, and click OK to close the dialog box.

6 In the Document window, select the jump menu object, and delete the Jump Menu event for it in the Behaviors panel.

ON THE VIRTUAL CLASSROOM CD-ROM Forms are an important part of many Web sites. In Lesson 5, "Creating Forms," the instructor demonstrates the process of inserting form fields and customizing them for logical and intuitive use by site visitors.

Working with Frames

Frames are intricate stuff. They demand a small mental shift for the beginning Web designer because a page designed with frames isn't just one page, it's a number of pages, all displayed in a single screen (see Figure 8-1). A site using frames needs a page for each frame's content and another page that defines the frames themselves. In other words, if there are three frames displayed on the screen, there are four HTML documents required to make it happen. Don't let this intimidate you, though. Dreamweaver makes that mental shift nearly painless. It allows you to visually build a frame-based site from the ground up, or apply predefined frames and add your content afterward.

FIGURE 8-1

A simple, frame-based page

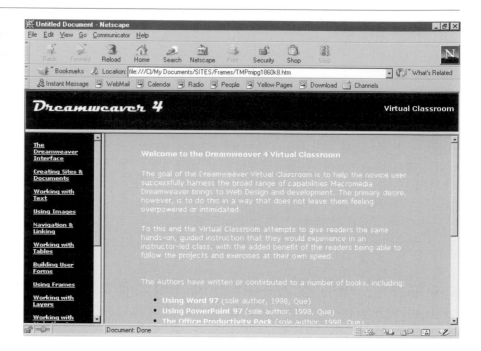

UNDERSTANDING FRAMES AND FRAMESETS

As I said, when you are looking at a frame-based Web page, you're looking at a number of documents simultaneously. The governing document is the *frameset*. It defines the number of individual frames and their attributes, as well as which documents to display inside them. The frameset document is more a set of instructions than a Web page, since what is actually seen in the browser window is the other documents it references. Indeed, a frameset has no `<body></body>` tags at all, so it can't display any content of its own other than the borders of the frames it describes. In a sense, a frameset is like a grand table whose rows and columns contain entire documents.

Like tables, a frameset's column widths and row heights can be set as fixed pixel amounts or as percentages of the browser window they are displayed in. Unlike tables, however, you can also set the size of a frame relative to the other frames in the frameset. Using this relative measurement allows you to set a fixed or percentage value for some frames, leaving a relative frame to fill the remainder of the browser window. A relative measurement also lets you set one frame dimension in proportion to another—effectively saying that regardless of the size of the browser window, one frame should always be so many times larger or smaller than another one.

Frames are predominantly used as a navigational strategy. You can create a page of links in one frame that, when clicked, will open new documents in another. This allows you to maintain consistency by keeping certain content permanently on the screen while other content is swapped out. Because you can control a frame's ability to scroll, you can fix those permanent frames in place while allowing the others to scroll based on the amount of content inside them.

INSERTING A FRAMESET

You can create a frameset by using the Frame Border visual aids and dragging frame borders into your document, or by dividing the Document window using commands from the menu bar.

To make frame borders visible, select View | Visual Aids | Frame Borders from the menu bar. This will add a visible border around the interior of the Document window (as shown here), which you are then free to manipulate with your mouse.

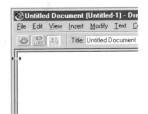

To create a new frameset, use either of the following methods:

▶ With your mouse, drag any of the frame borders to divide the screen horizontally or vertically (see Figure 8-2). Dragging from a corner will create four frames (as shown in Figure 8-3).

FIGURE 8-2

Drag any of the frame borders to divide the screen.

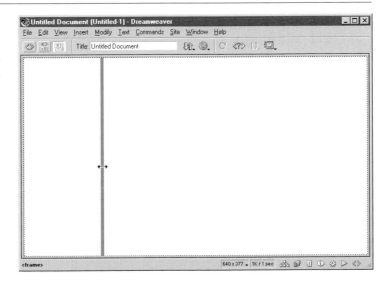

FIGURE 8-3

Dragging from a corner will
create four frames.

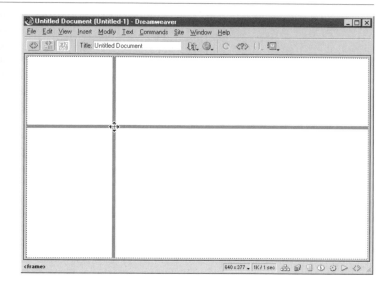

▶ Select Modify | Frameset | Split Frame, and choose Left, Right, Up, or Down.

You can use your mouse to position the frame border anywhere you like. Once
you've placed the initial borders, you can make new frames inside the frameset
by holding down the ALT key and dragging an interior frame border. You can
remove frames by simply dragging borders back off the Document window or
by dragging one border into another.

USING PREDEFINED FRAMESETS

Dreamweaver gives you the ability to insert a full frameset by simply
selecting a predefined configuration from the Objects Panel or the
Insert menu.

To insert a predefined frameset, use either of the following methods:

▶ Select the Frames category from the Objects Panel menu (shown here),
  and click the button of the frameset you want to use.

▶ Select Insert | Frames, and select Left, Right, Top, Bottom, Left and
  Top, Left Top, Top Left, or Split. These choices mimic identically the
  buttons on the Objects Panel, working left to right, top to bottom.

In the Frames Objects Panel, you will notice the buttons have a color
coding scheme. When you insert a frameset in this manner, Dreamweaver

incorporates the present document in the Document window, placing it inside the blue frame represented on the Insert button. The white frames represent the new frames that are added.

NESTING FRAMESETS

A nested frameset is just a frameset placed inside another one. After you've initially divided a page into two frames, each time you split an existing frame using the commands from the Modify menu, you are actually inserting a new frameset inside the existing frame. In HTML parlance, it is said the original frameset has spawned a *child*. That makes the original frameset the *parent*.

To nest a frameset, place the cursor in the frame in which you want a new frameset nested and use any of the following methods:

▶ Click the frameset button of your choice from the Objects Panel.

▶ Select Modify | Frameset | Split Frame Left, Right, Up, or Down.

▶ Select Insert | Frames and then select Left, Right, Top, Bottom, Left and Top, Left Top, Top Left, or Split.

If you want to nest the initial frameset inside an outer one, simply CTRL-drag any of the outside frame borders.

FORMATTING FRAMES AND FRAMESETS

When formatting the various frame and frameset properties, it's easy to get a little confused. There are so many things you can modify in a frames-based site. There are borders, scrollbars, row heights, and column widths. Not to mention adding content to the pages and targeting links from one frame or another. Don't panic. Dreamweaver makes this child's play.

SELECTING ELEMENTS WITH THE FRAMES PANEL

Like everything else in Dreamweaver, in order to format something you have to be able to select it. Dreamweaver provides an excellent tool specifically for selecting frame elements: the Frames Panel (see Figure 8-4). A miniature representation of your frameset's structure, it allows you to quickly select individual frames and nested framesets with a click of the mouse.

To open the Frames Panel, use either of these methods:

▶ Select Window | Frames from the menu bar.

▶ Press SHIFT-F2.

SETTING COLUMN AND ROW DIMENSIONS

You set the dimensions of your frameset's rows and columns in the Frameset Properties Inspector (see Figure 8-5). From here you can select the individual row or column and apply a fixed pixel value, a percentage, or a relative scale.

Relative units are commonly used in conjunction with pixel values so that while one frame stays fixed, the other expands to fill the rest of the browser window. You can also use relative units to create fractional heights and widths. For example, in a three-column frameset, by entering a value of 1 for each column and setting them to relative units, each frame will always occupy a third of the screen. In other words, 1 + 1 + 1 = 3 units. You could set the values in a progression, 1 unit, 2 units, and 3 units, and divide the screen in 1/6, 2/6, and 3/6 sections. For those of you who were good with fractions, this is your chance to show off.

FIGURE 8-4

The Frames Panel

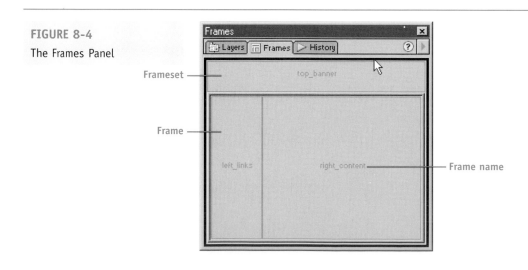

FIGURE 8-5

The Frameset Properties
Inspector

To Modify COLUMN WIDTHS AND ROW HEIGHTS:

Column tabs

Row tabs

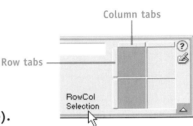

1 Select the frameset you want to modify.

2 Select the row or column you want to resize in the Properties
Inspector using the tabs of the RowCol Selection box (as shown here).

3 Enter a value in the Value field and select a unit of measure
from the Units drop-down menu.

FORMATTING BORDER PROPERTIES

Borders, and what you do with them, are the linchpins in a frame-based design.
They can be left to their own devices, free to be moved about by visitors for their
viewing convenience. Borders can be locked down to enforce a specific boundary.
You can change their color, change their thickness, make them flat, or conceal
them altogether.

SETTING BORDER STATES

There are three possible values for the border
attribute:

▶ Yes Displays borders as gray, three-dimensional
bars, approximately five pixels thick, unless
another value is entered in the Border Width field.

▶ No Flattens the borders. Internet Explorer
displays them approximately two pixels wide
when no value has been entered in the Border
Width field. Netscape simply flattens them.

▶ Default Leaves it to the browser, which usually
defaults to Yes.

TIP **Freedom can spawn excess. Less
can be more. Subtlety is a virtue.
Granted, sometimes less is just less, but
the point I'm trying to make is that just
because you can do something is no positive reason to do it. Twenty-seven individual frames in one frameset with
shocking pink borders and fuchsia background colors will only get you a listing
in the book *Web Pages that Suck*. Of
course, that might be your intention,
but you get the idea.**

Border properties can be set in both the Frame and Frameset Properties Inspectors (see Figure 8-6). Be aware that any border property assigned to a frame will override those assigned to the frameset.

SETTING BORDER WIDTH

In the Frameset Properties Inspector, directly below the Borders drop-down menu, is the Border Width field. Entering a value will set the pixel width of each border in that frameset. If you set the border width to 0, Netscape Navigator will hide the borders completely. Internet Explorer requires that you also set the Border state to No to achieve the same thing.

> **TIP** When setting the border attribute at the frame level, realize that one frame's borders can't be set to No while the adjacent frame is set to Yes and achieve any success. In other words, frames that share a common border can't have conflicting border attributes.

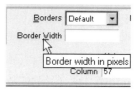

PREVENTING THE RESIZING OF FRAMES

By clicking the No Resize checkbox in the Frame Properties Inspector, you can prevent visitors from dragging the selected frame's border in the browser window. This can help you enforce your design intentions, and prevent visitors from accidentally hiding parts of the page content and navigation interface. Enabling the No Resize attribute does not prevent you from moving borders while working in the Document window, however.

FIGURE 8-6

The Borders drop-down menus in both Frame and Frameset Properties Inspectors

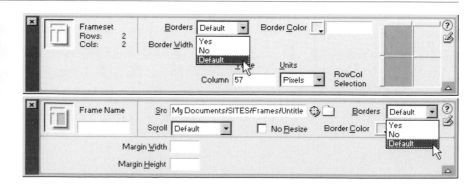

SETTING BORDER COLORS

To assign a border color, enter a hexadecimal value in the Border Color field or use the color well to select a color from the palette. Border colors also can be set at both the frame and frameset level (see Figure 8-7). Again, frame settings will override a frameset value.

SETTING SCROLLBAR PROPERTIES

Scrollbars get added by default if a frame's page content exceeds its viewable dimensions. To set the scrolling attribute, select the frame you want to modify and choose any of these options from the Scroll drop-down menu in the Properties Inspector:

▶ **Yes** Displays scrollbars regardless of the amount of content in the frame.

▶ **No** Disables scrollbars entirely.

▶ **Auto** Displays scrollbars if the amount of content requires them.

▶ **Default** Leaves the scrolling attribute undefined, letting the browser decide if it requires them. In most cases, this is equivalent to Auto.

> **TIP** Scrollbars cut into the viewable space of a frame, subtracting from your content's real estate. Because text, borders, and application windows display differently across browsers, operating systems, and monitor resolutions, your layout can vary from visitor to visitor. Before you set the scrolling attribute to No, be sure to test your site across as many browsers and platforms as you can.

FIGURE 8-7

Both Frame and Frameset Properties Inspector Border Color tools

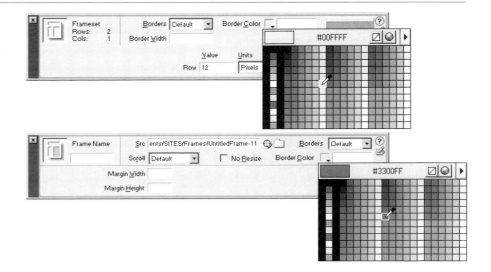

SETTING FRAME MARGINS

In an ordinary document, you'd apply margin settings through the Page Properties dialog box, which would write attributes to the `<body>` tag. This presents a small problem with frames—there *is* no `<body>` tag. Not to worry. In frames, there are two margin attributes you can modify:

▶ **Margin Width** Defines the pixel distance between a frame's contents and its left and right frame borders.

▶ **Margin Height** Defines the pixel distance between a frame's contents and its top and bottom frame borders.

> **TIP** Don't just set a value for one margin attribute and leave the other alone. It makes the undefined attribute default to 0, which will slam your content flush to whichever margin you didn't define. Also be aware that some old browsers don't recognize margin attributes and will simply ignore your settings.

To set the margin width and margin height of a frame, simply select the frame you want to edit, and enter pixel values into the fields provided in the Properties Inspector.

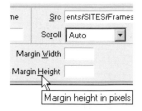

TARGETING FRAMES

If you want the links in one frame to open the documents they point to in another frame, you need to add an extra piece of information to your link. You need to make the one frame aim its links at, or *target,* the other frame. This is a two-step process: first, you give each of the frames in your frameset a unique name, then you reference these names when creating your links. With Dreamweaver, once you've named your individual frames, adding the target information is simple.

Any Properties Inspector that displays a Link field also has a Target field right beside it. When you assign names to the frames in your frameset they are added automatically to the Target drop-down menu. To target a frame you just select its name from the Target field drop-down menu in the Properties Inspector, as shown in Figure 8-8.

Be aware that for all intents and purposes, a frame is a little browser window unto itself. Any untargeted links simply open inside the frame they're in, so if you target a link to open another site inside one of your frames, that site's links will conveniently continue to open inside that frame. On the flip side, say you've for-

FIGURE 8-8

If you can assign a link to it in the Properties Inspector, you can assign a target as well.

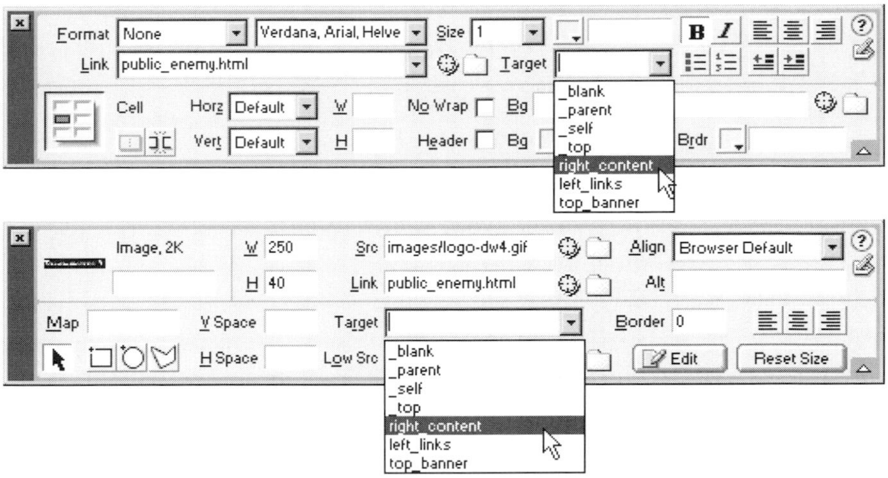

matted one frame in your layout to be a narrow, non-resizable frame to hold navigation links and you forgot to target one of them. When that link is clicked and a full-size document appears inside the same frame with 90 percent of the viewable content obscured, your visitors will be less than pleased.

To Name A FRAME:

1 Select a frame using any of the methods described in this chapter.

2 Enter a unique name in the Frame Name field of the Properties Inspector.

To Target A FRAME:

1 Select the text, image, or other object you want to assign a link to in any of the frames in your layout.

2 In the Properties Inspector, create a link to the document or other site you want it to open.

3 Locate the Target drop-down menu in the Properties Inspector, and select the name of the frame you want the document or other site to be opened in.

SPECIAL TARGET NAMES

Besides the frame names you defined, the Target drop-down menu also holds default target names:

▶ **_blank** Opens the document in a new browser window.

▶ **_parent** If the link is in a nested, child frameset, this target opens the document in the link frame's parent frameset.

▶ **_self** Opens the document in the current frame. This is equivalent to not defining a target at all.

▶ **_top** Displays the new document in the entire browser window, replacing the frameset altogether.

SETTING A BASE TARGET

If you've got the gumption to write a little HTML, you can tell a document to target a specific frame by default, without assigning individual targets to each link, by setting a base target.

To Set A BASE TARGET:

1 Click anywhere inside a frame to select the document.

2 Click the Code View or Code And Design Views button on the toolbar to view the HTML. If necessary, scroll to the top of the code:

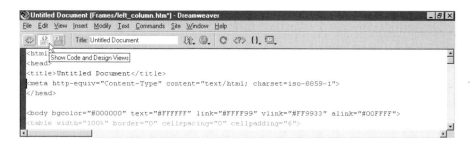

3 Place the cursor directly after the closing `</title>` tag and press enter to insert a new line.

```
<html>
<head>
<title>Untitled Document</title>

        I

<meta http-equiv="Content-Type" content="text/html; charset=iso-8859-1">
</head>

<body bgcolor="#000000" text="#FFFFFF" link="#FFFF99" vlink="#FF9933" alink="#00FFFF">
<table width="100%" border="0" cellspacing="0" cellpadding="6">
  <tr>
```

4 Enter **<base target=**_"your-frame-name-here"_**>**, **where** _your-frame-name-here_ **represents your unique frame name. Be sure to include the quotation marks.**

```
<html>
<head>
<title>Untitled Document</title>

<base target="right_content">

<meta http-equiv="Content-Type" content="text/html; charset=iso-8859-1">
</head>

<body bgcolor="#000000" text="#FFFFFF" link="#FFFF99" vlink="#FF9933" alink="#00FFFF">
<table width="100%" border="0" cellspacing="0" cellpadding="6">
  <tr>
```

Using the base target tag can create a situation where the _self target might come in handy. With a base target defined, that target is now the default frame for all links in that document, so you'd use the _self target when you needed a link in that document to open inside its own frame.

TARGETING LINKS IN OTHER DREAMWEAVER INTERFACE ELEMENTS

In Dreamweaver, there are a number of navigation elements where you define links through dialog boxes—for example, navigation bars, as discussed in Chapter 5, and the jump menu covered in Chapter 7. Each of the dialog boxes has fields for assigning targets, but doesn't necessarily inform you that's what they're for.

To assign a target frame to a link in a navigation bar:

▶ In the Insert Navigation Bar dialog box (see Figure 8-9), use the drop-down menu to the right of the Browse button in the When Clicked, Go To URL field, and select Main Window to open the file in the same window, or select an appropriate frame name.

To assign a target frame to a link in a jump menu:

▶ In the Insert Jump Menu dialog box (see Figure 8-10), use the Open URLs In drop-down menu and select Main Window to open the file in the same window, or select an appropriate frame name.

SAVING YOUR WORK

A frameset is made up of a number of related files, so saving files has a few more options than saving an ordinary document. Initially, the frameset and frames have

FIGURE 8-9

Use the Insert Navigation Bar dialog box to assign a target frame to a link in a navigation bar.

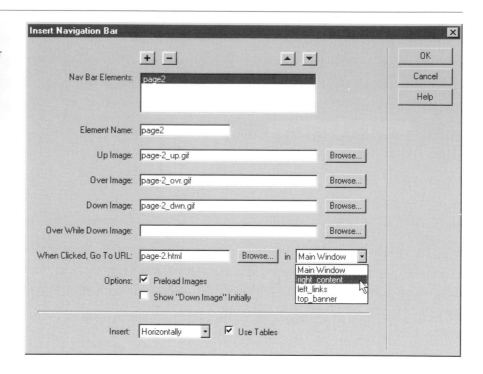

FIGURE 8-10

Use the Insert Jump Menu dialog box to assign a target from to a link in a jump menu.

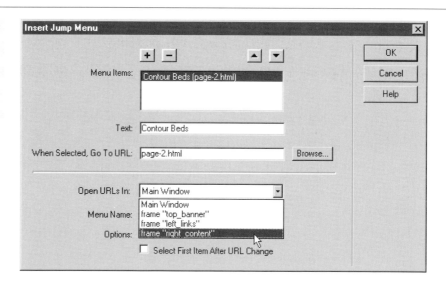

temporary Untitled file names just like ordinary documents. The frameset is called UntitledFrameset-1.htm, and each frame will be called UntitledFrame-1, UntitledFrame-2, and so on. The original document in the Document window (before the frameset was created) is put inside a frame, but simply remains Untitled.htm until given a proper file name.

To save a selected frameset, use any of the following methods:

▶ Select File | Save Frameset from the menu bar.

▶ Choose File | Save Frameset As to save the frameset as a different file.

To save a selected frame document:

▶ Select File | Save Frame, or File | Save Frame As.

To save all the associated files in a frameset:

▶ Select File | Save All Frames. The Save As dialog box will cycle through all
the associated files, allowing you to save them with a specific name. The
Document window will highlight each frame with a thick, dashed outline
as you are asked to save them.

ADDING PAGE TITLES TO A FRAMESET

Because the parent frameset document is the home page from a frame-based site,
it's the one you want to define a title for in order to display appropriate text in a
Web browser's title bar.

To title the parent frameset document, select it and use either of these methods:

▶ Enter the page title into the Title field of the Toolbar.

▶ Select Modify | Page Properties from the menu bar and enter a page title into
the Title field of the Page Properties dialog box (see Figure 8-11).

ADDING FRAME CONTENT

We've discussed the mechanics of frames and their formatting, but there's been
no discussion of how to actually put stuff in the pages themselves. This is because
adding content to frames pages is almost a no-brainer. However, Dreamweaver
does have some nice options that bear mentioning.

The simplest way to add content to a frame is to just click inside it and start working. Each frame is like its own little document window, and the same general rules

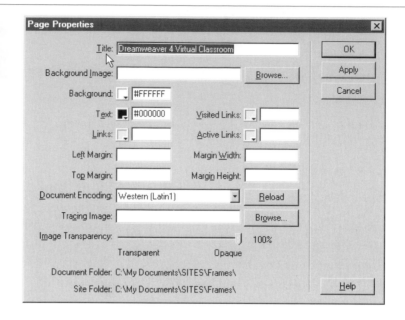

FIGURE 8-11

The Page Properties dialog box

apply. You can edit the document directly inside the frame using all the same formatting options you normally would. You can also open an existing document inside a frame, and voilà—instant content.

To open an existing document in a frame, select the frame in which you want to open a document, and use any of the following methods:

▶ In the Properties Inspector, drag the Src field point-to-file icon to a file in the Site window.

▶ Enter the path or URL of a document into the Src field. Use the Browse button to locate the file manually.

▶ Select File | Open In Frame from the menu bar, and choose a file or enter a URL with the Select HTML File dialog box.

ACCOMMODATING OLDER BROWSERS

A small portion of visitors may have browsers that do not support frames, in which case you want to define some content they'll be capable of viewing. This is referred to as creating noframes content,

> **TIP** There's no real way to view the NoFrames content of your frameset unless you can test it in a browser that doesn't support frames. What you can do instead is copy and paste the content from the NoFrames Document window into an ordinary document, save it, and test it from there.

because you are entering the equivalent of a regular Web page between
`<noframes></noframes>` tags at the bottom of the HTML code.

To Create CONTENT FROM NON-FRAME BROWSERS:

1 Select Modify | Frameset | Edit NoFrames Content from the menu bar. This displays the NoFrames screen in the Document window.

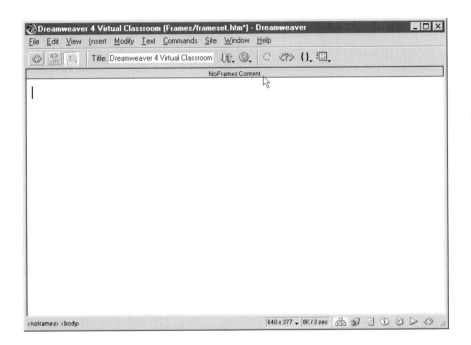

2 Insert content as you would in an ordinary document.

3 To return to your frameset, select Modify | Frameset |Edit NoFrames Content a second time.

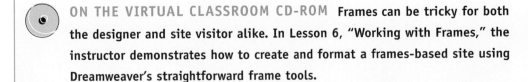

ON THE VIRTUAL CLASSROOM CD-ROM Frames can be tricky for both the designer and site visitor alike. In Lesson 6, "Working with Frames," the instructor demonstrates how to create and format a frames-based site using Dreamweaver's straightforward frame tools.

9

Working with Layers

When you think of layers, what do you picture?

Something on top of something else, right? The word "layer"

speaks for itself. Whether you're thinking winter clothes,

coats of paint, layer cakes, or onion skins, the concept is

basically the same.

With Web page layers, you define separate levels of page content that can be

▶ Stacked in front of each other

▶ Given an exact position anywhere on the screen

▶ Revealed independently, while other layers remain hidden

▶ Animated to move around the screen or be moved by visitor actions

This is fairly cutting-edge stuff, however, so these effects can only be displayed in Netscape and Internet Explorer versions 4.0 and later. And even then, support is not 100 percent consistent.

CREATING LAYERS

Creating layers in Dreamweaver is a nearly effortless process. Layers can be drawn in the Document window just like layout tables, inserted with menu commands or dragged onto the page from the Objects Panel. There is no limit to the number of layers a document can contain, and like tables and frames, layers can be nested inside one another.

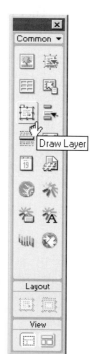

To create a layer, use any of the following methods:

▶ Click the Draw Layer button on the Objects Panel, then click and drag the cursor across an area of the Document window, as shown in Figure 9-1.

▶ Position the cursor in the Document window, and select Insert | Layer from the menu bar.

▶ Drag the Draw Layer button onto the Document window.

The Window Size pop-up menu on the Status bar displays the dimensions of your layer as you draw it in the Document window. By holding down the CTRL key while drawing layers, you can draw as many as you want without returning to the Objects Panel or Insert menu.

An anchor point icon appears in the Document window for each layer you create on a page. If you do not see the icon, be sure you have visual aids turned on by selecting View | Visual Aids | Invisible Elements from the menu bar. If you still don't see the icon, select Edit | Preferences, and choose Invisible Elements from the Category list, then make sure the Anchor Points For Layers checkbox is marked.

Because invisible element icons take up screen real estate in the Document window, they can force your page content to shift a bit to make room for them. Don't worry. These

FIGURE 9-1

Just like layout tables, you click and drag the cursor to draw a layer anywhere in the document.

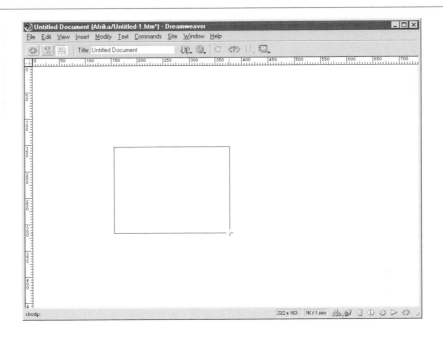

icons are for reference purposes only and are not in any way part of your actual document. They have no impact on the way your page displays in the browser window.

WORKING WITH THE LAYERS PANEL

When working with layers, you'll want some way to quickly pinpoint which layers are visible, the order in which the layers are stacked, and which layers are nested. Dreamweaver, of course, provides just the tool for the job: the Layers Panel.

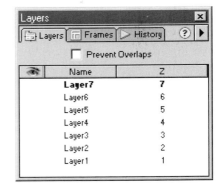

To access the Layers Panel, use either of these methods:

▶ Select Window | Layers from the menu bar.

▶ Press the F2 key.

The Layers Panel provides a list of the layers in your document, displaying the first layer you created at the bottom and the most recently created layer at the top. This list represents the layer's *stacking order*.

Imagine layers as physical, three-dimensional entities, like transparency sheets dropped on an overhead projector. The stacking order would correspond to where each layer sits in relationship to the glass (see Figure 9-2). The layer at the bottom of the list would be right on the glass itself, while the one on top is the farthest

FIGURE 9-2

Layers bring three dimensions to a two-dimensional medium. Notice the layers and their stacking order, and how that affects their placement on the page.

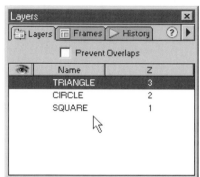

from it. The attribute that defines a layer's place in the stacking order is called the Z-index. This is the number displayed in the right column of the Layers Panel. The lower a layer's Z-index number, the lower its position in the stack.

To modify a layer's stacking order using the Layers Panel, use either of the following methods:

▶ Click on the layer name and drag it to the desired position in the stacking order.

> **TIP** By default, Dreamweaver will name your layers Layer 1, Layer 2, and so on as you create them. You can name them anything you like by either double-clicking on the name in the Layers Panel and entering a name of your choice, or entering a name into the Layer ID field in the Properties Inspector.

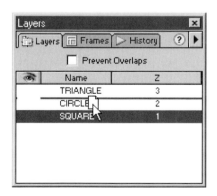

> **TIP** Z-indexes don't need to be unique to each level. If you have a number of layers that don't overlap, they can share a Z-index if you so choose. If, however, two layers with the same Z-index do overlap, the layer that appears first in the HTML code will be displayed on top.

▶ Click the layer's Z-index number and enter a new value.

You can also assign a new Z-index number to a layer using the Properties Inspector. To do so, select a layer using either the Document window or Layers Panel and enter a new value in the Z-index field (as shown on the next page).

FORMATTING LAYERS

Up to this point, element formatting has been strictly two-dimensional, and element placement mostly a matter of relative alignment. With layers, however, elements can be placed in exact positions three-dimensionally: left to right, top to bottom, and front to back. You can even control a layer's visibility, turning the layer on or off. Of course, before you can implement any of these changes, you need to be able to pick individual layers out of the pack.

SELECTING LAYERS

Selecting a layer is basically just a matter of clicking on it, and there are a number of places in which to do this.

> TIP **You can select multiple layers by holding down the SHIFT key while clicking on layer borders in the Document window or on layer names in the Layers Panel.**

To select a layer, use any of the following methods:

▶ Click on a layer's border in the Document window.

▶ Click a layer name in the Layers Panel.

▶ Click a layer's anchor point icon in the Document window.

Once selected, the layer will display individual resize handles on all sides and corners, as well as a larger selection handle on the upper-left corner.

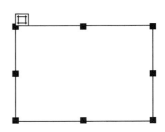

To place the cursor inside a layer so you can insert content, simply click inside the layer border. This keeps the selection handle visible with the cursor flashing in the upper-left corner of the layer.

NESTING LAYERS

Just like nesting tables or framesets, nesting a layer is simply a matter of placing one layer inside another one. To nest a layer, place the cursor inside an existing layer and use any of the following methods:

▶ Click the Draw Layer button on the Objects Panel and hold down the ALT key while drawing a new layer within the existing layer's border.

▶ Drag the Draw Layer button and drop it inside the existing layer.

▶ Select Insert | Layer from the menu bar.

To Nest AN EXISTING LAYER:

1 In the Layers Panel, select the layer you want to nest from the Name column.

2 Press and hold the CTRL key and drag the selected layer on top of the layer in which you want it nested.

3 Release the mouse to nest the layer.

When you drag the layer name, a small document icon appears under the mouse. Once the cursor is in the correct position over the layer you want to nest inside, a box appears around the layer name and Z-index number, at which point you can release the mouse. The nested layer will appear indented beneath its parent layer in the Layers Panel, as shown here.

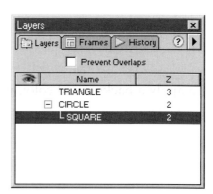

RESIZING LAYERS

Layers can be resized one at a time, or you can resize a group of selected layers to give them all the same dimensions.

To resize a selected layer, use any of the following methods:

▶ Drag any of the layer's resize handles.

▶ In the Properties Inspector, enter values for width (W) and height (H) in the appropriate fields.

▶ Press and hold the CTRL key, and use the UP and DOWN arrow keys to adjust the layer height, and the LEFT and RIGHT arrow keys to adjust the layer width.

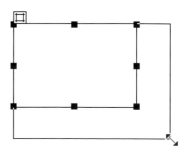

To resize a number of selected layers, use either of the following methods:

▶ Select Modify | Align | Make Same Width (or Height) from the menu bar. This method makes each selected layer conform to the last layer selected, which is displayed with black resize handles.

▶ In the Properties Inspector, enter values for width and height in the appropriate fields.

SETTING LAYER BACKGROUNDS

You can apply a color or image to a layer's background in the same way you would a table cell's by using the appropriate tools in the Properties Inspector.

To apply a background color, use either of these methods:

▶ Click the color well and choose a value from the color swatch.

▶ Enter a hexadecimal value directly into the field provided.

To apply a background image, use either of these methods:

▶ Click the folder icon beside the Bg Image field to browse for an image from your hard drive.

▶ Enter the path and file name of the image directly into the Bg Image field.

POSITIONING LAYERS

Positioning is what makes layers special. You can put any content you like inside a layer and specify exactly how many pixels from the left of the browser window and how many pixels from the top of the browser window that layer should be.

To position a selected layer, use either of the following methods:

> **TIP** The default unit of measurement for both layer size and layer position is pixels, and you'll notice that unlike other elements such as images and tables, an abbreviation (px) follows the number values. This is because you can specify different units of measure when working with layers. For example, centimeters (cm), inches (in), millimeters (mm), percentage (%), picas (pc), and points (pt). When entering values in the Properties Inspector, the abbreviation must follow the number value without any spaces, like so: 300px.

▶ Drag the selection handle and release the mouse when the layer is in the desired position. By watching the L (left) and T (top) fields in the Properties Inspector, you can choose an exact location.

▶ Enter exact pixel values into the L (left) and T (top) fields in the Properties Inspector.

If the layer is nested, the left and top pixel values will be in relation to the parent layer's top and left side. If you want to prevent layers from overlapping, click the Prevent Overlaps checkbox on the Layers Panel.

By default, Dreamweaver inserts a JavaScript function whenever you create layers. The function addresses a bug in Netscape 4.x generation browsers that causes the browser to lose the positioning coordinates when the visitor resizes the browser window. This script forces the page to reload whenever the browser window is resized to reestablish those coordinates.

When positioning layers, the Document window rulers come in handy. To view the rulers, select View | Rulers | Show from the menu bar. If possible, try to use the same unit of measure on the rulers that you're using to define your layer positions.

USING THE GRID

The Document window grid can be a helpful guide when positioning your layers. The grid also comes in handy when drawing or resizing your layers. Layers also do something no other element in Dreamweaver can do: snap to the grid. By this I mean that the layer will jump to a grid line if you release the layer within a certain distance of the gridline. To view the grid, select View | Grid | Show Grid from the menu bar.

To Make LAYERS SNAP TO THE GRID:

1 Select View | Grid | Snap To Grid.

2 Drag a selected layer to a grid line until it sticks.

> TIP Once you turn the Snap To Grid feature on, snapping will occur whether the grid is visible or not.

To Modify THE GRID SETTINGS:

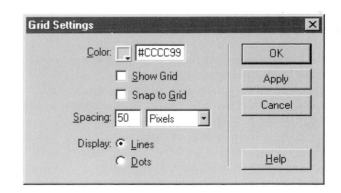

1 Select View | Grid | Edit Grid from the menu bar. This displays the Grid Settings dialog box.

2 To change the grid color, click the color well to select a color from the palette or enter a hexadecimal value in the field provided.

3 Click the Show Grid checkbox to display the grid in the Document window.

4 Click the Snap To Grid checkbox to turning snapping on.

5 Enter the amount of grid spacing you want in the field provided and select a unit of measure from the drop-down menu.

6 Using the Display radio buttons, select lines or dots for the grid lines.

7 Click Apply to display the changes in the Document window.

8 Click OK to close the dialog box.

ALIGNING LAYERS

It's possible to select a range of layers and then align all of them to one of the layer's four sides. To do this, select two or more layers in your document, selecting the layer you want the others to align to last. From the menu bar, select Modify | Align, and then one of the following options:

▶ Left Aligns the layers with the left side of the last selected layer.

▶ Right Aligns the layers with the right side of the last selected layer.

▶ Top Aligns the layers with the top of the last selected layer.

▶ Bottom Aligns the layers with the bottom of the last selected layer.

SETTING LAYER VISIBILITY

You can set a layer's initial visibility so that the layer is either visible or hidden when the page opens. You can then reveal or hide the layer using Dreamweaver behaviors discussed in Chapter 12.

There are four possible values that be assigned to a layer's visibility attribute:

▶ **Default** Sets no visibility attribute, leaving it up to the browser. Most browsers' defaults are equal to Inherit.

▶ **Inherit** Makes the layer inherit its visibility from its parent element. In other words, if the layer is nested, it inherits its visibility from the layer in which it is nested. If a layer is not nested, the parent element is the document itself (which is, of course, always visible).

▶ **Visible** Will always make a layer visible regardless of any parent element's visibility setting.

▶ **Hidden** Hides a layer regardless of any parent element's visibility setting.

Layer visibility can be set using the Properties Inspector or the Layers Panel.

> **TIP** You can set the visibility for all layers simultaneously by clicking the eye icon header at the very top of the column.

To Set LAYER VISIBILITY USING THE PROPERTIES INSPECTOR:

1 Select the layer whose visibility you want to modify.

2 Select one of the four possible values from the Vis (visibility) drop-down menu.

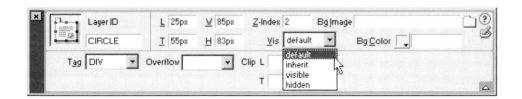

When setting layer visibility with the Layers Panel, visibility is adjusted by clicking in the first column on the left under the eye icon header. By clicking in this column, you toggle among three possible states:

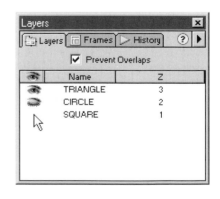

▶ A closed eye means the layer is invisible.

▶ An open eye means the layer is visible.

▶ No eye icon means the layer inherits visibility from its parent element.

CONTROLLING LAYER OVERFLOW

What happens if the contents of a layer exceed the dimensions you set for it? You get layer *overflow*. There are four possible values you can set for the overflow attribute:

▶ **Visible** Displays the full contents of the layer, regardless of actual layer dimensions. This is equivalent to not defining a value at all.

▶ **Hidden** Obscures any content that falls outside of the layer dimensions.

▶ **Scroll** Maintains the layer's dimensions, adding scrollbars to accommodate the expanded content. Scrollbars are added regardless of whether the content exceeds the layer's dimensions. Netscape Navigator does not support scrollbars in layers, and treats Scroll as Hidden.

▶ **Auto** Adds scrollbars only when the contents exceed the layer's dimensions. In Netscape, Auto is equivalent to Hidden. Internet Explorer treats it as Scroll.

To set a value for the overflow attribute, simply select one of these choices from the Overflow drop-down menu in the Properties Inspector.

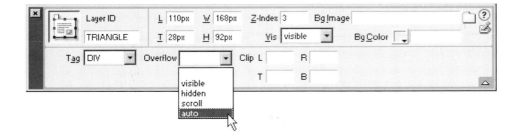

Dreamweaver will always display the entire contents of a layer in the Document window. The settings you choose for layer overflow are only viewable when the page is previewed in a browser. If you set no value for this attribute, the browser will show the full contents of the layer regardless of the dimensions you set for it.

SETTING A CLIPPING AREA

The clipping area defines the visible region of a layer, obscuring the content around a layer's edges. By entering pixel values into the L (left), R (right), T (top), and

B (bottom) fields of the Properties Inspector, you mark off a rectangular region of the layer that remains visible to the visitor. The L and R values get measured from the left edge of the layer, while the T and B values are measured from the top edge, as shown in Figure 9-3.

> **TIP** By default, any clipping area values are considered pixels. You can use centimeters by including a lowercase cm directly next to the number.

USING LAYERS FOR TABLE LAYOUT

Dreamweaver lets you create your layout using layers and then convert them into tables, effectively mimicking the tools of Layout view covered in Chapter 6. This probably seems a little redundant, but realize that Layout view is new to Dreamweaver 4 and its functionality is more likely the result of expanding upon concepts taken from the layer tools than the other way around. Dreamweaver has this layer/tables conversion ability primarily due to layers' inability to be seen in 3.0 version browsers, which were still in wide use when layers were first introduced. By using this tool, you can design in layers, convert the design over to a table format, and by inserting a browser detection behavior, direct the visitor to the proper page for the browser they're using. To learn more about Dreamweaver behaviors, see Chapter 12.

CONVERTING LAYERS AND TABLES

Each layer, when converted, becomes a cell in the new table. Consequently, you must make sure that your layers don't overlap, since table cells obviously can't.

FIGURE 9-3

Clipping does not delete content, it only hides it. Any images in a layer you apply clipping to still retain their original file size and affect download time the same way.

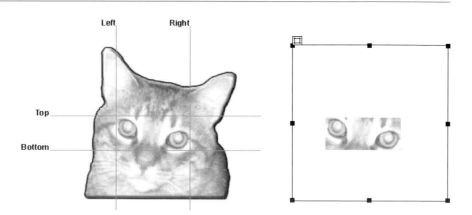

By checking the Prevent Overlaps checkbox at the top of the Layers Panel, you prevent any layer from being placed over or nested inside another one. Dreamweaver won't automatically fix any overlapping or nested layers if you turn this option on after you've created them. Simply move any offending layer until it's in the proper place. You can also select Modify | Arrange | Prevent Layer Overlaps from the menu bar to implement the Prevent Overlaps option.

Once you have your layout in place, the conversion process is quite simple.

To Convert LAYERS TO A TABLE:

1 Save your layers-based document.

2 Select Modify | Convert | Layers to Table from the menu bar.

3 The Convert Layers To Table dialog box will appear.

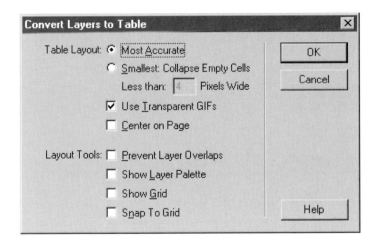

Choose the layout options you want enabled:

- Most Accurate Generates a table cell for each layer in your document, adding extra cells if they're required to maintain accurate spacing.

- Smallest: Collapse Empty Cells Creates a table with the fewest cells possible, deleting any cells that would be smaller than the pixel width you enter. This will create a table that contains all of your layer content, but will not duplicate your layout exactly.

- **Use Transparent GIFs**   Like the Layout view, this option inserts transparent GIFs to maintain exact column widths. Without this option turned on, the table may display differently from browser to browser.

- **Center on Page**   Aligns the created table in the center of the document. When this option is turned off, the table is left-aligned.

4 Choose the layout tools and grid options you want enabled, and click OK.

To Convert A TABLE TO LAYERS:

1 Select Modify | Convert | Tables To Layers from the menu bar.

2 In the resulting dialog box (shown here), choose the layer and grid options you want enabled.

3 Click OK.

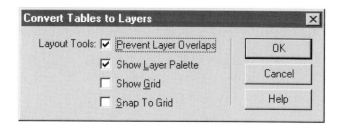

CONVERTING TO 3.0 BROWSER COMPATIBILITY

You can also convert a layers-based page to a table using the 3.0 Browser Compatible command, which generates a separate table document, leaving the original layers-based page intact.

To Convert TO 3.0 BROWSER COMPATIBILITY:

1 Select File | Convert | 3.0 Browser Compatible from the menu bar.

2 In the resulting dialog box (shown here), select from the following conversion options:

- **Layers to Table**   Like the Most Accurate option, this creates a cell for each layer and inserts any additional layers required to maintain proper spacing.

- **CSS Styles to HTML Markup** Replaces any Cascading Style Sheet markup with standard HTML wherever possible, and removes any that can't be converted.
- **Both** Will create cells for each layer, as well as replacing any CSS markup with standard HTML.

3 Click OK.

The newly generated table-based page is opened in a new Document window. If you try to convert a page that has animated layers, the layer animation is removed, since one cell of a table obviously can't jump out and move around. Any animation you might have in the document that isn't specifically related to a layer will remain.

SEE ALSO To learn more about Cascading Style Sheets, see Chapter 10. To learn more about layer animation and behaviors, see Chapter 12.

 ON THE VIRTUAL CLASSROOM CD-ROM Layers can be powerful tools for the Web designer, allowing for the exact placement of page elements. In Lesson 7, "Working with Layers," the instructor will demonstrate the process of creating and populating layers on a Web page.

Working with Style Sheets

Style sheets make it fast and easy to give all the pages in your site a consistent look-and-feel. When you look at the pages of this book, for example, you notice that all the chapter headings are formatted in a specific way, as are the all the tips, figure captions, and, of course, the page text. Now imagine that this book is a Web site. Using the methods you've learned so far, you'd probably bring the text into a blank Dreamweaver document by importing it or doing a copy and paste, then you'd go through and format each of the elements I've mentioned using the Properties Inspector. Once the site was finished and sitting on the Web somewhere, what would you do if you needed to change the font and color of all the headings? You'd have to go in and change each and every one manually, page by page. Unless you used style sheets.

UNDERSTANDING STYLE SHEETS

Remember back in Chapter 3 when you learned to format text? Remember all the different things you could do to it? You could set the font, the size, and the color, and modify a whole slew of other attributes to make text appear nearly any way you wanted. Imagine rolling all those different attribute settings into a single unit. This is exactly what a style does. It bundles a number of different formatting options and assigns them to either a specific HTML tag or a custom style called a *class*. Then, whenever that tag or class is used to mark up a selection of text in a Web page, all those formatting attributes get applied automatically.

A style sheet is simply a separate document that contains all your styles. When you assign a style sheet to a number of Web pages, they all share the same text formatting information. Think how useful this approach can be when you need to make changes. Say you apply a style class to a number of text blocks throughout your site. If you want to change the formatting to those text blocks, you only have to modify that style class in the style sheet to update the formatting across the entire site.

CSS styles fall into three categories:

▶ **Custom styles (or classes)** Create a unique style that can be applied to a range or block of text.

▶ **HTML tag styles** Assign new default formatting attributes to a specific HTML tag.

▶ **CSS selector styles** Assign new default formatting for a specific combination of tags—for example, creating a style that applies to a bold tag only when it appears inside a table cell.

Obviously, two of these styles are directly related to specific HTML tags. If you're new to HTML, check out Appendix A for an overview of how tags work. Also, make use of the Reference Panel, which includes both the O'Reilly HTML and CSS references, as well as one for JavaScript.

To Access THE REFERENCE PANEL:

1 From the toolbar, click the Reference button to launch the Reference Panel (see Figure 10-1).

2 Select the reference you want to use from the Book drop-down menu.

Be forewarned, style sheets are not equally supported by Netscape and Internet Explorer, and neither supports 100 percent of the CSS specifications outlined by the World Wide Web Consortium. You can still make great use of style sheets, however, by investigating what each browser is capable of and keeping your use of style sheets simple.

FIGURE 10-1

Use the Reference Panel for full descriptions of HTML tags and CSS attributes.

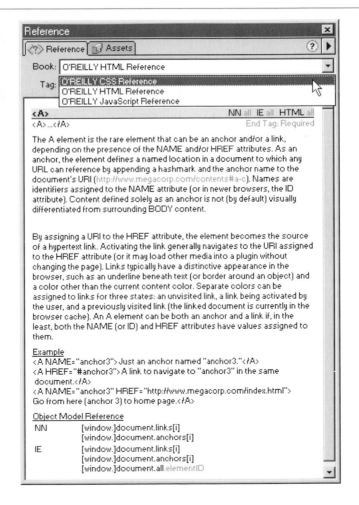

WHAT'S CSS MEAN, ANYWAY?

CSS stands for Cascading Style Sheet, which seems odd when you say CSS style sheet, doesn't it? But the question of acronyms aside, the one word to take to heart out of all of it is "cascade." Cascade means to flow or tumble down from one level to the next. With styles, cascading refers to the ability of the specific style to take precedence over the general style. So the closest style—for example, one affecting a single word—would override a style applied to the paragraph that word was in. The style applied to that paragraph would override a style applied to the entire body of the document.

HOW CSS STYLES GET APPLIED

Just as there are three types of styles, there are also three types of style sheets:

▶ **External style sheets** Separate documents that contain the styles you create. This allows them to be referenced by many Web pages, making it easy to perform sweeping format changes by editing a single file.

▶ **Internal style sheets** Create a list of styles within the code of a particular Web page. Styles created in this way can't be linked to other pages. Any changes made to these styles will only affect the single Web page they are a part of.

▶ **Embedded style rules** Insert a style into an HTML tag using the style attribute. In this instance, there is really no style *sheet* at all, only the application of style sheet formatting syntax to a particular tag. This method requires you to know style sheet syntax and enter it directly into the HTML code.

CREATING A CSS STYLE

Creating styles in Dreamweaver involves answering some questions about the type of style you want to create, and then entering the formatting rules you want the style to possess. It helps if you've given it a little thought before you start clicking buttons and filling in dialog boxes. Is this going to be a style *class* you can assign anywhere, or are you going to redefine a particular HTML tag? Or is your style going to apply only to a tag when it is under the influence of another tag? Then you need to decide if this new style is going to be specific to this one page, or if it needs to be part of an external style sheet so that other pages can access it as well. Once you have a handle on these questions, it's time to start tinkering.

FIGURE 10-2
The CSS Styles Panel offers tools to create and edit your page and site styles.

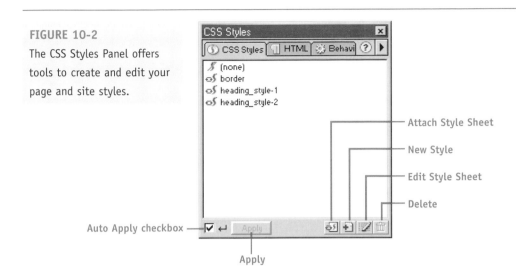

Attach Style Sheet

New Style

Edit Style Sheet

Delete

Auto Apply checkbox

Apply

The CSS Styles Panel, shown in Figure 10-2, is Dreamweaver's central tool for working with styles. From here, you can begin the style creation process, edit styles you've made, attach style sheets you've created to the current document, and apply any available custom style classes. To display the CSS Styles Panel, click the CSS Style button on the Launcher or Launch bar, or select Window | CSS Styles from the menu bar.

The body of the CSS Styles Panel is devoted to a list of the custom style classes you create in a particular site. Redefined HTML tag styles and CSS selector styles are not visible because they can't be applied; they are displayed in the Document window automatically whenever the tag or selector is used.

To Create A NEW STYLE:

1 Click the New Style button on the CSS Styles Panel to display the New Style dialog box.

2 Select the type of style you want to create from the options provided:

• Make Custom Style (Class) **Enter a short, descriptive name for your style class in the field provided, preceded by a period. If you forget the period, Dreamweaver will enter one for you.**

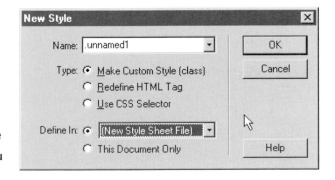

- **Redefine HTML Tag** Select the tag you want the style attributed to from the Tag drop-down menu.
- **Use CSS Selector** Enter the HTML tag combination you want the style attributed to in the Selector field. Dreamweaver provides four predefined selectors that apply specifically to text links.

2 Select where you want the new style to be defined—either in a new external style sheet file or within the current document. Click OK to display the Style Definition dialog box (see Figure 10-3). If you elect to define the style in an external style sheet, you will be asked to save the style sheet first.

3 In each category of the Style Definition dialog box, select and enter the formatting settings you want included in the new CSS style. Attributes you don't want to define in your style can be left empty. See the following section for a discussion of the various attribute options.

> **TIP** When naming custom style classes, it's best if you don't use spaces in their names. If you must have a separator, use dashes or underscores.

4 When you are finished, click OK to add the style to the style sheet. Clicking will also apply to the current selection in the Document window.

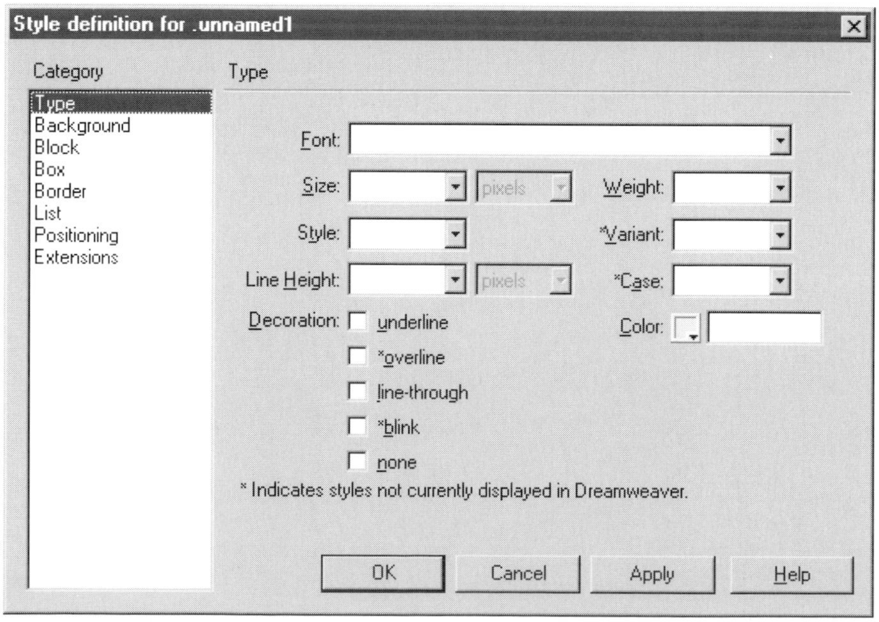

FIGURE 10-3

There are eight different categories of style attributes you can define in Dreamweaver.

DEFINING STYLE ATTRIBUTES

You define your style's attributes by entering values in one or all of the possible categories in the Style Definition dialog box, shown previously in Figure 10-3. Unfortunately, not all the available CSS attributes can be displayed in the Document window. Each attribute that can't be displayed is consequently marked with an asterisk (*) on the various category panels.

TYPE ATTRIBUTES

The Type Panel is the first category displayed in the Style Definition dialog box and is shown in Figure 10-3. Use this category to define basic typographical settings for your style. You can select from the following options:

▶ **Font** Just like selecting a font in the Properties Inspector, this drop-down menu defines the font family of your style.

▶ **Size** Defines the font size for your style. You can select a unit of measure from the drop-down menu immediately to the right. Pixel measurements tend to display with a higher level of fidelity across a range of browsers.

▶ **Style** Defines whether the type face is Normal, Italic, or Oblique. Normal is the default setting.

▶ **Line Height** Defines the amount of space between lines of text.

▶ **Decoration** Allows you to place a line under, over, or through the text. There is also an option to make text blink. The blink attribute is only supported by Netscape.

> **NOTE** The Oblique style is similar to Italic. In the serif font families, the italic and oblique differ in the shape of the serif and may look entirely different. Sans serif families often display oblique and italic the same.
>
> What's serif and sans serif? Serif fonts have little flourishes on the ends of their letters, while sans serif fonts don't. For example, the font used for this note is sans serif, while the general text used out on the page is serif.

▶ **Weight** Defines the boldness of the text. You can use relative settings (light, bold, bolder, or boldest) or specific amounts. Normal is 400; bold is 700.

▶ **Variant** Allows you to select between normal and small caps.

▶ **Case** Lets you capitalize the first letter of each word, or set the entire word to upper- or lowercase.

▶ **Color** Defines the color of the text. Enter a hexadecimal value or choose a color using the color well.

BACKGROUND ATTRIBUTES

Plain old HTML limits you to a single background color or one background image tiled across the entire browser window. CSS backgrounds, on the other hand, offer you much greater control. Background colors and images can be attributed not only to the page, but also to individual tags. Background images can be set to tile vertically, horizontally, or not tile at all. To define background attributes for your style, click Background in the Category field of the Style Definition dialog box (see Figure 10-4) and choose from the following options:

▶ **Background Color** Defines the background color for the style.

▶ **Background Image** Defines the background image for the style.

▶ **Repeat** Defines how or if a background image will tile:

  ● **No repeat** Displays the image once in the upper-left corner of the applied style.

  ● **Repeat** Tiles the image both horizontally and vertically.

  ● **Repeat-x** Tiles the image horizontally.

  ● **Repeat-y** Tiles the image vertically.

▶ **Attachment** Determines whether the background image is fixed or scrolls along with the rest of the page's content. Ordinarily, when you have to scroll

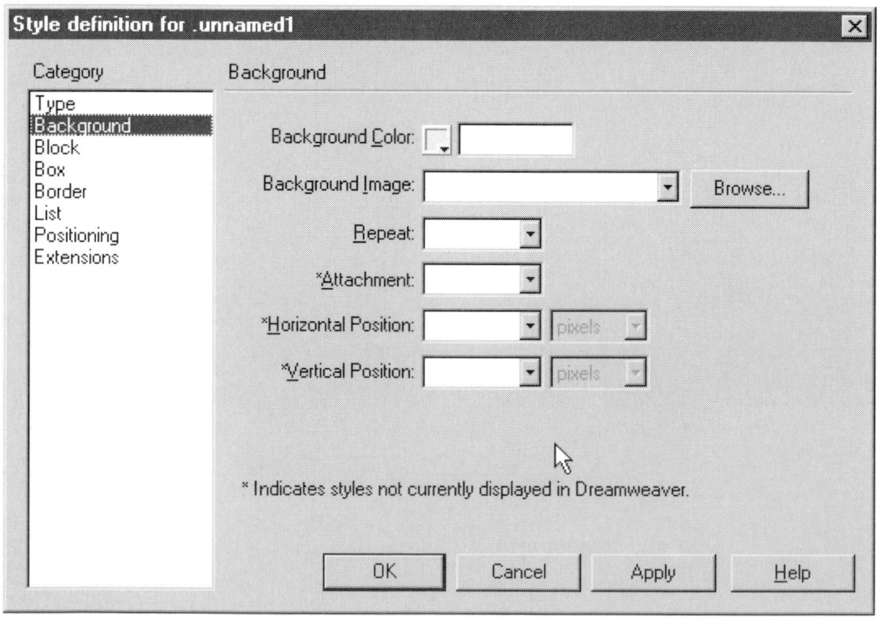

FIGURE 10-4
CSS background attributes allow a far greater level of control over background colors and images than traditional HTML.

Style definition for .unnamed1

Category
Type
Background
Block
Box
Border
List
Positioning
Extensions

Background

Background Color:
Background Image: Browse...
Repeat:
*Attachment:
*Horizontal Position: pixels
*Vertical Position: pixels

* Indicates styles not currently displayed in Dreamweaver.

OK   Cancel   Apply   Help

down in a document, the background image scrolls along with the rest of the page. When the fixed attribute is used, the background image appears to stay put while only the page content scrolls.

▶ **Horizontal and Vertical Position** Control the positioning of the background image in relation to the page element the style gets applied to. If the attachment attribute is set to fixed, the position becomes relative to the Document window.

BLOCK ATTRIBUTES

Block attributes deal with the alignment and spacing of words and characters— for example, text justification, which is text displayed as a solid block like the paragraphs in a column of text in a newspaper. Justified text is only one of the options available in the Block category (see Figure 10-5). As with any of the definition categories, you can leave blank any attribute that is not important to your style. The Block options include:

▶ **Word Spacing** Adjusts the amount of space between words. Spacing can be increased or decreased using positive or negative values, but the ability to display them depends on the browser viewing the page. Select the unit of measurement from the drop-down list immediately to the right. Be aware that word spacing can also be affected by selecting the Justify in the Text Align field.

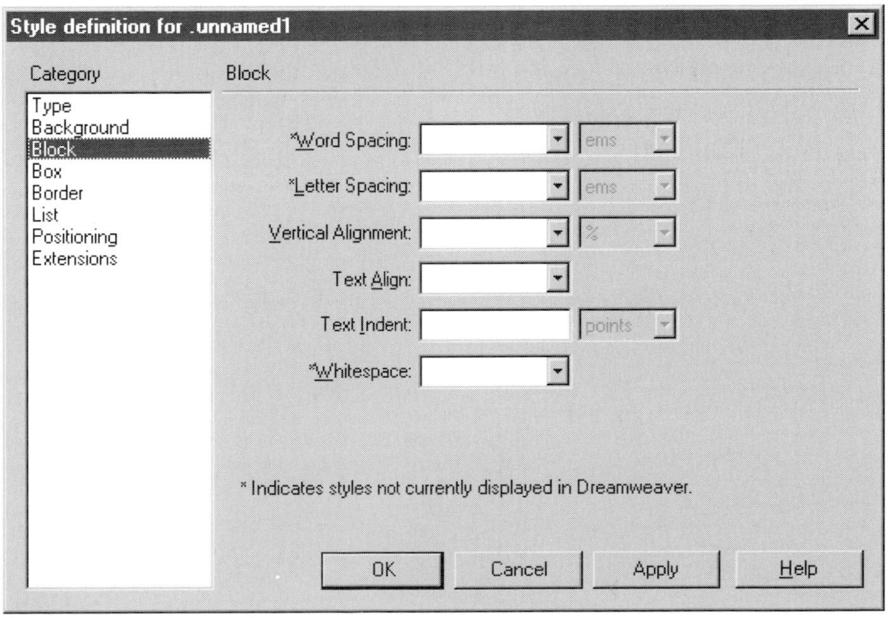

FIGURE 10-5
Block attributes provide a much higher level of control over text spacing.

Style definition for .unnamed1

Category
Type
Background
Block
Box
Border
List
Positioning
Extensions

Block

*Word Spacing: ems
*Letter Spacing: ems
Vertical Alignment: %
Text Align:
Text Indent: points
*Whitespace:

* Indicates styles not currently displayed in Dreamweaver.

OK   Cancel   Apply   Help

▶ **Letter Spacing** Adjusts the amount of space between characters. Again, the spacing can be increased or decreased by using positive or negative values. Space created using letter spacing takes priority over any extra space between letters caused by text justification. The letter spacing attribute is only supported by Internet Explorer.

▶ **Vertical Alignment** Defines the vertical alignment of the style. This attribute isn't displayed in the Document window except when the style being created is redefining the image tag, `<img>`.

▶ **Text Align** Defines the alignment of text for the style: Left, Right, Center, or Justified.

▶ **Text Indent** Defines how far the first line in a block of text is indented when the style is applied to it. Hanging text can be created by using a negative number, but again, the ability to display this depends upon the browser.

▶ **Whitespace** Directs how spaces and tabs are displayed. Your choices are normal, pre, and nowrap. Normal collapses whitespace; pre, just like preformatted text tags (`<pre></pre>`), maintains whitespace; nowrap prevents text from wrapping. This attribute is only supported by Netscape.

BOX ATTRIBUTES

The box attributes you define in the Style Definition dialog box (see Figure 10-6) give styles many of the same attributes you are familiar with from working in tables, such as width, height, and padding. When using box attributes in a style, picture the page element you apply the style to as gaining an invisible box around it. The box attributes you define will control the placement of the page element within this imaginary box. Box attributes are primarily used for styles being applied to images and layers. The box attribute options include:

▶ **Width and Height** Define the dimensions of the element affected by the style. Dreamweaver only displays these attributes in the Document window when they are applied to the image tag or to layers.

▶ **Float** Places the element affected by the style in either the left or right margin, wrapping any text in the page around it.

▶ **Clear** Defines which sides of an element to which you apply this style won't allow layers. If a layer occurs on the clear side, the element with the clear style applied to it is moved behind the layer. Dreamweaver only displays this attribute when it is applied to the image tag.

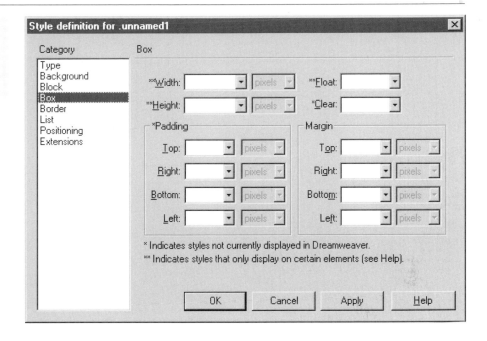

FIGURE 10-6

Box attributes help define element placement in your Web page.

▶ **Padding** Similar to the cell padding attribute used in tables, this defines the amount of space between the element the style is applied to and its border. If no border is defined, the margin is used. See the following section, "Border Attributes."

▶ **Margin** Defines the amount of space between the border and the element to which the style is applied. If no border is defined, the padding is used. This is only displayed in the Document window when the style is applied to block-level elements such as paragraph tags (`<p>`), heading tags (`<h#>`), and lists (`<ul>`, `<ol>`).

BORDER ATTRIBUTES

Border attributes, an extension of box attributes, have their own panel in the Style Definition dialog box (see Figure 10-7). With them, you can define border attributes independently for each side of an element: top, bottom, left, and right. Border options include:

▶ **Width** Defines the thickness of a border.

▶ **Color** Defines the border color.

▶ **Style** Offers particular border styles. As with many aspects of style sheets, however, the ability to display each of these styles varies from browser to browser.

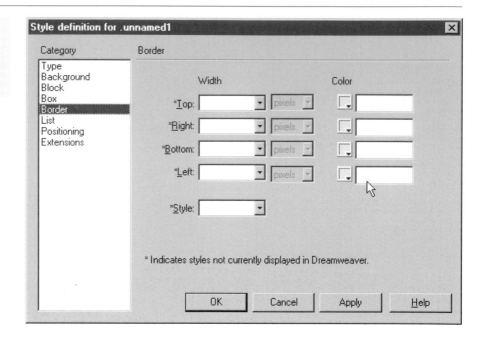

LIST ATTRIBUTES

List attributes pertain to styles that redefine the numbered and bulleted list tags (ol and ul). The List Panel of the Style Definition dialog box, shown in Figure 10-8, provides the following options:

▶ **Type** Defines how bullets and numbers are displayed.

- Order lists use decimal (1, 2, 3), lower-roman (i, ii, iii), upper-roman (I, II, III), lower-alpha (a, b, c), and upper-alpha (A, B, C).

- Bulleted lists use disc, circle, and square.

▶ **Bullet Image** Allows you to apply an image for list bullets. Click Browse to locate an image on your hard drive or enter the image's pathname.

▶ **Position** Defines how list item text wraps onto the next line. Outside wraps text directly beneath the list item, indenting it from the number or bullet. Inside wraps text beneath the number or bullet itself.

POSITIONING ATTRIBUTES

Positioning attributes convert the tag or block of selected text into a layer, as discussed in Chapter 9. You can only use these attributes when creating a custom

FIGURE 10-8
List attributes let you define how numbered and bulleted list are displayed.

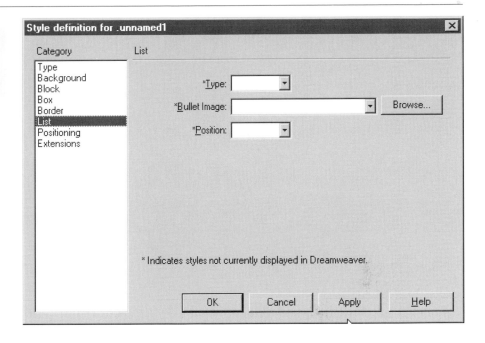

style class. The Positioning Panel of the Style Definition dialog box, shown in Figure 10-9, provides the following options:

▶ **Type** Selects the positioning method to be used by the browser:

- **Absolute** Positions the layer using the coordinates you enter in the Placement fields relative to the top-left corner of the browser window. These are exactly the same as those used in the Properties Inspector for positioning layers.

- **Relative** Positions the layer using the coordinates you enter in the Placement fields relative to its parent container, such as a table cell or other layer.

- **Static** Simply places the layer at its location within the text flow of the document, just like an image would be.

▶ **Visibility** Just like setting layer visibility in the Layers Panel or Properties Inspector, this defines the initial display state of the layer.

- **Inherit** The layer gets its visibility from the parent element, such as another layer. If there is no parent element, the layer is visible.

- **Visible** Makes the layer visible, regardless of the visibility of the parent element.

- **Hidden** Hides the layer, regardless of the visibility of the parent element.

FIGURE 10-9

The Positioning Panel of the Style Definition dialog box is essentially another interface for defining layers.

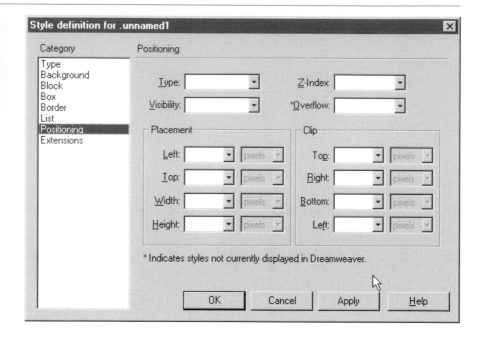

▶ **Z-Index** Sets the stacking order of the layer. As discussed in Chapter 9, the higher the number, the higher a layer's position in the stacking order.

▶ **Overflow (CSS layers only)** Determines what happens if the contents of a layer exceed the dimensions you set for it.

• **Visible** Displays the full contents of the layer, regardless of actual layer dimensions. This is equivalent to not defining a value at all.

• **Hidden** Obscures any content that falls outside of the layer dimensions.

• **Scroll** Maintains the layer's dimensions, adding scrollbars to accommodate the expanded content. Scrollbars are added regardless of whether the content exceeds the layer's dimensions. Netscape Navigator does not support scroll-bars in layers, and treats Scroll as Hidden.

• **Auto** Adds scrollbars only when the contents exceed the layer's dimensions. In Netscape, Auto is equivalent to Hidden. Internet Explorer treats it as Scroll.

▶ **Placement** Defines the layer's dimensions and location. The positioning attribute type settings determine how the browser interprets the location. Width and height values are overridden if layer content exceeds these dimensions. This is where overflow settings come into play.

▶ **Clip** Defines the clipping area of a layer. By entering pixel values into the Left, Right, Top, and Bottom fields provided, you mark off a rectangular region of the layer that remains visible to the visitor. The Left and Right values get measured from the left edge of the layer, while the Top and Bottom values are measured from the top edge.

APPLYING A CUSTOM STYLE

Once you've gone to all the trouble to create your styles, you'll want to employ them. Custom style classes are the only kind of styles you can apply to any text in your Web page, regardless of the HTML tags that control it. When you create custom style classes, their names are displayed in the CSS Styles Panel, and this is where you apply them from. As mentioned previously, styles that redefine HTML tag styles and CSS selector styles are not applied, but occur when the specific tags are used within the document.

To Apply A CUSTOM STYLE CLASS:

1 Select the text to which you want to apply the style. If you want to apply the style to a specific tag governing the selected text, click that tag in the Document window tag selector.

2 Click on the style name in the CSS Styles Panel. If the Auto Apply checkbox is not checked, select the style name and click the Apply button.

Custom styles can also be applied by right-clicking the selected text in the Document window and choosing CSS Styles and then the style name from the context menu.

AVOIDING STYLE CONFLICTS

You can get some really funky results if you apply two styles with conflicting attributes to the same selection of text. Which style wins out? Just remember cascading precedence and you'll be all right. As you recall from the discussion of cascading at the beginning of this chapter, the closest or most specific style will take precedence.

For example, imagine you have two styles: a custom style that changes text color to blue and another style that redefines the paragraph tag so that all text in paragraphs is red. If you apply that custom style to a word inside a paragraph, the word will be one color, while the text around it is another.

CREATING AND LINKING TO EXTERNAL STYLE SHEETS

As mentioned previously, an external style sheet is a separate document that contains the styles you've created. The benefit of linking to an external style sheet is that you can have multiple pages, or even sites, receiving their formatting information from this style sheet. When you need to update a formatting style, you only have to do it in the external style sheet to make the change across all the pages that link to it.

The style sheet document is a text file that is saved with the extension .css, for example, *my_styles.css*. When you link to the style sheet, Dreamweaver inserts a line of code into the Web page that looks like this:

```
<link rel="stylesheet" href="my_styles.css" type="text/css">
```

Instead of being a clickable hyperlink like the ones you create to navigate your site, this line of code simply instructs your Web page to connect with this file to get required information, letting your page know what the relationship between the two files is (`rel="stylesheet"`), what file should be referenced for this relationship (`href="my_styles.css"`), and what this file's format is (`type="text/css"`).

You create an external style sheet when you create a style and select Define In: New Style Sheet File from the New Style dialog box. When you click OK, the Save Style Sheet File As dialog box is displayed (see Figure 10-10), which allows you to save the file somewhere within your site. Dreamweaver then inserts the link reference to this style sheet into the document you are currently working on. From this point on, when you create a style while working on this site, this external style sheet will be one of the options available in the Define In drop-down menu, shown here. With this new external style sheet in place, you can now attach it to pages you create whenever or wherever you choose.

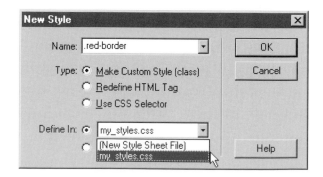

FIGURE 10-10
Save your style sheet
somewhere within your
present site.

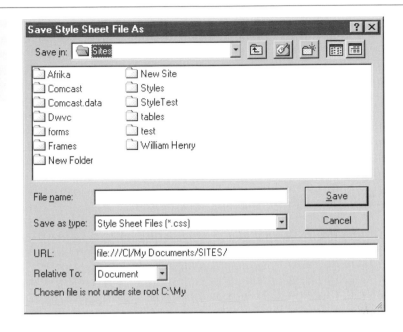

To Attach AN EXTERNAL STYLE SHEET TO A NEW DOCUMENT:

1 In the CSS Styles Panel, click the Attach Style Sheet button. This displays the Select Style Sheet dialog box.

2 In the Select Style Sheet dialog box, browse for the external style sheet you want, or enter the file name in the field provided.

3 Click Open to attach the style sheet to your document. All custom styles within the external style sheet appear in the CSS Styles Panel.

EXPORTING STYLES

You can also export the internal styles you make to create an external style sheet.

To Export INTERNAL STYLES TO CREATE AN EXTERNAL STYLE SHEET:

1 Select File | Export | Export CSS Styles from the menu bar. This displays the Export Styles As CSS File dialog box.

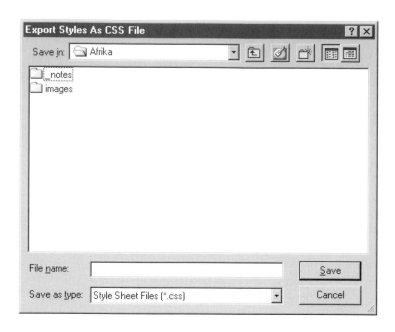

2 In this dialog box, enter a name for your new external style sheet.

3 Click Save to close the dialog box.

It's best to save this new file somewhere within your local site file for easy access.

EDITING EXTERNAL STYLE SHEETS

It's the ability to edit a single document to affect changes across a multitude of documents that makes external style sheets the powerful tool they are. Dreamweaver makes this editing process extremely easy.

To Edit AN EXTERNAL STYLE SHEET:

1 Open any document that is linked to the external style sheet you want to edit.

2 To access the Edit Style Sheet dialog box (shown here), either:

- Click the Edit Style Sheet button in the CSS Styles Panel.

- Choose Text | CSS Styles | Edit Style Sheet from the menu bar.

3 Select the external style sheet you want to edit and click the Edit button. A second Edit Style Sheet dialog box appears displaying the individual styles within the external style sheet. Select the style you want to edit, and click the Edit button. This displays the Style Definition dialog box.

4 Edit the style as you see fit (see "Creating a CSS Style," earlier in this chapter).

5 When you have finished editing your styles, click Save to close the dialog box.

> TIP You can edit a specific custom style class directly by right-clicking on its name in the CSS Styles Panel and selecting Edit style from the context menu.

WORKING WITH DREAMWEAVER HTML STYLES

The World Wide Web Consortium would prefer that everyone use CSS style sheets and never format a piece of text using HTML tags again. They have gone so far as to openly deprecate the use of HTML formatting in their HTML 4.0 specification released along with the CSS 2 specification in 1998. Don't get me wrong, I respect the W3C, but they can gripe until the cows come home. The fact remains that no browser fully supports the CSS specification, and older browsers think it's Greek. So what do you do when you need to keep your pages backward-compatible, but want as many of the advantages of CSS styles as you can get your hands on? Use Dreamweaver HTML styles.

WHAT'S AN HTML STYLE?

Dreamweaver's HTML styles essentially allow you to save a number of HTML formatting tags as a single unit which you can then use again and again. Granted, you can't update these HTML styles and have the changes reflected everywhere you've used the HTML style previously. They do cut down on the amount of time it takes to format your text, however, and you can be assured that the formatting will be the same each time the HTML style is applied.

CREATING HTML STYLES

Like CSS styles, HTML styles have their own panel (see Figure 10-11), which can be accessed in any of the following ways:

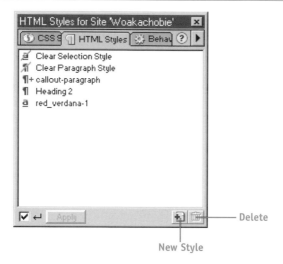

FIGURE 10-11

Reapply saved formatting to any text in any document using the HTML Styles Panel.

Delete

New Style

▶ Click the HTML Styles tab while in the CSS Styles Panel.

▶ Click the HTML Styles button in the Launcher or Launch bar.

▶ Select Window | HTML Styles from the menu bar.

To Create A NEW HTML STYLE:

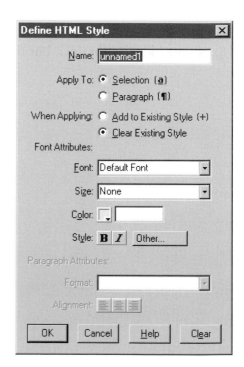

1 In the HTML Styles Panel, click the New Style button, or select Text | HTML Styles | New Style from the menu bar. This displays the Define HTML Style dialog box.

2 Enter a name for the new style. It's best to give the style a descriptive name that provides some indication of what the style does.

3 Choose whether to create a style that affects selected text or the entire paragraph by clicking either the Selection or Paragraph radio button.

4 Choose whether to apply the new HTML style along with any existing style, either CSS or HTML, or to have the style clear any existing styles.

5 Select the font attributes you want attributed to the HTML style, just as you would when formatting selected text in the Properties Inspector.

6 Click OK.

CREATING AN HTML STYLE FROM FORMATTED TEXT

If you've formatted a selection of text in the Document window using the Properties Inspector, it is a simple process to create a new HTML style based on that formatting. In the Document window, simply select the format you want to base the new style on and click the New Style button. This opens the Define HTML Style dialog box with the formatting of the selected text already entered into the various fields. From here, follow the same steps described in creating a new HTML style.

CREATING DUPLICATE HTML STYLES

You can base a new HTML style on an existing one by right-clicking on a style in the HTML Styles Panel and selecting Duplicate from the context menu. This opens the Define HTML Style dialog box with all the formatting of the selected style in place and the style name followed by the word Copy. You can then enter a new style name and make any changes you see fit, as described in creating a new style.

APPLYING HTML STYLES

This seems like a no-brainer, but there are a few things that should be mentioned anyway. When making your HTML styles, remember that they are either paragraph- or selection-based. You want to keep this in mind, because applying a paragraph-level HTML style to selection-level text can have unintended results.

For example, imagine you have five lines of text that aren't held within a set of paragraph tags (`<p></p>`), but instead employ line breaks (`<br>`) to separate each line. If you selected only one character in these five lines of text and applied a paragraph-level style to it, every bit of those five lines would be affected.

Of course, the reverse is not so much of a problem. Selection-level styles are designed to only affect the lone piece of selected text, so it doesn't matter where that text is located. It is all that will be affected.

To Apply AN HTML STYLE:

1. In the Document window, either click within the paragraph to which you want to apply a paragraph-level style, or select the text to which you want to apply a selection-level style.

2 Click the style name in the HTML Styles Panel. If the Auto Apply checkbox is not checked, select the style name and click the Apply button.

In the HTML Styles Panel, shown in Figure 10-12, paragraph-level styles are denoted with the traditional paragraph mark used in copy editing, like you've probably see on a word processor's toolbar. Selection-level styles display a lower-case *a*. When the style created adds to an existing style, these icons will be immediately followed by a plus (+) sign.

CLEARING HTML STYLES FROM A DOCUMENT

After having applied an HTML style, you may decide you want to remove it. This is what those two preexisting styles at the top of the HTML Styles Panel are for. Not only will they remove any HTML style you've applied, they remove any HTML formatting that's in place. They come in handy if you need to strip an area of any existing formatting before you imprint your own personal touch to an imported HTML document, for example.

To Clear ANY TEXT FORMATTING WITHIN A DOCUMENT:

1 Select the text from which you want to remove any formatting.

2 Click Clear Paragraph Style to remove formatting affecting the paragraph block. Click Clear Selection Style to remove formatting from the selected text only.

FIGURE 10-12

Notice the two styles at the top of the HTML Styles Panel? They are used to clear styles from your document. They cannot be removed from the panel.

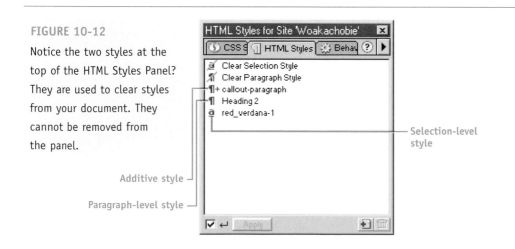

Additive style

Paragraph-level style

Selection-level style

EDITING HTML STYLES

Editing your HTML style is a simple proposition. Remember that when you edit an HTML style, Dreamweaver doesn't update any text in your documents to which you've previously applied the style.

To Edit AN HTML STYLE:

1 Right-click the HTML style you want to edit in the HTML Styles Panel.

2 In the Define HTML Style dialog box, modify your style settings as you see fit.

You can remove styles from the HTML Styles Panel altogether by simply selecting the style name and clicking the Delete Style button in the lower-right corner of the panel.

USING YOUR HTML STYLES IN OTHER SITES

Granted, you can't instantly update a site that uses HTML styles just by editing the HTML style itself, but you can use those same styles in other sites without having to rebuild them each time you create a new site.

Dreamweaver saves your HTML style information in an XML (Extensible Markup Language) file. You can copy this file and paste it into new sites you create, and voilà! You now have all those HTML styles at your disposal.

To Copy YOUR HTML STYLES TO OTHER SITES:

1 Click the Site button on the Launcher or Launch bar, or select Site | Site Files to open the Site window.

2 In the right pane of the Site window, locate and open the Library folder.

3 Find the styles.xml file, which maintains all of your HTML style information. Copy and paste it anywhere you like, either into another local site's Library folder or anywhere on your hard drive for future use.

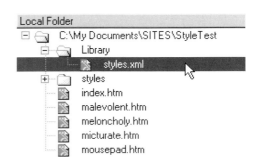

Working with
Multimedia Elements

Dreamweaver offers considerable tools for adding

multimedia to your Web pages, enabling you to add movies,

sounds, and special effects. You can add movies created in

Flash and Shockwave, as well those created with programs

beyond the considerable Macromedia arsenal. If there's a Java

applet that does something you'd like to use on your page—

a game, an interactive graphic, an interesting display feature—

Dreamweaver supports your addition of the object. In this chap-

ter, you'll learn how to insert and customize a vast array of

multimedia elements and to control many of them using the

Properties Inspector and the Behaviors Panel.

ADDING MULTIMEDIA OBJECTS TO YOUR WEB PAGE

The process of adding any sort of multimedia object to your page follows the same basic procedure you've used to insert most page content: positioning your cursor where the object should go and clicking the button for the desired multimedia object on the Objects Panel. Sound too easy? Well, this part is. It gets a little more complicated, or at least more detailed, as you move ahead, customizing the way elements work, when movies or sounds play, and so on.

Other options for inserting multimedia objects, which you'll find to be equally simple, include:

▶ With the Objects Panel displayed, drag the button for the desired object type onto your page, releasing it where you want the object to appear.

▶ Choose Insert | Media or Insert | Interactive Images. There are two different batches of multimedia objects, and they're listed in the two submenus that result from these two menu commands.

After you employ any of these three techniques, a dialog box will open, offering options for inserting the specific object type you selected. As shown in Figure 11-1, if you choose to insert a Flash movie, a standard Select File dialog box appears, through which you can select a Flash movie file to insert into the page.

As usual, when you add a multimedia object to your page, the required HTML code is added to the page as well. Because the Document window doesn't automatically, and in some cases can't, display dynamic content, the multimedia object will be represented by a placeholder graphic (as shown here) or an object-specific icon in Design view. Once inserted, you can customize the properties of media objects using the Properties Inspector, which will offer a variety of tools depending on the type of multimedia object that's selected on the page. To test how your media object functions in your document, preview your page in your Web browser.

FIGURE 11-1

Pick a file, any file—a Flash file, in this case.

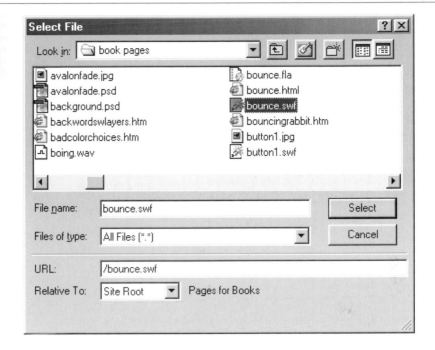

WORKING WITH FLASH CONTENT

Many people hear the word "Flash" with regard to the Web and think of content generated expressly using Macromedia's Flash software, which can create animated graphics as well as entire interfaces. With the inclusion of Flash text effects and premade Flash buttons in Dreamweaver 4, you can now incorporate Flash effects directly into your documents through the Dreamweaver interface, rather than having to know and use Flash to create the object.

If you are inserting content created natively in Flash it's important to understand the differences between the two file types Flash creates, as they play very different roles in the life of your content:

▶ **FLA** This is the format in which Flash movies are saved. This format can only be opened in the Flash application, not through Dreamweaver or a browser. If you want to play a Flash movie, you need the SWF format, which is created when you use the Publish command within the Flash application.

▶ **SWF** This is the Web-friendly Flash movie format, optimized for viewing on the Web. This is the file type you'll select when you choose a Flash movie to play on your page, and it's the format that Flash buttons and text use as well. This file format is limited, however, in that it cannot be edited in Flash. If you want to make changes to the movie, you'll have to open the FLA version of the file, make your changes, and then recreate the SWF version using the Flash Publish command. If you don't know Flash, don't panic. When it comes to Flash buttons and text, there is no need to open them in Flash—Dreamweaver gives you all the tools you need to make changes to their appearance and function.

CREATING FLASH BUTTONS

Flash buttons are images that you access by clicking Insert Flash Button on the Objects Panel, shown here, or choosing Insert | Interactive Image | Flash Button. There are more than 40 different button styles to choose from, in a wide variety of colors, shapes, and sizes. Some buttons have text that you specify and others are picture buttons such as arrows and buttons with symbols on them, like the play and rewind buttons on a VCR.

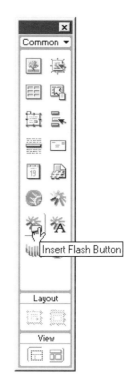

To Insert A FLASH BUTTON ON YOUR WEB PAGE:

1 If the page has not yet been saved, save it. If you don't, as soon as you issue the Insert Flash Button command, you'll be prompted to do so.

2 Click to position your cursor where you want the new button to be.

3 Click Insert Flash Button on the Objects Panel. You can also choose Insert | Interactive Images | Flash Button.

4 The Insert Flash Button dialog box opens, as shown in Figure 11-2. Scroll through the Style list, and click once on any styles you want to preview in the Sample box.

5 Type the text you want to appear on the button in the Button Text box. Keep the width of the button in mind as you type the text—try not to exceed 20 characters, including spaces.

6 Choose a font and size for the text. The size is in points, not pixels.

> **TIP** The Insert Flash Button dialog box includes a Get More Styles button. Click it to access the Macromedia Web site where new button styles can be downloaded. Once they've been copied to your computer, the new styles will be available through the Insert Flash Button dialog box.

FIGURE 11-2
The words "Button Text" will
be replaced by text you enter
into the dialog box.

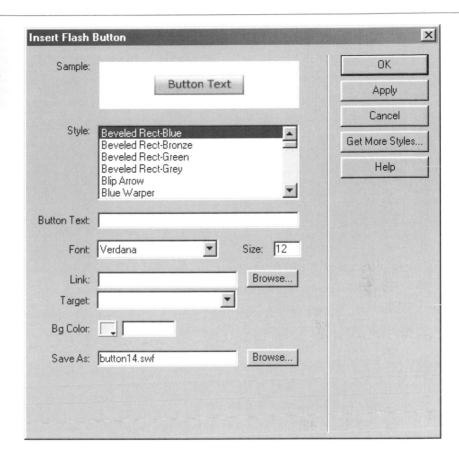

7 Enter the link for the button. This can be a Web address or a page within your site. You can also click Browse to select any other kind of file.

8 If working in a frame-based site, choose the appropriate target for the button. For a full discussion of targeting frames, see Chapter 8.

9 Choose a background color for the button, using the Bg Color color well.

10 If you know you'll use this particular button again (with the text you typed, in the font and size you selected), give it a name and save it by typing a name in the Save As box. Be sure to retain the .swf extension on whatever file name you enter.

11 Click OK to insert the button and close the dialog box. If you want to see the button in place and then make changes, click Apply, which keeps the dialog box open after inserting the button on the page. Figure 11-3 shows a Flash button in place.

FIGURE 11-3

Flash buttons with text tell the site visitor what will happen or what they'll see when the button is clicked.

Camp Runamoc

Summary 2001

Activities

Counselors

Special Events

CUSTOMIZING A FLASH BUTTON

Once the Flash button is in place, you can change it by double-clicking it. The Insert Flash Button dialog box will reopen, and you can pick a different button style, and change the font, size, or background color. You must also use the Insert Flash Button dialog box if you want to change the Link setting—you can't do that through the Properties Inspector, because the image is a Flash object and not a simple GIF or JPG graphic. To view what you can change through the Properties Inspector, click once on the button to select it. Your options appear, as shown in Figure 11-4.

In addition to making these basic changes, you can also use the Properties Inspector to adjust the V Space and H Space, increasing or decreasing the amount of white-

FIGURE 11-4

The Properties Inspector offers tools for changing the size, alignment, and background color of the button.

Camp Runamoc

Summer 2001

Activities

Counselors

Special Events

space above, below, and on both sides of the button. This is entered and measured in pixels. The rest of the options that appear in the Properties Inspector when a Flash button is selected—Quality, Scale, Parameters—don't need to be changed because the button doesn't move or play, it simply appears as a static object on the page.

There is a Play button in the Properties Inspector for the selected Flash button, which when pressed allows the flash button to interact with the mouse in the document window. You can use the Properties Inspector's Edit button to reopen the Insert Flash Button dialog box if you want to make changes to the style, text, font, or font size used in the button.

As is the case with any graphic element you add to your page, it's a good idea to check how it looks and works within the page by previewing your page through a browser. You can press F12 to open your active page in the browser you have set as the default, or you can pick which browser to use by choosing File | Preview In Browser and then select a specific browser from the list.

CREATING FLASH TEXT

Flash text is also a Flash movie, but rather than any animation occurring, the text simply responds to the visitor pointing to it and changes color. When you add Flash text to a Web page, you're really creating a rollover image, but you don't have to create two graphic images (one for the image when the page loads and the second to appear when someone points to the first image), and you don't have to go through the process of selecting two separate images. Instead, you'll simply type the text and pick the color it should turn when someone points to it.

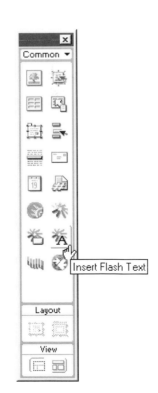

To Build FLASH TEXT:

1 If you haven't done so already, save the Web page document.

2 Click to position your cursor where the Flash text should appear.

3 Click the Insert Flash Text button on the Objects Panel (shown here), or choose Insert | Interactive Image | Flash Text.

FIGURE 11-5

Apply one of the hundreds of fonts you may have on your computer to your Flash text.

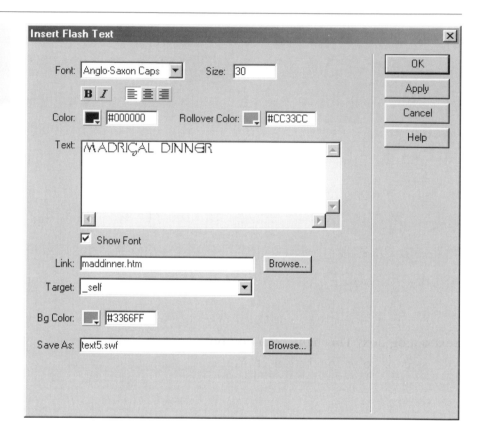

4 In the resulting Insert Flash Text dialog box (see Figure 11-5), choose the font your text should appear in. You're not restricted to any limited list of Web-friendly fonts—you can pick any font that's on your computer.

5 Pick a size for the text, apply bold or italic (or both) if you wish, and choose an alignment (left, center, or right) for the text.

6 In the Color field, pick the starting color (the color the text will be when the page loads and the Flash text first appears).

7 Pick the Rollover Color (the color the text will turn when someone points to it).

8 Type the text you want on the page. Flash text can be of any length, but single words or short phrases such as "View the Calendar" are the most effective use of Flash text.

9 In the Link field, type or click Browse to select the link for the text.

10 Adjust the Target setting as required.

11 In the Bg Color field, pick a background color for the text. This color will appear as highlighting behind the text.

12 If you want to save the Flash text for reuse exactly as you've set it up, type a new name in the Save As box. Be sure to leave the .swf extension intact or retype it when you insert the name.

13 Click OK to close the dialog box and insert the Flash text, as shown in Figure 11-6. If you want to keep tinkering with the text and to see it on the page first, click Apply rather than OK. The dialog box will stay open and you can continue to make changes to the text and its appearance.

CUSTOMIZING FLASH TEXT

Once your Flash text is inserted, you can double-click it to reopen the Insert Flash Text dialog box. Through the dialog box, you can adjust the text, and change the font, size, or color for the object. You can also change the Link and Target settings as desired—anything you set when you created the object can be changed.

When it comes to using the Properties Inspector to customize your Flash text, like Flash buttons, there are only a few options that really apply to Flash text:

▶ **Width and Height** These settings can be changed to make the Flash text object larger or smaller.

▶ **V Space and H Space** These settings can be adjusted to increase or decrease the amount of whitespace above, below, and on both sides of the text. This is entered and measured in pixels.

FIGURE 11-6

This Flash text has a yellow background and turns from black to red when a visitor points to the text.

▶ **Bg Color** The background color can be changed, just as it can through the Insert Flash Text dialog box. The effect of the background color for Flash text is much more dramatic than it is for a Flash button. On a button, the background color results in what appears to be a colored border, most of the background being obscured by the button itself. The background color for Flash text fills the space behind and around the text, and you should pick a color that isn't the same as the rollover color, unless you want the text to disappear when someone points to it.

▶ **Edit** This option will reopen the Insert Flash Text dialog box.

PREVIEWING YOUR FLASH TEXT ROLLOVER EFFECT

To test your Flash text, preview the page in a Web browser. When you point to the text, it should change color, switching to the color you specified in the Insert Flash Text dialog box.

ADDING MOVIES TO YOUR PAGE

Using Flash, Shockwave, or other format movies on your Web pages is at the very least a way to add some visual interest by virtue of motion: text and/or images moving within a portion of the page. We're not talking here about Web pages that are movies. Those are created through Flash and are an entirely different animal. Rather, what we're discussing here are movies that play within a Web page. If simply adding some movement is the least a movie can do, at its best a movie can share information, create excitement, and keep people coming back to your site. Depending on what was built into the movie—such as text, interactive buttons, and sound—the movie can be the most compelling part of your page.

The process of adding a movie to your document is relatively simple. You can click the Insert Flash Movie or Insert Shockwave button on the Objects Panel, or choose Insert | Media | Flash (or Shockwave), and then select the movie file (choosing the movie in its SWF format) from the resulting Select File dialog box.

Once inserted, you can preview the movie by clicking the Play button on the Properties Inspector, or you can preview the page in a browser and watch the movie play there automatically. While you're in Design view, unless the movie is playing, it is represented by a placeholder graphic.

Remember that download time is crucial to the success and effectiveness of a Web page. If you know that most of your site's audience is using a dial-up connection to the Web, don't use large movie files that will take forever to load and may not play smoothly on the page. If, on the other hand, your audience is likely to be connecting to the Web at work (and would then have faster access through a network and the network's connection to the Web), you can loosen up a little and add larger, longer-running movies to your site.

INSERTING A FLASH MOVIE

From start to finish, the process of inserting a Flash movie into your Web page should only take a minute, assuming you have the movie file available (in SWF format) and you know where you want it to appear in the page. With the movie file stored on your local drive (preferably in a folder within your site's designated images or multimedia folder), you can begin the process of inserting a Flash movie:

To Insert A FLASH MOVIE:

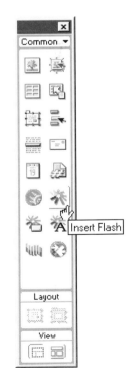

1 Click to place your cursor at the spot where the movie should appear.

2 Click Insert Flash on the Objects Panel, shown here, or choose Insert | Media | Flash. The Select File dialog box opens.

3 Choose the Flash movie file (in SWF format) by double-clicking it or click the file once and then click the Select button.

4 The movie appears, represented by the media placeholder, which is shown in Figure 11-7.

INSERTING A SHOCKWAVE MOVIE

With the exception of the button you click on the Objects Panel, the process for inserting a Shockwave movie is identical to the process you use to insert a Flash movie. Simply position your cursor where the Shockwave movie should appear, and click the Insert Shockwave button on the Objects Panel, or choose Insert | Media | Shockwave. The Select File dialog box opens, through which you pick the movie (again, in the SWF format) that you want to use on the Web page.

FIGURE 11-7

So you can design around the movie's dimensions, the placeholder is the same size as the movie's canvas.

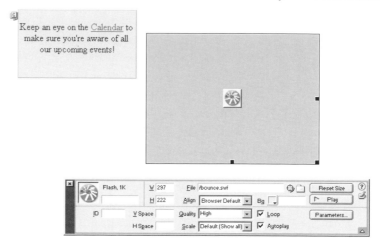

SETTING FLASH AND SHOCKWAVE MOVIE PROPERTIES

Unlike Flash text and buttons, Flash movies don't have their own dialog box through which content changes can be made. If you want to change something in the movie, you have to reopen the FLA version of the file in Flash and edit it there. If you want to edit a Shockwave movie's content, you need to reopen the movie file in Macromedia Director and then resave the file after making your changes. Within the Dreamweaver interface, your only options for adjusting the appearance and functioning of Flash and Shockwave movies are through the Properties Inspector, where the following options can be used:

▶ **Name** Allows you to give the movie object a name that will help you spot references in the HTML code and identify the movie for scripting.

▶ **W and H** Represent the current width and height of the movie in pixels. You can enter new values by typing them, or you can drag the object's handles to resize it manually. Be careful to maintain the current aspect ratio (proportionate width and height) or the movie's content will be distorted.

▶ **File** Can be used to change which movie plays in this spot on the page. Click the Browse To File button to reopen the Select File dialog box and choose a different movie.

▶ **Align** Controls the placement of the movie on the page. The drop-down menu gives you the following choices:

- **Browser Default** Varies by browser in terms of its effect on movie placement, but it normally means that the movie will sit on the baseline, the bottom of the image.

- **Top** Aligns the movie to the top of the tallest object on the current line.

- **Middle** Aligns the movie to the middle of the line, relative to anything else on the line.

- **TextTop** Aligns the movie with the top of the tallest character on the line, if there is text on the same line as the movie.

- **Absolute Middle** Aligns the movie to the absolute middle of the current line.

- **Absolute Bottom** Aligns the movie to the absolute bottom (which includes any descenders, as in the letter y or g) with the bottom of the selected object.

- **Left** Positions the movie on the left margin, and any text on the same line wraps around it to the right. If left-aligned text appears before the movie on the same line, it pushes the left-aligned movie to a new line.

- **Right** Puts the movie along the right margin, and any text on the same line wraps around the object to the left. If right-aligned text precedes the object on the line, it generally forces right-aligned objects to wrap to a new line.

▶ **Bg** A color well you can use to pick a background color for the movie area. This color also appears while the movie is not playing, while the movie is loading, and after it plays.

▶ **V Space and H Space** Represent the number of pixels of whitespace above, below, and on the left and right sides of the movie.

▶ **Quality** These settings control the level of anti-aliasing applied when the movie plays through a browser. The drop-down menu gives you the following choices:

- **High** Results in the best-looking image, but requires the user to have a faster processor.

- **Low** Results in the movie playing more quickly, but it doesn't look as good.

- **Auto Low** Emphasizes speed at the beginning, but the appearance improves if the user's computer and browser support it.

- **Auto High** Pays equal attention to both speed and quality when the movie first loads, but appearance will suffer for speed if it becomes necessary.

▶ **Scale** Controls the space within which the movie plays. Your choices are Exact Fit, No Border, and Show All.

▶ **Autoplay** If turned on, sets the movie to play automatically when the page loads.

▶ **Loop** If turned on, makes the movie play over and over indefinitely.

▶ **Reset Size** Returns the selected movie to its original size if you've resized the movie placeholder.

WORKING WITH SOUND

Sound files can be set to play as soon as someone visits your page or when a particular link is clicked. Many people who use sound set it to play as soon as the page loads, so the visitor takes a passive role in the multimedia experience. No motivation on the visitor's part is assumed, and none needs to be cultivated.

The process of playing a sound on a Web page requires that JavaScript be added to the page's HTML code. If you don't know how to write JavaScript, don't panic. Dreamweaver creates the script for you as soon as you choose the sound and set it to play at a desired time, such as when the page loads or when a visitor clicks a button.

The tool used to add sound to a page is the Behaviors Panel (shown here), which is displayed by clicking the Behaviors button on the Launcher or Launch bar, by selecting Windows | Behaviors from the menu bar, or by pressing SHIFT-F3.

Dreamweaver uses the word "behavior" to describe the JavaScript-based effects it allows you to create, such as the image rollovers, navigation bars, and jump menus you learned about in previous chapters. With regard to sound, the Behaviors Panel allows you to insert a sound in your document and control when and how it is played. A complete discussion of Dreamweaver behaviors can be found in Chapter 12.

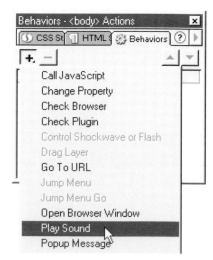

The process of adding a sound to your page with Dreamweaver is simple. Just display the Behaviors Panel and click the Plus (+) button to display a list of potential behaviors, as shown here. Choose Play Sound and the Play Sound dialog box will appear. You can type the path to and file name of the sound file that you want to be played, or you can browse to find the file if you're not sure of its name and location.

As soon as you pick a sound and click OK to add it to your page, the JavaScript is created. By default, assuming you have nothing selected in the Document window, the sound is set to play *onLoad*, meaning when the page is loaded in the visitor's browser window. If the file is a simple WAV file, the visitor will hear it as soon as the page and the sound file itself are downloaded. For this reason, you want to use small sound files so the download time isn't so long that the visitor gets bored and moves on before the sound ever plays. You can change the event associated with your sound by selecting the behavior in the Behaviors Panel and clicking the drop-down menu arrow that appears beside the event. This displays the Event Handler menu (shown in Figure 11-8), from which you can choose the event you want.

There are other sound file formats, some requiring plug-ins (which many people already will have, just from visiting other sites with the same sound file types in use), and others that are more obscure and require additional software beyond a simple plug-in. Some popular sound file format choices (in addition to WAV) are:

▶ **MIDI (.mid)** These files are supported by nearly all browsers, and don't require a plug-in. The files tend to be small, so download time is reduced. The sound quality is quite good. The downside to this file type is significant: MIDI files are created with a computer, using special hardware and software, unlike WAVs, which can be created with a microphone and software that comes with Windows. You can't play a song into your microphone or read a script and save as a MIDI-format file.

▶ **MP3** Even if you're never played one, you've probably heard about MP3 files because their availability online has been in the news for the last year or so. MP3 files are very small, and the sound quality is good. To create them, you need special software, and to play them, you also need special software and a plug-in, such as RealPlayer or the Windows Media Player. Most people have these plug-ins, so this isn't a huge stumbling block.

▶ **RAM, RPM (.ram, .rpm, RealAudio)** These formats create very small files, which is great for Web use. You can stream the files so that the music starts before all the page images are finished loading, which is very convenient. While the sound quality isn't great, it's fine for a page "soundtrack"—mood music while your page is onscreen—so RAM files are quite popular. To record and play them, you need to download and install RealPlayer (go to http://www.realplayer.com/ to get the software).

▶ **AIF (.aif)** This format is very similar to WAV format. AIF files have good sound quality, are supported by most browsers, and visitors won't need a plug-in to play them. You can record AIF files from a CD, tape, or microphone, making it very simple to create the files. One drawback: the large file size makes it hard to use all but the shortest sound clips without significantly lengthening the load time for your page.

If you want your sound to play at another time—say, when the visitor moves their mouse, resizes the window, or uses the scrollbar—you can change the event associated with the sound. Using the Behaviors Panel, select the sound you've added, and click the drop-down arrow next to the current event (as shown in Figure 11-8). A list of the events with which the sound can be associated appears. To make sure the proper events for the browsers you expect your visitors to be using are displayed, click the Show Events For command at the foot of the Events menu, as shown in Figure 11-9.

FIGURE 11-8

Click the drop-down triangle and pick an event.

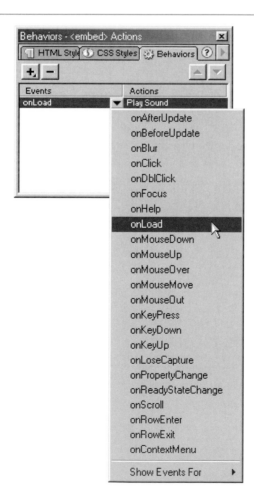

FIGURE 11-9

Choose to see a list of events associated with a different browser or version thereof.

SETTING UP SOUND FILE LINKS

Linking to a sound file is a much simpler way to go if you want sound on your page or if you want to share sound files with your visitors. By making the sound accessible through a link, you're allowing the visitor to choose whether or not to download and play the sound file. In the case of larger files, your visitors will appreciate your putting the choice in their hands. This approach also makes your page available to the largest audience. Rather than the sound playing directly on the page, which might require a plug-in (depending on the file type), the visitor can skip the sound link entirely if they know they don't have the plug-in to play that particular file.

To Set Up A SOUND FILE LINK:

1 Click once on the text or graphic that will serve as the link to the sound file.

2 Using the Properties Inspector, click inside the Link box and type the path and file name of the sound file, or click the Browse To File button to open a Select File dialog box through which you can find and select the sound file.

Pretty simple, right? When the visitor clicks the link, their browser will display a prompt telling them they're about to download a file. They can choose to Open or Save the file (as shown in Figure 11-10).

Whenever the visitor chooses to play the file—immediately upon download or later, double-clicking the sound file from within their My Computer or Windows Explorer windows—a player window will open. If the sound file requires a plug-in the user doesn't have, a prompt will appear. The user can then download the plug-in or delete the file if they don't want to get the plug-in required.

FIGURE 11-10

Let the visitor choose to play the sound now or to play it later after saving it to their local drive.

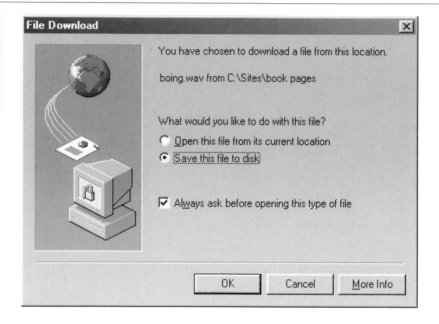

EMBEDDING SOUND IN YOUR PAGE

As a sort of compromise between a sound that plays automatically when a page loads and one that the visitor must download by choice after clicking a link, Dreamweaver offers the ability to embed a sound file into your page. Like any embedded content, a program (in this case, a sound player) is added to the page, set to play a specified sound. If you've ever used the Insert | Object command in a word processor or spreadsheet program to add a chart or table from another application, you've embedded a file. The concept is not unique to Dreamweaver or to Web design.

Some things to consider about embedding files:

▶ Not all browsers support the embed tag and some will therefore ignore it. Always preview your page with embedded sound before uploading it to the Web.

▶ If the sound file requires a plug-in, the visitor won't be able to play the sound unless they have that plug-in.

▶ The player window becomes part of your page design, and you need to accommodate it within your page. You can place the player inside a table cell, layer, or frame, or place it anywhere on an unstructured page. Figure 11-11 shows a player centered underneath the organization's logo.

FIGURE 11-11

Embedding a sound makes
the player window an integral
part of your page.

To Embed A SOUND FILE IN YOUR PAGE:

1 Click to place your cursor where the embedded file (and player window) should appear.

2 Click the Plugin button on the Objects Panel. You can also choose Insert | Media | Plugin.

3 Using the Properties Inspector, click in the Link box and type the path and file name of the sound you want to play, or click the Browse To File button to choose a file through the Select File dialog box.

4 Tinker with the Width and Height settings in the Properties Inspector. Unlike working with a graphic that might be distorted by your changing these settings, you are adjusting the space in which the player window will sit. You want to make sure all of the necessary parts of the window—play and stop buttons, for example—are visible. The illustration here shows a player window that is reduced to just the control buttons for  playing, rewinding, and fast-forwarding through the sound. Unlike the slightly larger player in Figure 11-11, this small bar can fit discreetly anywhere on the page.

It's important to test your page in both Internet Explorer and Netscape to make sure that the player window appears properly in both. You may end up having to display more of the player window than you wanted to, just to make sure that the essential parts are visible to users of both browsers.

UNDERSTANDING PLUG-INS AND ACTIVEX CONTROLS

The purpose of plug-ins and ActiveX controls is to make it possible for site visitors to open and view and/or play files of varying formats. For example, if there is Flash content on a Web page, visitors will need a Flash plug-in to experience the movie. If the visitor doesn't have the plug-in, a prompt appears, telling them they need to obtain a plug-in to open the file in question.

Netscape pioneered the use of plug-ins, using them to extend the effectiveness of their browser. Microsoft's answer to plug-ins, for use with their Internet Explorer browser, is ActiveX controls. By adding plug-ins and ActiveX control objects to your Web page, you're making it easier for visitors to your site to obtain these tools if they need them. Further, through the use of the Check Plugin behavior, you can add JavaScript to your page that will check the visitor's computer for the plug-in or control needed for a particular file type. If they don't have it, they will be sent to a Web site where they can download the plug-in or control they need.

WORKING WITH NETSCAPE PLUG-INS

Plug-ins enhance Netscape Navigator, helping users play and view multimedia files in a wide variety of formats. It's very easy to add a plug-in to your page, making it possible for your visitors to download a plug-in they need to view multimedia content from your site.

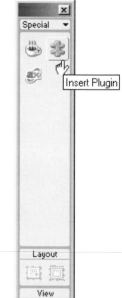

To Add A PLUG-IN TO YOUR PAGE:

1 Click to place your cursor where you want the plug-in to appear.

2 Click the Insert Plugin button on the Objects Panel.

3 In the resulting Select File dialog box, select the plug-in file by double-clicking it. The plug-in appears on the page, represented by a placeholder, shown here.

CUSTOMIZING NETSCAPE PLUG-INS

You can use the Properties Inspector to adjust the settings for the plug-ins you add to your page. When you click the plug-in placeholder, the

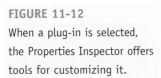

FIGURE 11-12

When a plug-in is selected, the Properties Inspector offers tools for customizing it.

Properties Inspector changes to offer a set of tools pertaining to plug-in content (see Figure 11-12).

Your options are as follows:

▶ **Name** Allows you to create a recognizable label for your plug-in as it appears in your HTML code and related script.

▶ **Width and Height** Used to adjust the size of the plug-in on the page, measured in pixels.

▶ **Src** This is the plug-in file. If you want to change to a different file, click the Browse To File button and select a new file. You can also type a path to and file name for a different file in the Src box.

▶ **Plg URL** The Web address where visitors can go to download the plug-in. If the visitor doesn't have the needed plug-in, their browser will automatically go to this URL and attempt to download the file.

▶ **Align** Offers several choices for the position of the plug-in on the page: Browser Default, Top, Middle, TextTop, Absolute Middle, Absolute Bottom, Left, and Right. These choices are similar to those listed in the section "Setting Flash and Shockwave Movie Properties," earlier in this chapter.

▶ **V Space and H Space** Represent the amount of whitespace above, below, and on the left and right sides of the plug-in. The space is measured in pixels.

▶ **Border** Allows you to enter the width of the border around the plug-in, measured in pixels.

▶ **Parameters** Opens the Parameters dialog box, through which you can enter parameters to use with the Netscape plug-in.

TROUBLESHOOTING NAVIGATOR PLUG-INS

While plug-ins are fairly foolproof, there will be times when despite having the appropriate plug-in for a multimedia object on your page, the object won't play properly or won't play at all. If this happens, consider these potential solutions:

▶ Check to verify that the plug-in needed for the given multimedia object is in fact on your computer, and that you have the version required for the specific object. If you're not sure, download the plug-in and use the Browse To File button in the Properties Inspector (with the plug-in placeholder selected) to select the new plug-in you've just acquired. If you aren't sure where to find a particular plug-in, search the Web for "_____ plug-in," where the blank represents the name of the multimedia object you're trying to play. Figure 11-13 shows the Macromedia site and the page through which a Flash plug-in can be downloaded.

▶ Check to see if Dreamweaver supports the plug-in. To do this, locate the UnsupportedPlugin.txt file on your computer and open it in a text editor. This file contains a list of all the plug-ins Dreamweaver doesn't currently support. If your plug-in is listed, you've found your problem. The file is found in the Configuration/Plugins/ folder within the main Dreamweaver directory.

▶ Check your system resources to be sure you have sufficient RAM and disk space available to handle the extra drain. Plugins can use up to 5MB of extra memory to run effectively. Your computer will need enough memory to run the plug-in and the multimedia object itself. Also realize that if you do have the resources and playing the media object is still sluggish, there's a good chance site visitors will experience the same thing, and this is something you want to avoid.

FIGURE 11-13

Need a Flash or Shockwave plug-in? Go to the manufacturer, Macromedia.

WORKING WITH ACTIVEX CONTROLS

Just as Netscape needs plug-ins to expand its capabilities as a browser, Internet Explorer needs similar tools to give users the ability to view and play multimedia files. Instead of plug-ins, however, Internet Explorer uses ActiveX controls. The controls run in Internet Explorer with Windows, but don't work at all on the Macintosh or in Netscape Navigator. Dreamweaver provides an ActiveX object on the Special version of the Objects Panel, and a version of the Properties Inspector to help you customize the ActiveX control and how it will work in your visitor's browser.

INSERTING AN ACTIVEX CONTROL

ActiveX controls are very simple to add to your page—you'll recognize the procedure from the one you may have used to insert a Netscape plug-in. Just follow these steps:

To Insert AN ACTIVEX CONTROL:

1 Click to place your cursor where you want the ActiveX control to appear.

2 Click the Insert ActiveX button on the Objects Panel. You'll find it on the Special version of the panel. You can also choose Insert | Media | ActiveX.

3 An icon (similar to a placeholder, but it doesn't look like the Flash, Shockwave, or plug-in placeholders you've seen before) appears on the page.

CUSTOMIZING ACTIVEX CONTROLS

As soon as you insert the ActiveX control icon, you can begin setting up the control and how it will work. With the control selected, the Properties Inspector offers a set of options for everything from the simple (naming the control) to the more complex (setting parameters). It's important to note that there are no set standards for setting these options, certainly none that apply to all ActiveX controls. Your best bet is to consult the documentation for the ActiveX control you're using, and that can be found at the Web site where you obtained the control in the first place. Figure 11-14 shows the Properties Inspector as it appears when an ActiveX control icon is selected.

FIGURE 11-14
ActiveX settings vary and should be researched for the specific control you've inserted.

The Properties Inspector's ActiveX options are as follows:

▶ **Name** Helps you identify the ActiveX control by giving it a label that will appear in the HTML code and scripts related to the control.

▶ **Width and Height** Represent the size of the ActiveX control icon. You can adjust these numbers (measured in pixels) through the Properties Inspector, or you can drag the handles on the icon itself.

▶ **Class ID** Identifies the ActiveX control to the browser. You can enter an ID or choose one from the drop-down list. The browser uses this ID to locate the control, and if it's not found, it goes to the URL you set in the Base option (discussed later in this list) to find it.

▶ **Embed** Inserts an embed tag inside the object tag for the ActiveX control. If there's a Netscape Navigator plug-in that matches the selected control, the embed tag will activate that plug-in.

▶ **Align** Determines how the object is aligned on the page. The options include: Browser Default, Top, Middle, TextTop, Absolute Middle, Absolute Bottom, Left, and Right.

▶ **Parameters** Opens a dialog box for entering additional parameters to pass to the ActiveX object. This is one of the options you should investigate through the documentation for the specific ActiveX control you're using.

▶ **Src** Defines the Netscape Navigator plug-in to use if the Embed option is in use. If you don't enter anything here, Dreamweaver will try to figure out which plug-in goes with the selected ActiveX control.

▶ **V Space and H Space** Allow you to adjust the amount of whitespace above, below, and on the left and right sides of the object. This is measured in pixels.

▶ **Base** The Web address where the ActiveX control can be found. Internet Explorer downloads the ActiveX control from this URL if it is not found on the visitor's computer. If you don't enter anything here, and the visitor doesn't already have the ActiveX control on their computer, the browser can't display the ActiveX object.

▶ **Alt Img** Lists the image file that should be displayed if the visitor's browser doesn't support the object tag that was inserted via your entry in the Base option. Of course, Alt Img is available only when the Embed option is deselected.

▶ **ID** Defines the optional ActiveX ID parameter. This parameter is most often used to pass information between ActiveX controls and is another setting you should check on in the ActiveX control's documentation.

▶ **Data** Specifies a data file for the ActiveX control to load. ActiveX controls for Shockwave and RealPlayer don't use this parameter.

WHAT IS JAVA?

Java, not to be confused with JavaScript, is an object-oriented programming language used to create mini-applications, called applets, that run inside Web pages. You may have encountered Java applets in pages you've seen, without knowing that Java was at work. Some common Java applets include special effects such as scrolling text, interactive banners and buttons, and games. If you don't know how to write Java applets, that doesn't mean you can't have Java applets on your pages. You can download free, customizable Java applets from a long list of Web sites. Try http://www.javaboutique.internet.com/ or http://www.javapowered.com/. Figure 11-15 shows a Java applet demo running.

USING JAVA APPLETS

Java applets are supported by both Netscape and Internet Explorer, and their support goes back several versions. You can count on your Java applets working properly for visitors running Netscape back to version 2, and Internet Explorer back to version 3 (and of course the latest versions of both browsers continue to support Java applets).

Once you've created or downloaded a Java applet, you need to add it to your page. The process is very simple, and most of the customization tools are simple to use as well.

FIGURE 11-15

Test the applet online, and
if you like it, download it
to your computer.

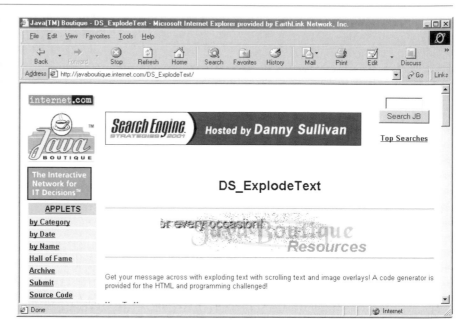

To Insert A JAVA APPLET ONTO YOUR PAGE:

1 Click to position your cursor on the page where you want the Java applet to appear.

2 On the Special version of the Objects Panel, click the Insert Applet button. (There's no shortage of coffee-related references to Java, as this button demonstrates.)

3 In the resulting Select File dialog box, choose the applet file you want to run on your page by double-clicking it. A Java applet icon, shown here, appears on the page.

WORKING WITH JAVA APPLET PROPERTIES

After you add the Java applet to your page, you can change its settings through the Properties Inspector, as shown in Figure 11-16. You may want to consult any documentation available about Java applets you've downloaded. Of course, if you wrote the applet, you'll know what settings it requires to run properly.

Your applet property options are as follows:

► **Name** A label you can apply to make it easier to spot references to the applet in your HTML code.

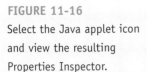

FIGURE 11-16

Select the Java applet icon and view the resulting Properties Inspector.

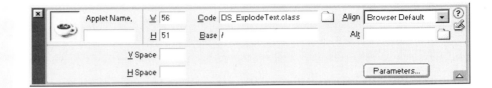

▶ **Width and Height** The dimensions for the area in which the applet will run.

▶ **Code** The source of the .CLASS file on your computer. You can click the Browse To File button to select one other than the one you chose when you inserted the applet originally. When you choose a source for your applet, the Base field (which follows) is filled automatically.

▶ **Base** The folder that contains the applet you chose to add to your page.

▶ **Align** Offers several choices for the position of the applet on the page: Browser Default, Top, Middle, TextTop, Absolute Middle, Absolute Bottom, Left, and Right.

▶ **Alt** The image file that will appear instead of the applet if the visitor's browser doesn't support Java applets or if the applet isn't working. You can also type alternative text in this box if you'd prefer that to an image.

▶ **V Space and H Space** Represent the amount of whitespace that surrounds the applet. This space is measured in pixels.

▶ **Parameters** Opens a dialog box for entering additional parameters to pass to the applet. You'll want to consult the applet's documentation before making any selections in the Parameters dialog box.

JavaScript and Dreamweaver: Behaviors and Animation

We've seen that Dreamweaver can write its own

JavaScript when making things like image rollovers, navigation

bars, and jump menus. Each of these effects takes advantage

of one or more Dreamweaver behaviors. *Behavior* is the term

Dreamweaver uses to refer to the JavaScript-based effects you

can insert directly through the Dreamweaver interface. Just as it does for layers, frames, and assets, Dreamweaver provides a convenient tool for adding and modifying JavaScript behaviors: the Behaviors Panel.

Behaviors allow you to manipulate layers, create effects triggered by mouse events, preload the images in your document for seamless display, and produce a slew of other effects without knowing any JavaScript. If you are JavaScript-savvy, you can create new behaviors that can then easily be inserted using the Dreamweaver interface whenever you need them.

By now I'm sure you're tired of hearing me repeat this, but not all browsers support each behavior. The nice thing about the Behaviors Panel is that you can target the browsers you want your page to be compliant with, such as 3.0 generation browsers, 4.0 generation browsers, and specific versions of Internet Explorer and Netscape Navigator.

THE BIG THREE: BEHAVIORS = EVENTS + ACTIONS

Dreamweaver behaviors are *actions* that take place in response to an *event*. For example, in the image rollover effect you learned about in Chapter 4, the event is the mouse moving over the initial image. In JavaScript, the event is processed by an *event handler*, in this case `onMouseOver`. The action taken in response to the event is the swapping of the first image for the second one. The action Dreamweaver inserts is prewritten JavaScript code, called a *function*.

The same event can be used to call multiple actions, and you can control which action takes place first. Be aware that different page elements support different events; for example, `onMouseOver` works with images and links, but does not work for regular text. Also, different browsers may require different event handlers to activate the same action.

Dreamweaver includes 23 actions that have been designed by the programmers at Macromedia to be compatible with as many browsers as possible. You can also download third-party actions from the Macromedia Web site.

THE BEHAVIORS PANEL

The Behaviors Panel, shown in Figure 12-1, is the perfect synthesis of form and function. The events are displayed in the list on the left of the panel, and the actions attributed to them appear on the right. When you select a page element, its corresponding tag is displayed in the Behaviors Panel title bar. To display the Behaviors Panel, click the Behaviors button on the Launcher or Launch bar, select Windows | Behaviors from the menu bar, or press SHIFT-F3.

The Behaviors Panel contains the following elements:

▶ **Add Action button (+)** When clicked, displays a menu of the available actions that can be attached to the element selected in the Document window.

▶ **Delete Action button (-)** Use this to remove an action from a selected page element.

▶ **Up and Down buttons** Can be used to change the order of actions that have the same event handler.

▶ **Event Handler menu** When the event is selected in the Behaviors Panel, a drop-down arrow appears beside it. Clicking it displays a list of the possible event handlers for the attached action. The available event handlers depend on the element selected in the Document window and browsers selected in the Show Events For submenu.

▶ **Show Events For submenu** Located at the bottom of the Event Handler menu and the Add Action menu, the selection you make from this menu determines

FIGURE 12-1

Use the Behaviors Panel to select your actions and event handlers.

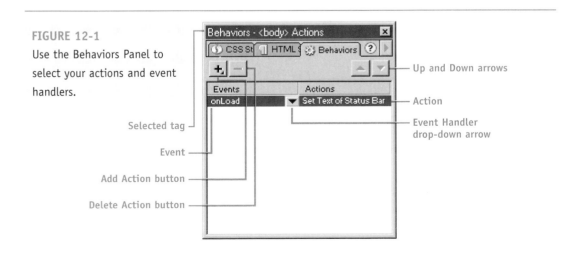

which events appear in the Events pop-up menu. For example, choosing 3.0 And Later Browsers displays only events available in all versions of Internet Explorer and Netscape Navigator version 3.0 and higher.

ATTACHING BEHAVIORS

The actual process of attaching a behavior is simple. Remember that your event and action choices are determined by the page element you select and the browsers with which you want to be compatible.

To Attach A BEHAVIOR:

1 In the Document window, select the element to which you want to attach your behavior. To attach a behavior that affects the whole page, such as Preload Images, select the <body> tag by clicking it in the Document window Tag Selector.

2 In the Behaviors Panel, click the Add Action (+) button and select the browser or set of browsers in which you want your behavior to function using the Show Events For submenu (see Figure 12-2).

3 Click the Add Action button again and select the action you want from the drop-down menu. Actions that are not available for the current selection are dimmed. Once you make a selection, a dialog box is displayed in which you enter values and parameters for the chosen action. Each action is discussed in detail later in this chapter.

4 Dreamweaver enters the default event handler for the action in the Events column. If you want to select a different event handler, select the event handler and click the drop-down arrow beside it, then select a new one from the drop-down menu.

Just like actions, available event handlers depend on the element selected in the Document window as well as the browser you choose from the Show Events For submenu.

USING NULL LINKS IN BEHAVIORS

If you attach a behavior to an image and check the possible event handlers, you'll notice that some of them are in parentheses. This means they can only be used for links. If you select one of them and the image doesn't already have a link,

FIGURE 12-2

Select the browsers for which you want your behaviors to be compatible.

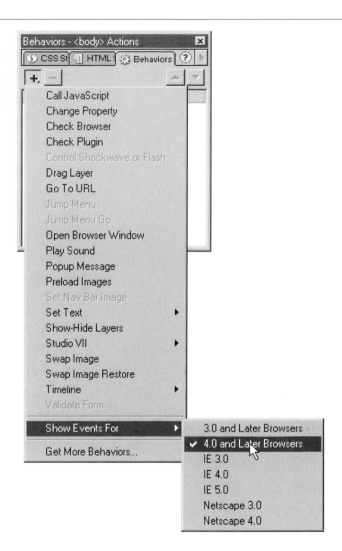

Dreamweaver will insert a *null link*—a link that leads nowhere—allowing you to use this event handler to trigger the action. This null link, instead of containing a document reference, will read javascript:; in the element's Properties Inspector link field. This little tidbit can put to a good advantage elsewhere.

Because you can't attach a behavior to text, but you can to a link, you can assign a null link to text and then attach a behavior to it. Granted, this will change the text color, as well as underline it, but you can change this using an embedded style, as described in Chapter 10.

To Attach A BEHAVIOR TO SELECTED TEXT:

1 Type javascript:; **into the Link field of the Properties Inspector.**

2 **In the Behaviors Panel, attach a behavior using the steps described in the previous section.**

There are other places where using a null link will come in handy when creating behaviors, and I've made an attempt to point them out in the discussion of the individual actions later in this chapter.

THE EVENT HANDLERS

Here is a list of all the event handlers Dreamweaver employs in its behaviors. The list also notes which browsers support each event handler. Remember, your choice of events is predicated on the page element you select.

EVENT HANDLERS	DESCRIPTION	COMPATIBLE BROWSERS	MOST COMMON ELEMENTS
onAbort	Occurs when the visitor prevents the browser from successfully loading, either clicking the browser's Stop button or pressing the ESC key.	NS3, NS4, IE4, IE5	Images, \<body\> tag
onAfterUpdate	Occurs after a form field's content changes and the cursor moves to the next field.	IE4, IE5	Links, images, \<body\> tag
onBeforeUpdate	Occurs after a form field's content changes, but before the cursor moves on to the next field.	IE4, IE5	Links, images, \<body\> tag
onBlur	Occurs when the visitor moves from one form element to the next. The form field they are in is considered "in focus." Once they move to the next field, it is now "blurred." See onFocus.	NS3, NS4, IE3, IE4, IE5	Text fields, text areas, lists/menus

Continued

EVENT HANDLERS	DESCRIPTION	COMPATIBLE BROWSERS	MOST COMMON ELEMENTS
onChange	Occurs when the visitor changes the default selection in a form field, for example, in a drop-down menu with initially selected text defined.	NS3, NS4, IE3, IE4, IE5	Form fields
onClick	Occurs when the visitor clicks the element to which the behavior is attached, then releases the mouse button.	NS3, NS4, IE3, IE4, IE5	Links, form buttons, checkboxes, radio buttons
onDblClick	Occurs when the visitor double-clicks the element to which the behavior is attached.	NS4, IE4, IE5	Links, images
onError	Occurs when there is a browser error while the document or image is loading.	NS3, NS4, IE4, IE5	Links, images, <body> tag
onFocus	Occurs when the visitor selects the form element to which the behavior is attached.	NS3, NS4, IE3, IE4, IE5	Text fields, text areas, lists/menus
onHelp	Occurs when the visitor clicks the browser's Help button or selects Help from the menu bar.	IE4, IE5	Links, images
onKeyDown	Occurs the moment the visitor presses any key on their keyboard.	NS4, IE4, IE5	Text fields, text areas
onKeyPress	Occurs when the visitor presses and releases any key on their keyboard.	NS4, IE4, IE5	Text fields, text areas
onKeyUp	Occurs when the visitor releases any key on their keyboard.	NS4, IE4, IE5	Text fields, text areas
onLoad	Occurs when a document or image finishes loading.	NS3, NS4, IE3, IE4, IE5	Images, <body> tag
onMouseDown	Occurs when the visitor presses the mouse button.	NS4, IE4, IE5	Links, images

Continued

EVENT HANDLERS	DESCRIPTION	COMPATIBLE BROWSERS	MOST COMMON ELEMENTS
onMouseMove	Occurs when the visitor moves the mouse.	IE3, IE4, IE5	Links, images
onMouseOut	Occurs when the visitor moves the mouse off of the element to which the behavior is attached.	NS3, NS4, IE4, IE5	Links, images
onMouseOver	Occurs when the visitor moves the mouse over the element to which the behavior is attached.	NS3, NS4, IE3, IE4, IE5	Links, images
onMouseUp	Occurs when the visitor releases the mouse button.	NS4, IE4, IE5	Links, images
onMove	Occurs when a window or frame is moved.	NS4	`<body>` tag `frameset` tag
onReadyStateChange	Occurs when page is loading.	IE4, IE5	Images
onReset	Occurs when the visitor clicks a form's Reset button.	NS3, NS4, IE3, IE4, IE5	`<form>` tag
onResize	Occurs when the visitor changes the size of the browser window or a frame.	NS4, IE4, IE5	`<body>` tag, `frameset` tag
onScroll	Occurs when the visitor uses the browser's scrollbars.	IE4, IE5	`<body>` tag
onSelect	Occurs when the visitor selects in the form field to which the behavior is attached.	NS3, NS4, IE3, IE4, IE5	Text fields
onSubmit	Occurs when the visitor clicks a form's Submit button.	NS3, NS4, IE3, IE4, IE5	`<form>` tag
onUnload	Occurs when the visitor leaves the browser's current document.	NS3, NS4, IE3, IE4, IE5	`<body>` tag

THE BEHAVIOR ACTIONS

This section outlines the implementation of the actions available through the Behaviors Panel. Actions applied by inserting page elements such as navigation bars, image rollovers, and jump menus are not repeated here, though you will see them displayed in the Behaviors Panel. It's best to insert and modify them using the methods discussed in their individual chapters.

Macromedia designed these actions to be compatible with Netscape Navigator's fourth generation browsers (4.0 through 4.7), and Internet Explorer 4.0 and above. Older browsers have less support for JavaScript, and in some cases, no support at all.

The descriptions provided here make the assumption that you have selected an appropriate element from the Document window and have chosen the browsers for which you want your behavior to comply. If there's a preferred page element or event handler for a specific action, I've tried to include them where appropriate. Refer back to "Attaching Behaviors" for a complete overview of the process.

CALL JAVASCRIPT

This action allows you to invoke a custom JavaScript function or a single line of JavaScript code when the specified event occurs. This requires that you have previous JavaScript experience and have written your own function or have included a function you gathered from an outside source and placed within your document.

To Add THE CALL JAVASCRIPT ACTION:

| Click the Add Action (+) button and select Call JavaScript from the drop-down menu. This displays the Call JavaScript dialog box.

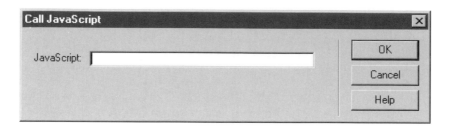

2 Enter the function name or line of JavaScript you want executed, and click OK.

Make sure the default event handler is the one you want to use; otherwise click the Event Handler drop-down arrow and select a new one.

CHANGE PROPERTY

This action allows you to change the properties of layers, images, forms, and form fields. The individual properties you have control over are dictated by the browser you initially selected. As with Call JavaScript, this action requires that you have a firm understanding of HTML and JavaScript.

To Add THE CHANGE PROPERTY ACTION:

1 Click the Add Action (+) button and select Change Property from the drop-down menu. This displays the Change Property dialog box.

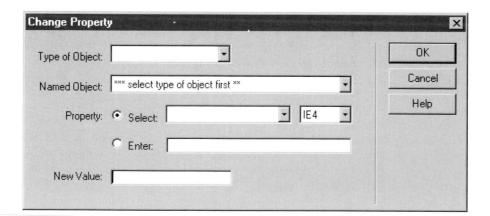

2 From the Type Of Object drop-down menu, select the type of page element whose property you want to change. This populates the Name Of Object field. If you haven't given a unique name to the element you want to change, go back and do so in the Properties Inspector.

3 In the Named Object field, select the page element you want to modify.

4 In the Property section of the dialog box, click Select and choose a property from the drop-down menu, as well as the browser you want this behavior to be compatible with. If the property you want to change is not listed in the drop-down menu, select the Enter radio button and type it in yourself.

5 In the New Value field, enter the property's new value to be inserted when the event occurs.

6 Click OK. Change the event handler if necessary.

The Type Of Object field lists the HTML tags this action can affect. If you don't know the tag, select the page element, click Design And Code View, and scroll until you find the highlighted code. The main tag will be the first few characters after the initial <, for example, `img`, `form`, or `select`.

CHECK BROWSER

The Check Browser action does exactly what it says. It checks to see what browser a visitor is using, and then sends them to a specific page based on what it discovers. Remember all the browser issues I've warned you about in past chapters? This action offers a way to work around them. You can have visitors with Netscape Navigator go to one version of your page and visitors with Internet Explorer go to another. Because you want this action to encompass the entire document, it's best to attach it to the `<body>` tag, and use the `onLoad` event handler.

To Add THE CHECK BROWSER ACTION:

1 Click the Add Action (+) button and select Check Browser from the drop-down menu. This displays the Check Browser dialog box, shown in Figure 12-3.

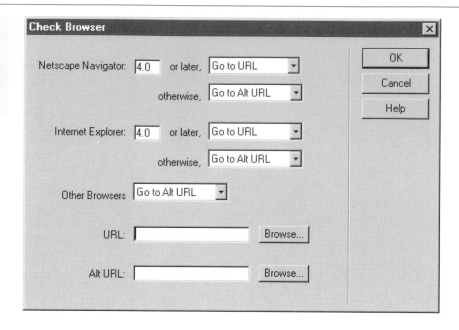

2 For each browser option (Netscape Navigator, Internet Explorer, or Other Browsers), select whether the visitor should go to one URL (Go To URL), an alternative URL (Go To Alt URL), or stay on this page. You can divide your visitors by browser, version number, or both.

3 Type the paths and file names you want used into the URL and Alt URL fields at the bottom of the dialog box. Use the Browse button to locate the files on your hard drive. To specify a URL outside your site, enter the entire address, for example, http://www.outside-site.com/.

4 Click OK. Change the event handler if necessary.

CHECK PLUGIN

Similar to the Check Browser action, this action allows you to redirect visitors depending on whether they have a specific plug-in installed. For example, if you've inserted Flash text effects into your site, you wouldn't want visitors not capable of viewing this content to see a page with gaping holes in it.

It is not possible to detect plug-ins in Internet Explorer with JavaScript. If you choose Flash or Director in the Check Plugin dialog box, however, Dreamweaver inserts the proper VBScript required to check for those plug-ins in the Windows OS. Internet Explorer for Macintosh does not support plug-in detection at all.

To Add THE CHECK PLUGIN ACTION:

1 Click the Add Action (+) button and select Check Plugin from the drop-down menu. This displays the Check Plugin dialog box.

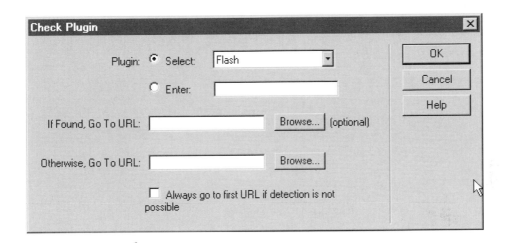

2 Select the plug-in for which you want to check from the Select drop-down menu. If the plug-in you want to check for is not in the drop-down menu, click Enter and type the plug-in name in the field provided.

3 Enter the page for visitors who have the plug-in in the If Found, Go To URL field.

4 For visitors without the plug-in, enter a URL in the Otherwise, Go To URL field. If you want visitors without the plug-in to stay on the present page, leave this field blank.

5 Click OK. Change the event handler if necessary.

CONTROL SHOCKWAVE OR FLASH

This action allows you to play, stop, rewind, or go to a specific frame of a Shockwave or Flash movie clip inserted in your page. For example, you can create the equivalent of VCR buttons in your favorite image editor, insert them into your document alongside your Flash or Shockwave movie clip, and then assign the appropriate command to each button.

To Add THE CONTROL SHOCKWAVE OR FLASH ACTION:

1 In the Document window, select the movie clip, and enter a name for it in the Properties Inspector.

2 Select the page element with which you want to trigger the action. In the example above, this would be one of the button images.

3 Click the Add Action (+) button and select Control Shockwave Or Flash from the drop-down menu. This displays the Control Shockwave Or Flash dialog box.

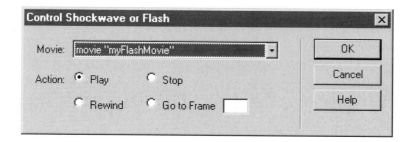

4 From the Movie drop-down menu, select the movie clip name you assigned in step 1.

5 Select the action you want performed using the Action radio buttons. If you select the Go To Frame action, enter the frame number you want the movie clip to start at in the field provided.

6 Click OK. Change the event handler if necessary.

The Go To Frame action is a bit confusing. Just attaching the Go To Frame action won't make the move start playing at that point when whatever event handler you chose triggers the action. You actually have to attach the Control Shockwave Or Flash action to the same page element, with the same event handler you used the first time, and choose the Play action, effectively giving the dual command "Go to Frame X, and Play" when the event handler occurs.

DRAG LAYER

This action produces one of the neater pieces of "eye-candy" modern browsers are capable of. Using the Drag Layer action, any content that can be placed in a layer can be dragged and dropped anywhere within the browser window by your visitors. You have a great deal of control over where and how layers can be dragged and what can happen to them in different circumstances once they are released. Obviously, you need to have layers in your document before attaching this behavior. The JavaScript needed to create this effect must be executed before the visitor drags the layer itself, so it's best to attach the behavior to the <body> tag and use the onLoad event handler. This way the effect is ready to go once the page finishes loading in the visitor's browser.

To Add THE DRAG LAYER ACTION:

1 Click the Add Action (+) button and select Drag Layer from the drop-down menu. This displays the Drag Layer dialog box.

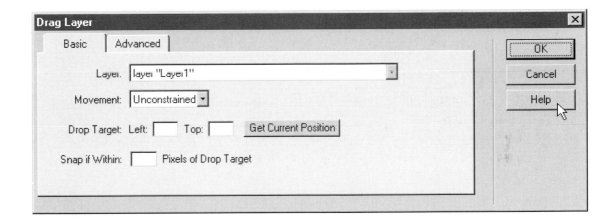

2 From the Layer drop-down menu, select the layer for which you want to enable dragging.

3 To allow the visitor to drag the layer anywhere within the browser window, select Unconstrained from the Movement drop-down menu. To limit the movement of the layer, select Constrained.

4 If you select Constrained, fields for entering movement values are displayed: Up, Down, Left, and Right. The pixel values you enter into these fields are relative to the starting position of the layer's upper-left corner. For example, to be able to drag the layer up 10 pixels from the starting point, enter 10 in the Up field.

- To constrain the layer's movement to a rectangular space, enter positive values into each field.

- To constrain the layer to only horizontal movement, enter 0 for Up and Down, and positive pixel values for Left and Right.

- To constrain the layer to only vertical movement, enter 0 for Left and Right, and positive pixel values for Up and Down.

5 If your page design requires the visitor to drag the layer to a specific location, you need to enter the location's coordinates in the Drop Target fields. The coordinates represent the position of the layer's upper-left corner relative to the upper-left corner of the browser window. To get the exact coordinates for the drop target, place the layer where you want it dropped, and click the Get Current Position button.

6 If you want the layer to snap to the drop target when the visitor releases the mouse button, enter a pixel value in the Snap If Within field. This says if the layer is within so many pixels of the exact drop target coordinates, it will snap automatically. Five pixels is usually a good number to start with. Test the effect in your browser to determine the optimal setting for your particular design.

7 Click the Advanced tab, shown here, to modify what area of the layer responds to the mouse, keep track of the layer's movement while it's dragged, and trigger another action once the layer is dropped.

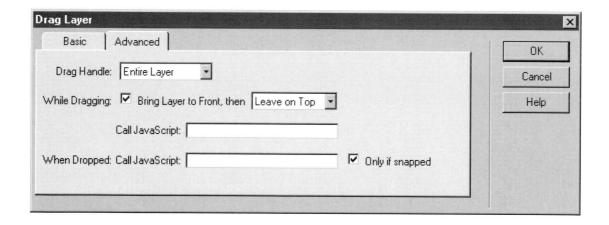

- From the Drag Handle drop-down menu, first select Area Within Layer to define a specific area within the layer that will respond to the visitor's mouse. This choice will cause four new fields to be displayed. Enter coordinates in the L (left) and T (top) fields to define the drag handle area's starting point, and pixel values in the W (width) and H (height) fields to define its physical dimensions. Finally, to make the entire layer respond to the visitor's mouse, select Entire Layer from the drop-down menu.

- Check the While Dragging checkbox and choose Bring Layer To Front to move the layer to the top of the stacking order while it is being dragged. After selecting this option, use the drop-down menu to determine if the layer remains at the top of the stacking order or gets returned to its original Z-index.

> SEE ALSO To brush up on Z-indexes and a layer's stacking order, see Chapter 9.

- Type a JavaScript function name or single line of code into the Call JavaScript field if you want the dragging event to trigger this action. Place the function name or line of code in the When Dropped: Call JavaScript field if you want the dropping event to trigger the action. Check Only if Snapped if you want the JavaScript executed only when the layer reaches the drop target. If your JavaScript skills aren't where you think they should be, leave this feature for future experimentation.

8 Click OK. Change the event handler if necessary. The `onMouseDown` and `onClick` event handlers can't be used with this action.

Go To URL

Use the Go To URL action to open a new page in the browser window or a specific frame. This is a nice action for making a link change the contents of two frames simultaneously.

To Add THE Go To URL ACTION:

1 Click the Add Action (+) button and select Go To URL from the drop-down menu. This displays the Go To URL dialog box.

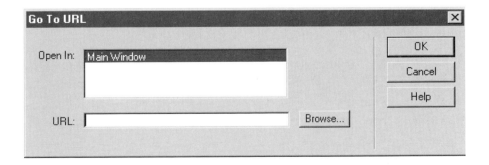

2 In the Open In field, select the main browser window or individual frame name in which you want the URL to open. If you aren't attaching this action within a frames-based site, only the Main Window option is available.

3 Click Browse to locate the document you want to open from your hard drive. Alternatively, enter the URL in the field provided.

4 Repeat steps 2 and 3 for each frame in which you want this action to open URLs.

5 Click OK. Change the event handler if necessary.

OPEN BROWSER WINDOW

This action is similar to Go To URL, except that instead of opening the new document in the existing browser window, it opens in a new one. You can specify the window's dimensions and control various window attributes, such as the presence of menu bars, navigation buttons, and scrollbars, to name only a few.

When used sensibly, this can create nice Web site interfaces. In the wrong hands, this action creates those annoying pop-up windows that keep opening and opening when you try to close your browser or move to a new site. Be kind to your fellow Netizens, and you can guarantee return visitors. Make your site a nightmare by attempting to keep visitors at your site involuntarily, and you can bet they will never return.

To Add THE OPEN BROWSER WINDOW ACTION:

1 Click the Add Action (+) button and select Open Browser Window from the drop-down menu. This displays the Open Browser Window dialog box, shown in Figure 12-4.

2 Click Browse to locate the URL you want displayed in the new browser window.

3 Enter the height and width of the new window in the fields provided. Leaving them blank creates a window with the same properties as the window the action is launched from.

4 Select the individual attributes you want the new window to have:

- Navigation Toolbar Adds the traditional Back, Forward, and Home button bar. Each browser's button set varies slightly.

FIGURE 12-4

The Open Browser Window action should be used sparingly, and only when it accentuates part of your design.

```
┌─ Open Browser Window ──────────────────────────────────────── [×] ─┐
│                                                                      │
│  URL to Display: [_____]  [ Browse... ]   ┌────────┐ │
│                                                              │   OK   │ │
│                                                              └────────┘ │
│  Window Width: [_____]      Window Height: [_____]           ┌────────┐ │
│                                                              │ Cancel │ │
│       Attributes:  ☐ Navigation Toolbar    ☐ Menu Bar        └────────┘ │
│                                                              ┌────────┐ │
│                    ☐ Location Toolbar       ☐ Scrollbars as  │  Help  │ │
│                                               Needed         └────────┘ │
│                    ☐ Status Bar             ☐ Resize Handles          │
│                                                                      │
│  Window Name: [_____]                            │
│                                                                      │
└──────────────────────────────────────────────────────────────────┘
```

- ● Location Toolbar **Adds the address field bar. Again, each browser has different options available on this item.**

- ● Status Bar **Located along the bottom of the browser, this bar displays messages concerning items remaining to be downloaded and the URLs of links when they are moused over.**

- ● Menu Bar **Adds the File, Edit, View, etc. menu bar common to most applications. This is a physical part of the window in Windows applications, whereas Macintosh's menu bars run along the top of the desktop.**

- ● Scrollbars As Needed **Will include scrollbars in a window if content is sufficient to warrant them.**

- ● Resize Handles **Will allow the visitor to manually resize the window.**

- ● Window Name **Like adding names to the elements in your page using the Properties Inspector, naming a window object allows you to manipulate it using JavaScript.**

5 Enter a unique name for the window in the Window Name field to allow the window to be manipulated by any custom JavaScript you choose to create. Make sure there are no spaces or special characters in the name. Dreamweaver will prompt you if there are any syntax problems.

6 Click OK. Change the event handler if necessary.

In most cases, you'll be attaching this behavior to a null link, as described earlier in this chapter. If you're using text to trigger this action, create a null link for it in the Properties Inspector, and then go about attaching the behavior. If you use an image, you can just attach the behavior and select onClick for the event handler, which will appear in parentheses on the Events drop-down menu. Dreamweaver creates the null link automatically.

POPUP MESSAGE

This action allows you to display a JavaScript Alert box, shown here, when the specified event occurs. You enter the message you want displayed in the alert box using the Popup Message dialog box. If you know JavaScript, you can enter function calls, properties, or other valid JavaScript expressions along with any text by placing them inside curly braces, like this: {expression}.

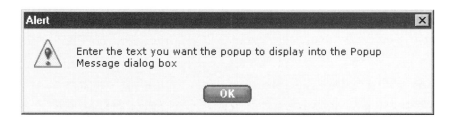

To Add THE POPUP MESSAGE ACTION:

1 Click the Add Action (+) button and select Popup Message from the drop-down menu. This displays the Popup Message dialog box.

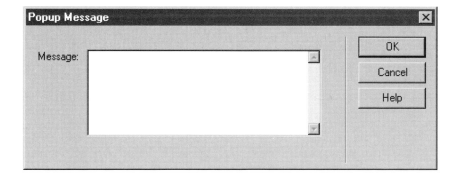

2 Enter the message you want displayed in the Message field.

3 Click OK. Change the event handler if necessary.

SET TEXT OF FRAME

On the Actions drop-down menu is a submenu titled Set Text, from which you can select any of four related actions. This first Set Text action is quite a powerful piece of JavaScript. With it, you can dynamically generate the content of a specified frame, literally writing all the HTML code for the frame contents using JavaScript. By using this approach you can make links in one frame actually write the pages in another frame on the fly, instead of maintaining a number of frame documents. This action is probably best applied to null links in a given frame, using the `onClick` event handler to trigger it. See the section "Using Null Links in Behaviors" earlier in this chapter.

To Add THE SET TEXT OF FRAME ACTION:

1 Click the Add Action (+) button and select Set Text Of Frame from the drop-down menu. This displays the Set Text of Frame dialog box.

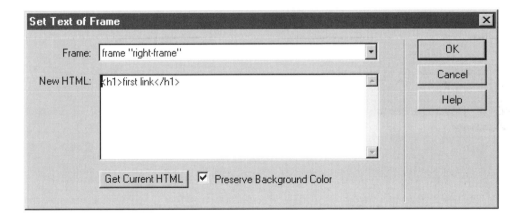

2 From the Frame drop-down menu, select the target frame whose contents you want to create dynamically.

3 Enter the HTML for the content you want to appear in the selected frame in the New HTML field. To keep the basic code of the frame you originally created, click the Get Current HTML button, and modify only what you wish to change.

4 To keep the background and text, and link attributes from the original frame document, click the Preserve Background Color checkbox.

5 Click OK. Change the event handler if necessary.

If your HTML skills are not where you think they should be, don't worry. Open a new page and create the content you want the action to write. When you've got the content you want, switch to Code view and copy all the HTML between the opening and closing body tags, `<body>` and `</body>`. Paste the code into the Set Text Of Frame dialog box, and you're finished.

> **SEE ALSO** See Appendix A for more information about HTML.

SET TEXT OF LAYER

This action takes existing content and formatting on a layer and replaces it with content you choose, including any valid HTML code. When the content and formatting are replaced, the layer's attributes are maintained, which includes the current color selection. To format the new content, use the New HTML field in the Set Text Of Layer dialog box to include HTML tags.

To Add THE SET TEXT OF LAYER ACTION:

1 Click the Add Action (+) button and select Set Text Of Layer from the drop-down menu. This displays the Set Text Of Layer dialog box.

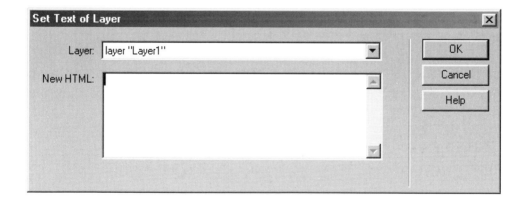

2 Click the Layer drop-down list to choose the target layer for this action.

3 Type a message in the New HTML field.

4 Click OK. Change the event handler if necessary.

SET TEXT OF STATUS BAR

This action displays a message on the status bar at the bottom of the browser window. You can use this action to describe where a link is going or to provide additional information about a graphic on the page. While text on the status bar can be informative to the user (and it's helpful to you to have this additional place to insert text), remember that many users may not notice it. If the information is integral to the visitor's use of your page, be sure to use the text in additional locations, such as in the Properties Inspector's Alt field for graphic.

To Add THE SET TEXT OF STATUS BAR ACTION:

1 Click the Add Action (+) button and select Set Text Of Status Bar from the drop-down menu. This displays the Set Text Of Status Bar dialog box.

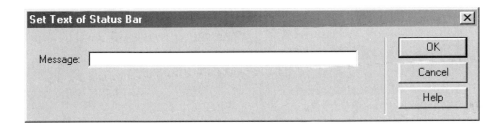

2 In the Message field, type the text you want to appear on the status bar.

3 Click OK and change the event handler if necessary.

It's a good idea to verify that the status bar text looks the way you want it and doesn't have any typos or misspellings in it. You can preview your page in a browser by pressing F12, at which point you can read the status bar text when you point to the link or graphic to which the status bar text refers and make sure it appears as desired.

If you need to make any changes, select the link or graphic, and then select the Set Text Of Status Bar action from the list of established behaviors and double-click the Action. This will reopen the Set Text Of Status Bar dialog box, and you can edit the message accordingly.

SET TEXT OF TEXT FIELD

You can use this action to replace the content of a text field in a form. By associating this action with an event such as onFocus, you can make form fields more interactive for your visitors. For example, your initial value for a text field might be United States (for a field requesting the user's country). You can set an onMouseOver action to change that initial value to "Click List to Select Another Country" or some other instructional text. A subsequent action can return the text to the initial value (United States) if the user mouses away before clicking the drop-down list to select a country.

To Add THE SET TEXT OF TEXT FIELD ACTION:

1   Click the Add Action (+) button and select Set Text Of Text Field from the drop-down menu. This displays the Set Text Of Text Field dialog box.

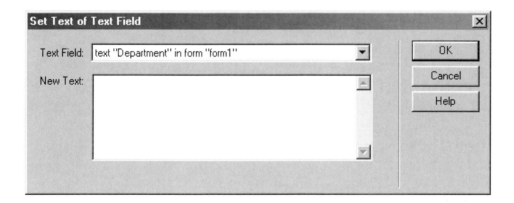

2   If the displayed field (in the Text Field text box) is not the field you want to adjust, click the drop-down list to select the correct field.

3   In the New Text field, type the text that should appear in the field when the selected event occurs.

4   Click OK and change the event handler if necessary.

SHOW-HIDE LAYERS

This action is used to control the visibility of layers, associating their appearance and/or disappearance with events such as onMouseOver or onClick. Show-Hide

Layers adds interactivity to your page, making it possible to have instructions appear when a user mouses over a particular link or graphic. For example, if your page includes a map, you can have layers appear when the user mouses over hotspots on the map. The layers can contain directions to locations within the area, or the phone number of a store or office in the area to which the visitor has pointed.

You can also use the Show-Hide Layers action to obscure the content of the page until all of it has loaded. Associate the action with the <body> tag (click <body> in the lower-left corner of the Dreamweaver workspace) and then add the Show-Hide action. You'll want to select the layer to be hidden, and make sure the event handler is onLoad.

> **TIP** If the Show-Hide Layers action is unavailable or doesn't show in the list at all, chances are you clicked and selected a layer before beginning the process of adding an action. Another reason the Show-Hide Layers action might be dimmed is the absence of a layer on the active page. Because layers don't accept events in both Internet Explorer 4.0 and Netscape 4.0, you want to select a different object, such as the <body> tag, before attempting to add an action.

To Add THE SHOW-HIDE LAYERS ACTION:

1 Click the Add Action (+) button and select Show-Hide Layers from the drop-down menu. This displays the Show-Hide Layers dialog box.

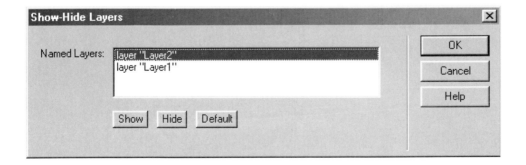

2 Select the layer you want to show or hide from the Named Layers list.

3 Click the Show or Hide button for the selected layer.

4 Repeat steps 2 and 3 for all the named layers that you want to show or hide.

5 Click OK and change the event handler as needed.

SWAP IMAGE

This action swaps one image for another by changing the source (src) attribute of the image tag for a selected graphic. You can create rollover effects (if you set the action to occur onMouseOver), or you can make several swaps occur simultaneously based on virtually any event handler.

When choosing the image that is swapped for the original, it's important that you pick an image that has the same dimensions as the original image. Why? Because if, for example, your first image is 150 pixels by 200 pixels and the second image is 100 pixels by 75 pixels, the image that is swapped in will be distorted—stretched to fit a 150 by 200 pixel space.

Another thing to consider when adding a Swap Image action is the Swap Image Restore action, which is added to the list of behaviors automatically. You can choose the event handler for Swap Image Restore, keeping in mind that if you want the original image to come back, you'll want the restore-related event to be something that occurs naturally. For example, if your Swap Image action is set to happen onClick, you might choose onMouseOut or onClick again for the event that triggers the Swap Image Restore action.

To Add THE SWAP IMAGE ACTION:

1 Click the Add Action (+) button and select Swap Image from the drop-down menu. This displays the Swap Image dialog box, shown in Figure 12-5.

FIGURE 12-5
Select the image that will replace the original when your selected event occurs.

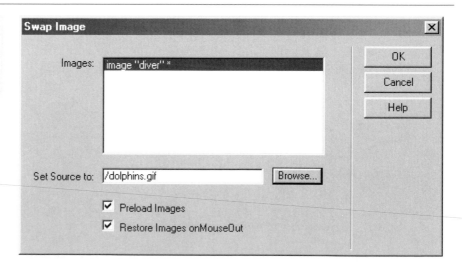

2 As needed, select a named image from the Images list. The one selected on the page should be selected, but you can pick a different one.

3 Click in the Set Source To text box, and type the path and file name of the image that should be swapped with the original. You can also click Browse to select a file.

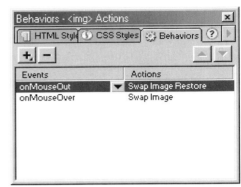

4 Click OK. Note that in the Behaviors Panel, two new actions appear: Swap Image Restore and Swap Image, as shown here. You can change the event handler associated with one or both of these actions.

SWAP IMAGE RESTORE

Because this action is added automatically whenever a Swap Image action is added, you don't need to add this one yourself. You can change the event handler for this action, choosing an event that is likely to occur on its own or that the visitor is likely to perform when the original image is swapped. You can remove this action if you don't want the original image to come back until or unless someone reloads the page.

GO TO TIMELINE FRAME

This action is used to control the looping or playback of an animation. By choosing a particular frame to Go To, you can make an animation jump to a particular point. You can also set more than one Go To Timeline Frame action, each associated with a different event handler, each resulting in a jump to a different frame of the animation.

For this action to be available, your page must contain a timeline—an animated layer, for example. You'll also want the Timeline Panel onscreen so you can see the frames involved in the animation and also see each frame's number to assist you in setting up the action. To learn more about timeline animation, see the section "Dreamweaver Timeline Animation" later in this chapter.

To Add THE GO TO TIMELINE FRAME ACTION:

1 Click the Add Action (+) button and select Go To Timeline Frame from the drop-down menu. This displays the Go To Timeline Frame dialog box.

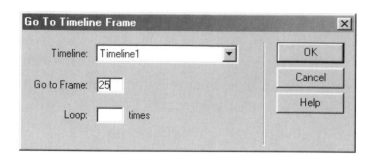

2 In the Go To Timeline Frame dialog box, select a timeline from the Timeline list. If your page has only one timeline, you can skip this step.

3 Enter the frame number you want the animation to jump to in the Go To Frame text box. You'll want to check the Timeline Panel to get the exact frame number.

4 Enter the number of times the animation should loop to this frame. Note that if your timeline is not set to loop, an error prompt will appear if you try to complete this process with a number in the Loop box.

5 Click OK and change the event handler as desired.

PLAY TIMELINE AND STOP TIMELINE

These two actions enable your visitors to click a button, graphic, or link to either play or stop a timeline. The most common use of this action involves a Play or a Stop button (or text) and the onClick event handler. Before adding this action, you should have selected the image or text you want to serve as the trigger, and there must be a timeline on the page for the action to be available in the Behaviors list.

To Add THE PLAY TIMELINE OR STOP TIMELINE ACTION:

1 Click the Add Action (+) button and select Play Timeline or Stop Timeline from the drop-down menu. This displays the Play Timeline or Stop Timeline dialog box.

2 In the Play Timeline or Stop Timeline dialog box, click the drop-down list to choose the timeline to be played or stopped by the action.

3 Click OK. You can change the event handler for this action as needed.

VALIDATE FORM

You can use this action to prevent a user from submitting a form with invalid or missing data in it. The action is associated with individual fields in a form, using the onBlur event to validate the fields as the user goes from field to field. To have the validation performed on multiple fields when the user clicks the Submit button, you'll use the onSubmit event handler.

To add this action, your page must have a form in it, and that form must contain text fields, as only text fields can be validated. If your form has not yet been created, build it first, and then proceed to add the Validate Form action to individual fields or to the entire form.

To Add THE VALIDATE FORM ACTION:

1 If you will be validating the entire form and not just an individual field, click the \<form> tag in the tag selector found in the lower-left corner of the Dreamweaver window. If you will be validating an individual field within the form, select that field before proceeding to step 2.

2 Click the Add Action (+) button and select Validate Form from the drop-down menu. This displays the Validate Form dialog box.

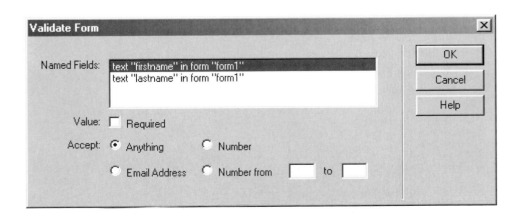

3 In the Validate Form dialog box, verify that the individual field you want to validate is selected. If it isn't, click once on it in the Named Fields list.

4 If the field cannot be left blank, click to place a checkmark in the Value Required checkbox.

5 To control the type of data entered, choose one of the options in the Accept section of the dialog box. If you choose Number From, enter the range of numbers, such as 200 to 300.

6 Repeat steps 3 through 5 for all the text fields you want to be validated, whether they'll be validated individually or you're validating the entire form.

7 Click OK and change the event handler as desired. The default for individual field validations is onBlur, and onSubmit will validate the entire form when the user clicks the Submit button. It's best to leave them at these default settings.

DOWNLOADING THIRD-PARTY BEHAVIORS

All these behaviors not enough for you? Need to expand your toolkit? Not a problem. The Macromedia Web site maintains a collection of third-party behaviors that expert users have been kind enough to create and share.

To Download NEW BEHAVIORS:

1 Click the Add Action (+) button and select Get More Behaviors from the drop-down menu. This will open your default Web browser and connect you to the Macromedia Exchange Web site.

2 Tour the site, download the Dreamweaver Behavior extensions you want, and follow the instructions for installing them.

DREAMWEAVER TIMELINE ANIMATION

You've seen how layers can be made to drag using the Drag Layer behavior, but you can also make Dreamweaver move the layer to create animation effects. Dreamweaver accomplishes this using a timeline. In addition to moving layers,

Dreamweaver timelines can also be used to trigger the various behaviors we've discussed.

Keep in mind these rules before you create a design that relies on timeline animation:

▶ Timeline animation is only possible in fourth generation browsers.

▶ Any page element you want to animate must be inside a layer. Dreamweaver will prompt you if you attempt to break this rule.

▶ A single timeline can have many animations within it, but no two animations in a timeline can affect the same layer simultaneously. You could have two separate timelines animating the same layer at the same time, but in all likelihood, they would wreak havoc with each other.

With that said, know that timeline animation is tightly integrated with layers and behaviors. You'll want to have a firm understanding of how each works before you get started, so make sure you've read the first part of this chapter, as well as Chapter 9.

THE TIMELINES PANEL

If you've ever made a flip book, you have a basic grasp of how the timeline works. Each page of a flip book contains an image that is slightly different from the page before it. When each page is flipped over in turn, the illusion of movement is created. Cartoons and movies work in similar fashion, except where the flip book has pages, motion pictures have frames. Dreamweaver timelines use a frames metaphor too. To display the Timelines Panel, shown in Figure 12-6, select Window | Timelines from the menu bar, or press SHIFT-F9.

The Timelines Panel consists of the following:

▶ **Playback head** Indicates which frame is currently being displayed.

▶ **Timeline drop-down menu** Shows the timeline currently being displayed in the Timelines Panel.

▶ **Animation channels** Hold the individual animation bars which represent the animation of layers and images.

▶ **Animation bars** Display the length of a given page element's animation.

FIGURE 12-6

The Timelines Panel provides a powerful interface for creating animation effects.

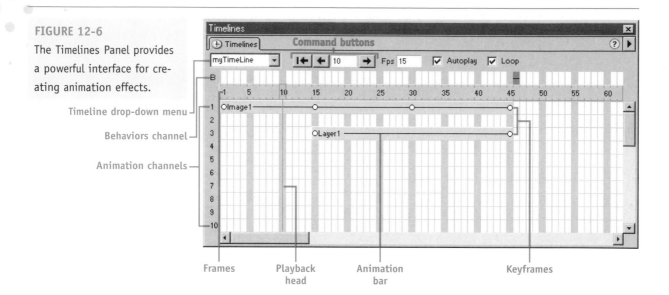

Timeline drop-down menu

Behaviors channel

Animation channels

Frames   Playback   Animation   Keyframes
            head   bar

▶ **Keyframes** Represent the frames of an animation bar in which specific properties have been defined for the page element. After you define these relative starting and ending points, Dreamweaver fills in the frames in between.

▶ **Behaviors channel** Adds behaviors so they get executed at specific frames in the timeline animation.

▶ **Frame numbers** Delineate the individual frames in the timeline.

Try thinking of the Timelines Panel as a VCR or cassette deck. Running along the top of the Timelines Panel, to the right of the Timeline drop-down menu, shown here, are a series of control buttons and checkboxes that will probably seem familiar to you:

Rewind   Play   Autoplay checkbox

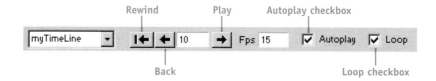

Back   Loop checkbox

▶ **Rewind** Returns the playback head to the beginning of the timeline.

▶ **Back** Moves the playback head back one frame to the left.

▶ **Play** Moves the playback head forward one frame to the right. Holding the Play button down will advance the playback head repeatedly through the animation.

▶ **Autoplay** Checking Autoplay makes the timeline start playing the moment the page loads.

▶ **Loop** Checking Loop makes the animation play continuously once the page loads.

CREATING TIMELINE ANIMATIONS

To create a timeline animation, you need to have layers in your document to animate. With that prerequisite out of the way, you then need to add the layer you want to move to the timeline itself. Once you have it there, you can start using the Timelines Panel to work with it.

To Create A TIMELINE ANIMATION:

1 Select the layer you want to animate.

2 Place your layer in the Timelines Panel using any of the following methods:

- Right-click in the Timelines Panel and select Add Object from the context menu.
- Select Modify | Timeline | Add Object To Timeline.
- Drag the layer directly into the Timelines Panel itself.

An animation bar representing the layer appears in the Timelines Panel with the layer name within it.

3 Click the circular keyframe marker at the end of the animation bar.

4 In the Document window, position the layer where you want it to be at the end of the animation sequence. A thin line appears marking the path the layer will follow.

5 To add additional keyframes between the starting and ending points of the animation sequence, CTRL-click in a frame on the animation bar, or select a frame and right-click, then choose Add Keyframe from the context menu. In each keyframe, you can reposition the layer to alter the course of its movement through the animation sequence.

6 Hold down the Play button to preview your animation in the Document window. Click the Preview/Debug In Browser button in the Document window menu bar to see how it plays in your browser.

7 Repeat these steps for each layer you want to add to the timeline.

RECORDING A LAYER'S PATH

Defining individual keyframes is fine when the path your layer is following isn't terribly complex, but think of how tedious adding a large number of keyframes could get if you were shooting for something really intricate. Fortunately, Dreamweaver allows you to drag the layer you want animated around the Document window while recording the path it follows.

To Record A LAYER'S PATH:

1 Select the layer you want to animate, and position where you want it to be when the animation sequence begins.

2 Select Modify | Timeline | Record Path Of Layer from the menu bar.

3 Begin dragging the layer along the path you want it to follow during the animation sequence. You will see a thick gray line following the layer as you drag it along.

4 Release the mouse where you want the animation to stop. Dreamweaver adds an animation bar with keyframes defined as needed.

5 Return the playback head to the first frame of the timeline and use the Play button to preview your animation.

EDITING TIMELINES

Once you've got a basic animation sequence in place, you can use the Timelines Panel to modify such properties as duration, speed, and start time.

To Modify THE DURATION OF AN ANIMATION SEQUENCE:

1 Drag the last keyframe to the left to shorten it, or to the right to make it longer. The intermediate keyframes reposition themselves to maintain their relationship to one another.

2 If you want the intermediate keyframes to remain in their original positions, press the ALT key while dragging the last keyframe. You can also choose Modify | Timeline | Add Frame or Remove Frame from the menu bar.

To Reposition AN INTERMEDIATE KEYFRAME:

▶ **Drag the keyframe to the desired position within the animation bar. You cannot drag a keyframe beyond the one on either side of it.**

To Reposition AN ENTIRE ANIMATION BAR:

▶ **Click the animation bar in a non-keyframe to select it, and drag it anywhere within the timeline. Use this method to change the start time of the animation sequence by dragging it forward or back. Drag the animation bar up or down to place it on a different animation channel.**

To add playback control behaviors, choose the appropriate method:

▶ Click Autoplay to make the timeline start playing when the page loads. This attaches a Play Timeline action to the `<body>` tag with an `onLoad` event handler. To learn how to attach this same action to other page elements, see the section "Play Timeline and Stop Timeline" earlier in this chapter.

▶ Click Loop to make the timeline play continuously. This adds a Go To Timeline Frame action to the Behaviors channel of the Timelines Panel in the frame immediately following the last frame in your animation sequence. To modify the loop properties, locate the Go To Timeline Frame action in the Behaviors Panel and double-click to display the Go To Timeline Frame dialog box. See the discussion of this action in "The Behavior Actions" earlier in this chapter.

▶ To use a behavior to stop a timeline, see the section "Play Timeline and Stop Timeline" earlier in this chapter.

If after checking your animation in a browser, it seems like something out of an '80s video game instead of the glossy Industrial Light and Magic production you envisioned, don't worry. The easiest way around this is to extend the overall length of the animation, and increase the frames per second at which it moves. Also, avoid animating huge graphic files. The browser already has to pull the thing in across whatever Internet connection the visitor has. Having to redraw the image from location to location is extremely hardware-intensive. Which brings up a good point: the biggest impact on how an animation sequence looks comes from the hardware viewing it. Most machines in the 500MHz and above range with 128MB of RAM or more, a quality graphics card, and a solid Internet connection should be able to handle just about anything you can dish out with Dreamweaver. I know this is sounding old by now, but remember, you want a site that is accessible to the widest audience possible. Keep animations small. Use them as accents, not the central theme of your site. "Less is more" is a good maxim here.

> **TIP** If the animation bug has bitten you hard, Macromedia has the perfect tool for the job: Flash 5. And guess what? The Virtual Classroom series has a book on the very subject, *Flash 5 Virtual Classroom,* by Doug Sahlin (Osborne/McGraw-Hill, 2001).

COPYING AND PASTING IN THE TIMELINES PANEL

After you've created an animation sequence, it's a snap to copy and paste it within the same timeline, different timelines, or entirely different documents. You can copy single animation bars, multiple bars, and behavior frames.

To Cut, Copy, Or Paste ANIMATION SEQUENCES:

1 Select the animation bars you want to manipulate. SHIFT-click to make multiple selections. Pressing CTRL-A selects all the animation bars.

2 To cut or copy the selected sequences, right-click on them and choose Cut or Copy from the context menu. Alternatively, use the keyboard shortcuts CTRL-X to cut and CTRL-C to copy.

3 Position the playback head within the current timeline where you want to place the sequences or create a new timeline in which to place them, either in this document or in a new one.

4 To paste the sequences, right-click and choose Paste from the context menu, or use the keyboard shortcut CTRL-V.

If an animation sequence you paste into a new document contains a layer with the same name, Dreamweaver applies the animation to the existing layer. To avoid this, make sure your layers have unique names. If you want to ascribe the new animation sequence to a different page element, right-click on the animation sequence and select Change Object from the context menu. This displays the Change Object dialog box. Select the page element you want to reassign the sequence to using the Object To Animate drop-down menu. You can use this process to reassign any animation you choose throughout your documents.

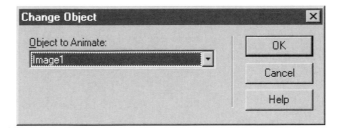

MODIFYING LAYER AND IMAGE PROPERTIES

You've seen how to make layers move around the browser window, and how to modify the basic properties of individual animation sequences, but there's more to animation than just moving an object from point A to point B. You can also make layers and images come and go from the screen, either by changing the source of an image or changing the visibility of a layer at a given point in the timeline.

> TIP You're better off placing your images in separate layers and then modifying their visibility than changing the source files back and forth. Changing source files requires the browser to download the new image each time, slowing down the overall animation. Placing the images in layers, whether visible or not, has the browser download all the required image files at once, so they're all in the visitor's cache waiting to be displayed.

To Change AN IMAGE'S SOURCE FILE IN A TIMELINE:

▶ Add the image you want to modify to the timeline using any of the methods described previously and select the keyframe in which you want the source file of the image to change. You can insert a new one as you see fit. Then use the Properties Inspector to change the source file of the image by clicking the folder icon beside the Src field and choosing a new file for the image. When the timeline plays, the new image will replace the original one at the appropriate frame in the timeline.

To modify layer properties in a timeline, use the appropriate method:

▶ To change the visibility of the layer, add the layer you want to modify to the timeline and choose the keyframe in which to change the layer's visibility. In the Visibility field of the Properties Inspector, change the visibility to Inherit, Visible, or Hidden, using the drop-down menu provided.

▶ To modify the stacking order of the layer, enter a new value in the Properties Inspector's Z-index field.

▶ To resize the layer, enter new values into the Properties Inspector's Width and Height fields, or drag the layer's resize handle. This effect is currently only supported by Internet Explorer.

WORKING WITH MULTIPLE TIMELINES

Depending on how you like to work, you may find using an individual timeline for each animated page element an easier proposition than a single timeline with a gazillion animation channels in it.

To create and manage multiple timelines, use the appropriate method:

▶ Select Modify | Timeline | Add Timeline to create a new one. This displays a new timeline in the Timelines Panel. To switch back to the original timeline, click the Timeline drop-down menu and select the timeline name you want to view. Default timeline names are Timeline 1, Timeline 2, and so on.

▶ To rename a timeline, right-click anywhere in the present timeline and select Rename Timeline from the context menu. Alternatively, you can rename a selected timeline by choosing Modify | Timeline | Rename Timeline from the menu bar.

▶ To delete a timeline, right-click anywhere in the present timeline and choose Remove Timeline from the context menu, or choose Modify | Timeline | Remove Timeline from the menu bar.

 ON THE VIRTUAL CLASSROOM CD-ROM Follow along with the instructor in Lesson 8, "Working with Behaviors," as he demonstrates how to use the Behaviors Panel to create a number of JavaScript effects.

13

Dreamweaver Power Tools: Assets and Automation

Remember that cache file you created when you set up a local site back in Chapter 2? We've seen how the cache file assists link management, keeping track of all your link relationships and helping you update them when files are moved, deleted, or renamed, but that's not all it keeps track of. Essentially, that little cache file acts as your own private secretary, keeping track of everything you put into the site of which it is a part. Every time you assign a color, insert an image or multimedia file, or create a link to a URL outside your site, Dreamweaver saves the information in its own panel from which you can quickly and easily recall them. This is the Dreamweaver Assets Panel.

The two most powerful elements in the Assets Panel are Dreamweaver templates and library items. Dreamweaver templates are complete Web page layouts you use to create new documents. In creating a template, you designate which areas of a new page will remain locked, unable to be edited, and which areas can be altered. The Dreamweaver library contains items you create that, instead of being whole page layouts, are individual page elements such as a navigation bar, a specific table, or a block of text you want to use repeatedly. The power of these two elements is that you only need to edit the individual template or library item to update each instance of the element wherever you've used it in your local site files.

Not only does Dreamweaver keep track of everything you put into your site, it remembers every step you take in a given document as well. These steps are recorded in the History Panel, from which they can be repeated, undone, saved as commands, and recorded as macros.

THE ASSETS PANEL

The Assets Panel may run a close second to the Properties Inspector as the most useful tool in the Dreamweaver workspace. It offers a convenient interface for managing your site's assets, from which they can then be quickly and easily deployed. To display the Assets Panel (see Figure 13-1), use any of the following methods:

▶ Click the Assets button on the Launcher or Launch bar.

▶ Select Window | Assets from the menu bar.

▶ Press F11 on your keyboard.

There are eight categories in the Assets Panel, encompassing all the different elements your site can possess. To view the assets within your site, simply click the button for the category you'd like to explore. These buttons run vertically down the left side of the Assets Panel and are (from the top down):

> **TIP** It might take a moment for the Assets Panel to display its contents because the site cache file has to be read first in order to create the list. Remember, you need to have defined a site and created a site cache before you can use the Assets Panel. To learn about setting up a local site, see "Creating the Local Site" in Chapter 2.

FIGURE 13-1
The Assets Panel automatically puts your site's assets in the appropriate category.

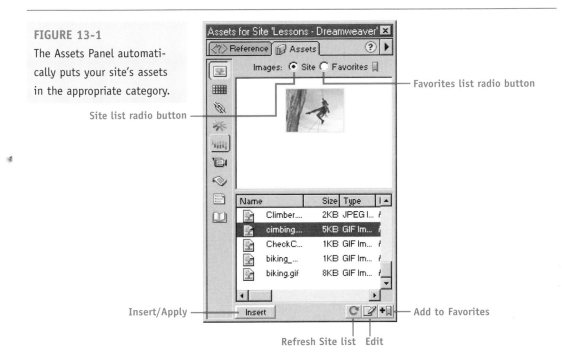

Site list radio button

Favorites list radio button

Insert/Apply

Add to Favorites

Refresh Site list   Edit

▶ **Images** Displays the GIF, JPG, and PNG files you've inserted in your site.

▶ **Colors** Displays each of the colors you've used in your site's documents and style sheets.

▶ **URLs** Displays the URLs of external sites you've linked to.

▶ **Flash** Displays the Macromedia Flash movie files in your site.

▶ **Shockwave** Displays the Macromedia Shockwave files in your site.

▶ **Movies** Displays the MPEG and QuickTime movies in your site.

▶ **Scripts** Displays JavaScript and VBScript files referenced in your site. Any scripting done within the HTML documents of your site—for example, Dreamweaver behaviors—is not referenced in the Assets Panel.

▶ **Templates** Displays each of the templates you've created within the site. When you modify a template, all pages based on that template are updated within the local site folder.

▶ **Library** Displays each library item created in your site. Like templates, modifying a library item updates each instance of the item used throughout your site.

As you're working on a site, adding pages and content, your site's cache file registers each asset in the appropriate categories. To see new items you've recently inserted in a document added to the Assets Panel, simply click the panel's Refresh button. By clicking a particular category button and selecting an asset from the resulting list, the asset is displayed in the preview area at the top of the Assets Panel. You can change the size of the preview area by dragging the border that separates it from the list of assets.

INSERTING ASSETS

Items in your Assets Panel are like ingredients in your kitchen cupboard. They're nearby and easily pulled down from the shelf for use in any recipe. Just drag them out of the Assets Panel and drop them on the page.

To Insert AN ITEM FROM THE ASSETS PANEL:

1 In the Document window, place your cursor where you want the item inserted.

2 Locate and select the asset you want to insert.

3 Use either of these methods:

- Drag the asset into the Document window from either the list or the preview area.
- Click the Insert button.

When applying color assets, you can select the text you want to apply it to and either drag the color onto the selection or click the Apply button (the Insert and Apply button are one and the same; it just swaps its name depending on the asset). URLs can be either applied to selected text or an image, or inserted to create a text link which states the URL itself.

PLAYING FAVORITES

The Assets Panel allows you to view assets in two ways:

▶ Via the Site list, which simply displays all the assets within your site

▶ Via the Favorites list, which is a collection of your chosen assets you've set aside for easy access

FIGURE 13-2

The Favorites list offers some options not available in the Site list.

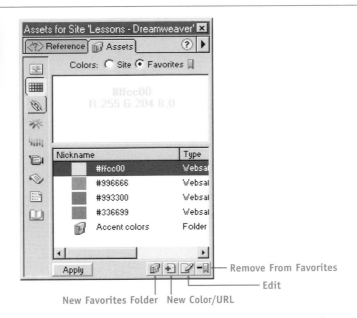

Remove From Favorites

Edit

New Favorites Folder   New Color/URL

To switch between the two views, just click the appropriate radio button at the top of the Assets Panel. You'll notice the buttons in the lower right corner change to reflect the new options available to you in the Favorites list (see Figure 13-2).

Because the Site list displays all the assets within a site, the list can be awkward to navigate when sites become large. By adding your most frequently used assets to the Favorites list, you no longer need to hunt and peck for them. The nice thing about Favorites is that you can group related assets together in folders. You can also give your favorite assets descriptive nicknames so you can immediately tell what they do.

To add an asset to your Favorites list, use any of the following methods:

▶ Select an asset from the Site list, and click the Add To Favorites button. You can select multiple assets within a category by holding down the SHIFT key. Use the CTRL key to select nonadjacent assets.

▶ Right-click any page element in the Document window and select the Add To Favorites command from the context menu. The menu command will always indicate which category the element will be placed in. For example, a selected graphic's context menu would say Add To Images Favorites.

▶ In the Site window, right-click on any number of selected graphic or movie files and select Add To Favorites from the context menu. Files that don't fit into a category are ignored.

Be aware that the Templates and Library categories don't have Favorites lists. If, for some reason, you decide to remove an asset from your Favorites list, simply select the Favorite and click the Remove From Favorites button in the lower-right corner of the Assets Panel. Removing an asset from the Favorites list will not remove it from the Site list.

CREATING NEW COLOR AND URL FAVORITES

In most cases, a favorite is simply a regular asset that's been singled out from the Site list for special treatment. However, with colors and URLs you can create favorites from scratch without them having to be part of the original Site list.

To Create A NEW COLOR OR URL FAVORITE:

1 Select the Favorites List, and click either the Colors or URLs category.

2 At the bottom of the Assets Panel, click the New Color or New URL button.

3 Do one of the following:

- Select a new color with the color picker.

- Enter a URL and nickname in the Add URL dialog box, and click OK.

ASSIGNING NICKNAMES TO FAVORITES

Creating a nickname for a favorite asset makes it much easier to identify. If you give an asset a descriptive label, even if it's halfway down in a category list, you'll know right away what it does without having to see it first in the preview area.

To assign a nickname to a favorite asset, use either of these methods:

▶ Right-click the asset in the Favorites list, and select Edit Nickname from the context menu. This creates a box around the highlighted name with a cursor blinking next to it. From here, enter a nickname of your choice.

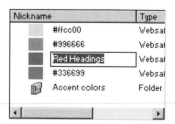

▶ Click the asset's name once to select it, pause, and click it once again to display the box and cursor with which to edit it.

CREATING FAVORITES FOLDERS

Favorites folders allow you to group related assets together for easier access. For example, if you have a number of URLs you use repeatedly that link to external Web design resource sites, you can put them in a folder called WebResourceLinks. Now you'll have them all in one spot the next time you need them.

To Create A FAVORITES FOLDER:

1 In the Favorites list, select the category in which you want to create a new folder.

2 Click the New Favorites Folder button in the lower-right corner of the Assets Panel. This displays a new untitled folder icon within the category's Favorites list.

3 Enter a name for the new folder.

4 Drag the individual assets from the Favorites list into the new folder.

EDITING FAVORITES

Editing certain kinds of assets, such as images and different types of movie files, opens the asset in an external editor. These types of assets can be edited in either the Site or Favorites list because you're actually editing a separate file, as opposed to an attribute value. Colors and URLs, being values (and having the ability to be created from scratch), can also be edited in the Favorites list. This won't affect their values in the Site list, so you don't have to worry about losing any information.

To Edit AN ASSET IN THE FAVORITES LIST:

1 Select the asset and click the Edit button.

2 Edit the asset as you see fit, either in the external editing application or with Dreamweaver's formatting tools if the asset is a color or URL.

SHARING ASSETS BETWEEN SITES

Dreamweaver lets you copy assets from one site to another. This way you can easily share assets between sites instead of having to recreate them with each new site you design. You can copy a single asset, groups of assets, or entire Favorites folders. You'll need to have another site already defined before you can copy assets to it.

To Copy ASSETS TO ANOTHER SITE:

1 Right-click the selected assets you want to copy.

2 From the context menu, select Copy To Site and choose the site name you want the assets copied to from the submenu.

The assets are copied to the site you choose and placed in their appropriate locations within the site root folder. The new assets join both the Site and Favorites lists in the new site's Assets Panel. If the asset copied was a URL or color, however, it only goes to the Favorites list because these two asset types don't possess corresponding files.

DREAMWEAVER TEMPLATES AND LIBRARY ITEMS

Dreamweaver templates and library items are known as "linked" assets. This means that, like CSS style sheets, you can update all the pages that make use of the linked asset by editing the asset directly. You can see how this makes maintaining a large site easier. Imagine a truly huge site of 100 pages or more that uses a different template for each of its four primary sections. Need to update the look of one section? Modify a single template file and a quarter of the site gets an instant facelift. Compare that with modifying the same site one page at a time. Have a single navigation bar running through all 100 pages? Edit a single library item and your work is finished. Templates and library items also increase the speed of site development, as well as maintain the consistency of your design. Create your base layout once, and then apply that layout across multiple pages.

CREATING DREAMWEAVER TEMPLATES

Templates can be created from existing documents or from scratch. Each template you create is saved within your local site in a folder called Templates which Dreamweaver generates for you when you save your first template file. These files end with the extension .dwt. Whatever you do, don't remove your templates from the Templates folder, or remove the Templates folder from the local site folder. If you do, you'll break the paths between the templates and the files that are based on them, removing their ability to be updated.

To Create A TEMPLATE FROM AN EXISTING DOCUMENT:

1 Open the file you want to use as a template.

2 From the Document window menu bar, select File | Save As Template. This displays the Save As Template dialog box.

3 Select the site you want to save this template in from the Site drop-down menu, and enter a name for the template in the Save As field. Any existing templates are shown in the Existing Templates field.

4 Click Save to close the dialog box.

Dreamweaver saves the new template, which now replaces the original HTML file in the Document window, ready to be edited. You'll always know you're working with a template because the Document window title bar will display "`<<Template>>`" followed by the template name in parentheses.

To Create A BLANK TEMPLATE FROM SCRATCH:

1 In the Assets Panel, click the Templates button.

2 Click the New Template button in the lower-right corner of the Assets Panel. This adds a new, untitled template to the Templates list. The preview window displays a message informing you this is a blank template and how to begin editing it.

3 Enter a name for the template, and press ENTER, or click anywhere on the screen.

4 To open the template in the Document window for editing, double-click the template name or click the Edit button.

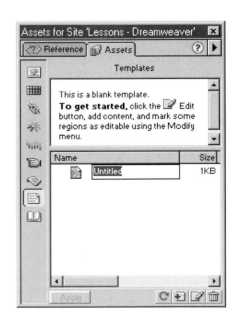

You can now create your template just as you would a regular document in the Document window.

CREATING EDITABLE REGIONS

When creating a template, you need to distinguish which areas of a new page will remain locked and which areas will accept new content. If you close the template file right after creating it, you'll see a dialog box warning you that your template contains no *editable regions*. What this means is that you have yet to define which areas of a document based on this template will be able to accept new content and which areas will remain locked. It's all right to save the template in this state; you will simply need to define editable regions at some point before you can put the template to good use.

To Define A TEMPLATE'S EDITABLE REGIONS:

1 In the template file, either select a range of text or content you want to make an editable region, or place the cursor in the spot you want the new editable region inserted.

2 Right-click and select New Editable Region from the context menu, or choose Modify | Templates | New Editable Region from the menu bar. This displays the New Editable Region dialog box.

3 Enter a unique name for the editable region. Don't use apostrophes ('), quotation marks ("), angle brackets (< >), or ampersands (&) in region names.

4 Click OK.

The new editable region appears in the Document window as a highlighted rectangle with the name you gave it in its upper-left corner and the content you selected inside it. If you didn't create an editable region from preexisting content, the region will simply repeat its name within brackets, as shown here. You can remove, or "relock," an editable region by right-clicking the region in the template and selecting Remove Editable Region from the context menu. You can also choose Modify | Templates | Remove Editable Region from the menu bar. The highlighted rectangle will disappear, leaving behind whatever content might have been in it as a fixed part of the template.

When you apply the template to a document, the entire page is outlined in a light yellow highlight, with the template name displayed in the upper-right corner of the Document window, as shown here. The editable regions you defined are present and will be the only place in which you can enter new

> TIP Choose Modify | Templates, and select the name of the region from the list at the bottom of that submenu to jump directly to that particular region.

content for the page. If the default highlight colors aren't to your taste, you can change it in the Highlighting category of the Preferences dialog box.

CREATING TEMPLATE-BASED DOCUMENTS

You can apply templates to both new and existing documents. To apply a template to a new document, use any of the following methods:

▶ Open a blank document, select the template you want to use from the Assets Panel, and click the Apply button.

▶ Drag the template from the Assets Panel onto a blank document in the Document window.

▶ Select File | New From Template from the Document window menu bar. This displays the Select Template dialog box (see Figure 13-3). From here, select the template you want to base the new document on and click Select.

When you apply a template via the Select Template dialog box, you'll notice the Update Page When Template Changes checkbox. By default, any document based

FIGURE 13-3
You can select a template from the current site or any site you've created templates in.

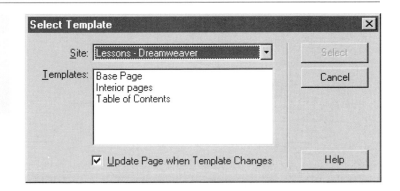

on a template will update to reflect any changes made to the template file. By dese-lecting this checkbox, the template ceases to function as a linked asset and simply creates an independent HTML file that uses the template as a design starting point.

To Apply A TEMPLATE TO AN EXISTING DOCUMENT:

1 In the document to which you want to apply a template, do any of the following:

- Select the template you want to use from the Assets Panel and click the Apply button.

- Drag a template from the Assets Panel into the Document window.

- Select Modify | Templates | Apply Template To Page. Choose a template from the Select Template dialog box and click Select.

Each of these methods displays the Choose Editable Region For Orphaned Content dialog box.

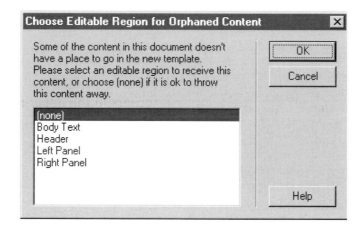

2 Select the editable region of the template in which you want the content of the exist-ing document to be placed.

3 Click OK.

If you apply a template to an existing document that is based on another template, Dreamweaver will try to place page content from the original template's editable regions into any regions of the new template with corresponding region names. If there are no matching region names, the Choose Editable Region For Orphaned Content dialog box asks which new editable region the content should be placed in.

You can detach a page from its template at any time. This will create a static document with the elements of the original template still in the page, only now the entire document is editable, and any update to the original template will have no impact on the page at all.

To Detach A PAGE FROM ITS TEMPLATE:

1 Open the document from which you want to remove the template.

2 Select Modify | Templates | Detach From Template.

EDITING TEMPLATES AND UPDATING PAGES

The ability to modify your templates and have those modifications reflected throughout the pages created from those templates is the primary reason to use them. You can assess a document's template in a number of ways:

▶ Open the document whose template you want to modify, and select Modify | Template | Open Attached Template from the menu bar.

▶ Select the template in the Assets Panel whose name appears in the upper-right corner of the current document and click the Edit button.

▶ Double-click the name of the template in the Assets Panel.

From here, you can edit the template in any way you choose. The updating process begins when you save the edited template. Dreamweaver displays the Update Template Files dialog box. To make updates now, click Update. If you want to perform the updates later, click Don't Update.

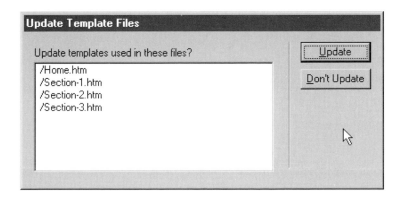

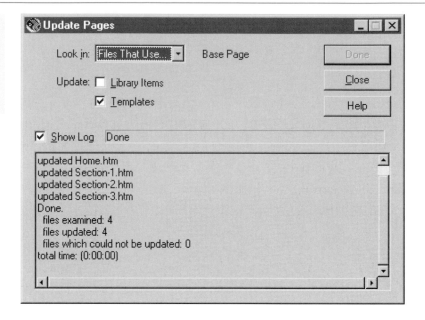

FIGURE 13-4
The Update Pages dialog box displays a log that indicates which files have been updated.

Clicking Update opens the Update Pages dialog box, shown in Figure 13-4, which allows you to update all the pages in the entire site. You can also update only those pages attached to the specific template by using the Look In drop-down menu.

If you choose to update your pages at a later time, simply select Modify | Templates | Update Pages from the Document window menu bar, which will display the Update Pages dialog box from which you can begin the updating process.

If you rename a template, the updating process is the same as if you had edited the template. You can rename a template by right-clicking a template name in the Assets Panel and selecting Rename from the context menu. You then can enter a new name of your choosing. You will see the Update Files dialog box, and the procedure continues as described.

PITFALL PREVENTION

Dreamweaver templates are a boon to the Web designer, but you need to keep a couple of thoughts in mind so they don't become a bane. A template-based page has the majority of its code marked as off-limits, and the only way to access the areas that are off-limits is by editing the template itself. Obviously, this can present problems if the things you want to change aren't things you want every document based on the template to share. What follows is a discussion of the major aspects of page design affected by using templates and strategies to prevent templates from becoming a hindrance instead of a help.

TEMPLATE PAGE PROPERTIES

Any modifications normally made to a document through the Page Properties dialog box are not available to you when working on a template-based document. This is because most of these page attributes are part of the `<body>` tag itself, and therefore not anything that can be included in an editable region. Dreamweaver does make one exception: the document title, which is an editable region created by default when you initially create the template.

In order to modify the page properties of a template-based document, you need to edit the template itself. This, of course, modifies the page properties of any document based on that template. To have pages with different page properties that rely on the same basic template, you need to create multiple copies of the same template, giving them new names. You can then make the necessary modifications you require and apply the different templates where you need them.

TEMPLATES AND HYPERLINKS

If you are going to have hyperlinks in a fixed region of a template, be sure to assign the links using the point-to-file icon, or by browsing for the file to link to with the folder icon of the Properties Inspector. Entering the link manually can cause a lot of grief later if the path isn't exactly right. If you think of the "mental" gymnastics required of Dreamweaver to keep track of a link that originates in a template inside the Templates folder, which is then attached to multiple documents that get saved in other parts of the site, you'll begin to get an idea as to why you want Dreamweaver to assign the link value.

INTERNAL CSS STYLES, TIMELINE ANIMATION, AND BEHAVIORS

Each of these elements places information between the `<head></head>` tags of a document. Because this section is locked when it is part of a template-based document, Dreamweaver can't insert these types of content. Consequently, these elements must be part of the actual template in order to function. Keep these suggestions in mind when designing a site that relies on templates:

▶ Use external style sheets instead of internal ones. Even though the template must contain the style sheet link reference, you won't have to update your pages to make a style change, and you won't be limited to using the exact same styles on every page that uses the template.

▶ Understand that any timeline animation must either be part of every page that uses the template, or detach the files that require timeline animation from their templates and update them manually. The same holds true for any behaviors you may want to assign.

LIBRARY ITEMS

The last of the Assets Panel categories is the Library. The individual library items consist of page elements you can select from existing documents or create from scratch. Library items are basically little snippets of HTML and JavaScript code that Dreamweaver copies into a document wherever you choose to insert them. The code that Dreamweaver inserts contains a comment line that is referenced each time you modify the library item. Dreamweaver then rewrites the segment of code in the document that represents the inserted library item and updates your file.

CREATING LIBRARY ITEMS

If it can appear in the Document window, you can turn it into a library item. As with templates, Dreamweaver saves your library item files inside a separate Library folder within your local site. The file extension for library items is .lbi.

To Create A LIBRARY ITEM FROM EXISTING PAGE CONTENT:

1 In the Document window, select a segment you want to save as a library item.

2 Use any of the following methods:
- Select the Library category of the Assets Panel, and click the New Library Item button.
- Drag the selection into the Library category of the Assets Panel.
- Select Modify | Library | Add Object To Library from the menu bar.

3 Enter a name for the new library item.

To Create A LIBRARY ITEM FROM SCRATCH:

1 In the Assets Panel, click the Library button.

2 Click the New Library Item button in the lower-right corner of the Assets Panel. This adds a new, untitled template to the Library list. The preview window displays a message informing you that this is a blank template and how to begin editing it.

3 Enter a name for the library item, and press ENTER or click anywhere on the screen.

4 To open the library item for editing, double-click the library item or click the Edit button.

You are now free to add any content you choose to the blank library item.

INSERTING LIBRARY ITEMS

Once you have your library items created, they can be inserted in new and existing documents as you need them.

To Insert A LIBRARY ITEM:

1 Place your cursor in the Document window where you want the library item to be inserted.

2 Use one of the following methods:

● Select the library item in the Assets Panel and click the Insert button.

● Drag the library item onto the document window.

The library item appears highlighted in the Document window. If you want the contents of the library item inserted without maintaining a link to the library item, hold down the CTRL key while dragging the library item into the Document window. The library item contents will appear without the highlight and are now simply a regular part of the document. They will not be updated if the library item is modified.

EDITING LIBRARY ITEMS

Like templates, library items can be edited, renamed, and detached from the document into which they've been inserted.

To Edit A LIBRARY ITEM:

1 Select a library item in the Assets Panel.

2 Click the Edit button in the lower-right corner, or double-click the library item's name in the category list.

3 Edit the library item as you see fit, and save your changes. This displays the Update Library Items dialog box.

4 Click Update to update your changes.

Clicking Update opens the same Update Pages dialog box shown when updating templates. Again, you can update all the pages in the entire site or just those pages that contain the specific library item. If you decide to update your pages later, select Modify | Library | Update Current Page or Update Pages from the Document window menu bar.

Renaming a library item is identical to renaming a template. Right-click the library item name and select Rename from the context menu. Once you rename the library item, the Update Files dialog box appears. From here, you can decide to update now or wait.

You can delete a library item by selecting its name in the category list and clicking the Delete button in the lower-right corner of the Assets Panel. This removes the file from the Library folder, but doesn't remove the instance of the library item from any of the pages you've inserted it in. The Dreamweaver reference is still in the HTML code of the documents, but now that the library item no longer exists you can't update any changes. To remove the library item reference from the document code, select the instance of the deleted library item in the Document window and click the Detach From Original button in the Properties Inspector, shown in Figure 13-5.

If after deleting a library item from the Assets Panel you wish to recreate the item, you need only select an instance of the old library item in the Document window and click the Recreate button in the Properties Inspector.

FIGURE 13-5

The Properties Inspector for a select library item allows you to recreate a deleted library item, open a library item for editing, and detach the item from the library.

THE HISTORY PANEL

Dreamweaver has another component that's extremely useful. It has a memory, remembering every step you take during a particular session using the software. This information is displayed in the Dreamweaver History Panel, shown in Figure 13-6.

The History Panel displays a list of every action you take in a document from the moment you open it. It gives you the ability to repeat steps you've taken, undo them, or save your steps as commands you can use again and again. To display the History Panel, use any of the following methods:

► Click the History button on the Launcher or Launch bar.

► Select Window | History from the menu bar.

► Press SHIFT-F10.

FIGURE 13-6

The History Panel allows you to automate repetitive tasks.

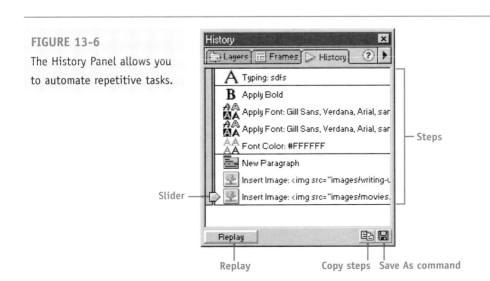

Almost any action you take during the course of working on a document can be replayed from the History Panel, whether it's inserting different objects such as tables or images, modifying object properties such as width and height, or entering and formatting text. Unfortunately, many actions performed with the mouse cannot be reused in the History Panel, such as dragging objects or making selections. However, as you are doubtlessly aware, there are keyboard shortcuts and menu commands for nearly every possible action you can take in Dreamweaver. If you plan on creating a command for a particular set of actions, there is nearly always a method of performing the required steps without the aid of the mouse.

REPEATING AND UNDOING STEPS

You can use the History Panel to repeat or undo both single and multiple steps. To repeat any single step in the History Panel, simply select that step by clicking on it and click the Replay button. If you perform an action and want to undo the most recent step, move the slider up one step in the

> **TIP** You can also repeat or undo any action you take immediately using the keyboard shortcuts CTRL-Y (repeat) and CTRL-Z (undo).

History Panel list. The step remains in the list in its proper order, but becomes grayed out, as shown here. The next action you take will replace it in the step list.

To Repeat A SERIES OF STEPS:

1 Select the steps in the History Panel using one of the following methods:

- Drag from one step to the next until you've selected the range of steps you want to repeat.

- Click the first step in the range you want to select, then hold down the SHIFT key while selecting the last step in the range.

- Hold down the CTRL key and select any number of nonadjacent steps.

2 Click the Replay button.

The power of the History Panel comes when applying steps to different objects in the Document window. For example, you may have performed a number of formatting steps to a piece of text which you wish to repeat. Simply select the object in the Document window you want to apply these past steps to, select the appropriate steps in the History Panel, and click the Replay button. You can apply steps to a single object or a series of objects.

COPYING AND PASTING STEPS

You can copy and paste History Panel steps between any number of open documents on your desktop. Be careful to avoid including steps that are themselves copy and paste commands.

To Copy And Paste STEPS:

1 Select any number of steps from a document's History Panel.

2 Click the Copy Steps button in the lower-right corner of the History Panel.

3 Open the document you want to paste the steps into if it isn't already open or click its Document window to select it.

4 Place the cursor in the Document window or select the object to which you want to apply the copied steps.

5 Select Edit | Paste from the Document window menu bar.

The copied steps are played back in the new document as they're pasted into the History Panel as a new step titled Pasted Steps.

CREATING COMMANDS

History Panel steps can be saved as a new command in the Commands menu.

To Create A NEW COMMAND:

1 Select any number of steps from the History Panel.

2 Click the Save As Command button. This displays the Save As Command dialog box.

3 Enter a name for the new command.

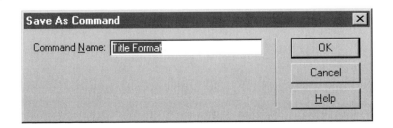

The new command is now available at the bottom of the Commands menu on the menu bar. You can use this just as you would any menu command whenever you like.

To Rename A COMMAND:

1 Select Commands | Edit Command List. This displays the Edit Command List dialog box, shown in Figure 13-7.

2 Click the name of the command you want to rename.

3 Enter a new name for the command, and click Close.

If you want to delete a command from the Edit Command List dialog box, click the Delete key.

RECORDING COMMANDS

If you've ever had occasion to record macros in a word processor, spreadsheet application, or other type of software that supports them, recording commands will not be new to you.

FIGURE 13-7

You can rename or delete commands from the Edit Command List dialog box.

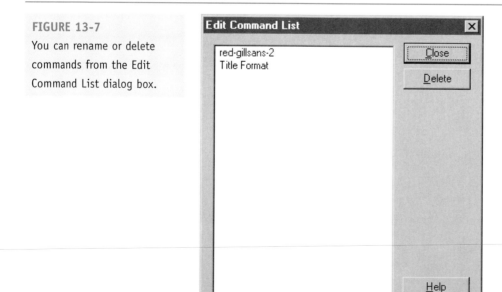

Dreamweaver allows you to record steps as they are performed so you don't need to save them from the History Panel afterward. As mentioned before, certain mouse actions cannot be repeated as steps and consequently cannot be recorded during this process. These actions will be unavailable to you during recording, so keyboard shortcuts and menu commands must be used instead.

You also can't switch between documents while recording, and any changes made to another document are not recorded. The mouse pointer changes to a cassette tape icon during recording, so if at any time the cursor changes back to its traditional pointer, you will know you are not recording the actions being taken.

You can only record one command at a time. If you begin recording another command, the first one is lost. You can save your recorded commands by playing them back and saving the playback action from the History Panel as a command, as discussed in the previous section.

To Record A COMMAND:

1 From the menu bar, select Commands | Start Recording, or press CTRL-SHIFT-X. The pointer changes to a cassette tape icon to indicate the recording process is underway.

2 When you have performed the actions you want to record, select Commands | Stop Recording from the menu bar, or press CTRL-SHIFT-X a second time.

3 Play back the recorded actions by selecting Commands | Play Recorded Command, or press CTRL-P. A step named Run Command appears in the History Panel.

4 Select the Run Command step and click the Save As Command button on the History Panel.

5 Enter a name for the new command in the resulting dialog box, and click OK.

Web Site Management and Maintenance

Think about the life of a Web site. The design and development

is just the fast, fun, and furious part at the very beginning.

Granted, this is usually the most gratifying part of the process,

but it's by far the shortest part as well. Much more time is

spent managing and maintaining a Web site. Macromedia

understands this, putting as much thought and effort into

Dreamweaver's site management tools as they put into the rest

of the application. The end result? Dreamweaver is a complete

site development *and* site management tool. When the site

is ready to go up on the server, there's no need to leave

Dreamweaver. The Site window introduced in Chapter 2 is fully capable of transferring files to and from your Web server. If you're working in a collaborative environment, Dreamweaver can also keep track of who is presently working with a particular file so folks don't overwrite each other's work.

SETTING UP YOUR REMOTE SITE

The first step in getting your local site up on the Web is configuring the Site window to connect to the remote site or Web server. First, you'll need to know some basic information about the server your site will be hosted on. For example:

▶ Will you be transferring files across an FTP (File Transfer Protocol) connection?

▶ Or is the Web server accessible as part of your local network?

If you aren't sure, check with your network administrator, Internet service provider, or the client you're building the site for to find out how to send your files to the Web server you'll be using. If you are connecting via FTP, you'll need to know the name of the FTP server, the host directory of your site, and the necessary login and password information. Once you have all this in hand, you're ready to begin the remote site setup process.

To Set Up YOUR REMOTE SITE FOR FTP ACCESS:

1 Access the Define Sites dialog box using either of the following methods:

- Select Define Sites from the Current Sites drop-down menu in the Site window.

- From either the Site or Document window menu bar, select Site | Define Sites.

2 Select the local site you want to work with and click Edit to display the Site Definition dialog box.

3 Click the Remote Info category, and select FTP from the Access drop-down menu (see Figure 14-1).

4 In the FTP Host field, enter the FTP address for the Web server, for example, ftp.your-hostname-here.com.

TIP If you're dialing in to the Web server from your home PC, you probably don't have a firewall in place. However, an employer's network probably does. Check with the network administrator to find out what firewall settings, if any, you will need to set up your remote site.

FIGURE 14-1

Dreamweaver remembers your user information so you don't need to enter it each time you log in.

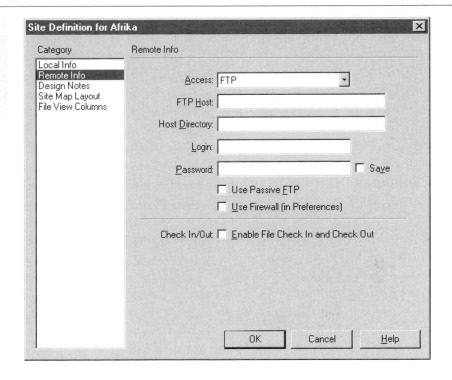

5 If necessary, enter the name of the root directory for your site in the Host Directory field. Check with your ISP or network administrator to get this information.

6 Enter your username and password for the FTP account in the appropriate fields. Check Save to have Dreamweaver remember this information.

7 Click OK.

8 To connect to the remote site, click the Connect/Disconnect button beside the Site drop-down menu on the Site window toolbar (see Figure 14-2).

FIGURE 14-2

The Site window toolbar

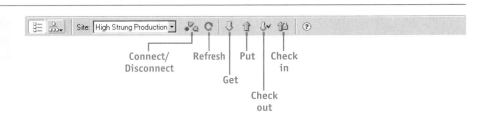

To Set Up YOUR REMOTE SITE FOR A LOCAL NETWORK:

1 Display the Site Definition dialog box for the site you want to work with, as described in the previous section.

2 In the Remote Info category, select Local/Network from the Access drop-down menu (see Figure 14-3).

3 Click the Folder icon beside the Remote Folder field to display the Choose Remote Folder dialog box. Choose Network Neighborhood from the Select drop-down menu and browse for the correct machine and folder, then click Select.

4 Click OK to close the Site Definition dialog box. This will return you to the Site window, with the remote site displayed in the right panel.

GETTING AND PUTTING FILES

Get and Put are the commands used to transfer files between local and remote sites. *Getting* a file means to download it from the remote server, and *putting* a file means to upload it to the remote server.

FIGURE 14-3

Accessing a Web server via a local network connection is just like accessing a folder on your own hard drive.

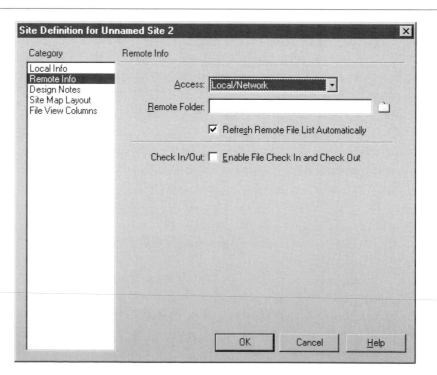

To Download FILES FROM THE REMOTE SERVER:

1 After connecting to the remote site, select the files you want to download in the Remote Site Panel.

2 From the Site window toolbar, click the Get button. Alternatively, you can right-click on the files and select Get from the context menu, or select Site | Get from the menu bar. You can also press CTRL-SHIFT-D. This displays the Dependent Files dialog box.

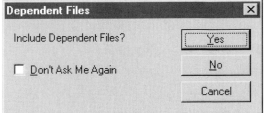

3 Click Yes to download dependent files, or No to ignore them. Check the Don't Ask Me Again option to disable the dialog box. Dependent files are all the outside files referenced in a page, such as its images, external style sheets, multimedia files, and in the case of framesets, all the individual frame documents as well.

If the files you download are in directories that don't exist in the local site, Dreamweaver creates the new directories for you. The same is true when uploading files to the remote server. You can stop a file transfer at any time by clicking the Stop Current Task button, shown here, in the lower-right corner of the Site window. You can also press the ESC key on your keyboard.

To Upload FILES TO THE REMOTE SERVER:

1 Connect to the remote site and select the files you want to upload in the Local Site Panel.

2 Click the Put button. Just like downloading files, you can right-click the files and select Put from the context menu, or choose Site | Put from the menu bar. The equivalent keyboard shortcut is CTRL-SHIFT-U.

3 If any of the files you are uploading have unsaved changes in them, Dreamweaver will ask you if you want to save the files first. Select Yes to save your changes and upload the files. Click No to upload the previously saved version of the files.

4 Again, you'll see the Dependent Files dialog box to which you can respond accordingly, as described in the previous section.

When transferring files via FTP, Dreamweaver records the transactions in the Site FTP log, shown in Figure 14-4. As with any type of information transfer across the Internet, errors can occur. If you've ever had an e-mail fail to get through, you understand. The FTP log can help you determine what the cause of the error might be. To view the FTP log, select Window | Site FTP Log from the Site window menu bar.

> **TIP** As long as you're connected to the remote site, you can upload or download the file you are currently working on by selecting Get or Put from the Document window Site menu, or using the keyboard shortcuts described in this section.

SYNCHRONIZING YOUR LOCAL AND REMOTE SITES

When you have both local and remote sites with identical files on them, it can get a little confusing as to which machine has the most current versions. This is particularly true when you aren't the only one working with the files. By using the Synchronize command, you can guarantee that the most current versions of each file are on both machines. You can also check which files are newer on either machine before you synchronize. After connecting to the remote server of the site

FIGURE 14-4

Use the Site FTP log to troubleshoot transfer errors.

```
FTP Log                                                    _ □ X
FTP Command:
226 Transfer complete.
RMD XYIZNWSK
250 RMD command successful.
PWD
257 "/users/sv011614" is current directory.
CWD /users/sv011614/www
250 CWD command successful.
PWD
257 "/www" is current directory.
PASV
227 Entering Passive Mode (209,196,33,254,211,153)
LIST
150 Opening ASCII mode data connection for /bin/ls.
total 200
drwxr-xr-x  11 11614   11614      4096 Feb 27 03:37 .
drwxr-xr-x  15 0        1         4096 Jan 17 00:39 ..
-rw-r--r--   1 11614   11614       350 Jan 17 00:40 .htaccess
drwxr-xr-x   2 11614   11614      4096 Jan 17 00:40 _private
drwxr-xr-x   4 11614   11614      4096 Jan 17 00:40 _vti_bin
drwxr-xr-x   2 11614   11614      4096 Jan 17 00:40 _vti_cnf
-rwxr-xr-x   1 11614   11614      1716 Jan 17 00:40 _vti_inf.html
drwxr-xr-x   2 11614   11614      4096 Jan 17 00:40 _vti_log
drwxr-xr-x   2 11614   11614      4096 Jan 17 00:40 _vti_pvt
drwxr-xr-x   2 11614   11614      4096 Jan 17 00:40 _vti_txt
drwxr-xr-x   2 11614   11614      4096 Jan 27 23:23 guestbook
drwxr-xr-x   2 11614   11614      4096 Feb 27 03:37 images
-rw-r--r--   1 11614   11614      1856 Jan 28 00:14 index.html
-rw-r--r--   1 11614   11614      2458 Jan 17 00:40 postinfo.html
drwxr-xr-x   2 11614   11614      4096 Feb 10 20:41 program
-rw-r--r--   1 11614   11614      1013 Feb 11 20:46 redux.html
-rw-r--r--   1 11614   11614     13823 Feb 11 20:47 redux.swf
-rw-r--r--   1 11614   11614      2432 Jun  6 2000 scrolledge10rule.jpg
-rw-r--r--   1 11614   11614     14575 Jan 28 00:15 splash.swf
lrwxrwxrwx   1 0        1          11 Sep 14 00:21 webstats -> ../webstats
226 Transfer complete.
NOOP
200 NOOP command successful.
```

you want to check, select Edit | Select Newer Local, or Edit | Select Newer Remote, from the Site window menu bar, depending on the pane in which you want the newest files to be highlighted.

To Synchronize YOUR FILES:

1 Select Site | Synchronize from the Site window menu bar to display the Synchronize Files dialog box.

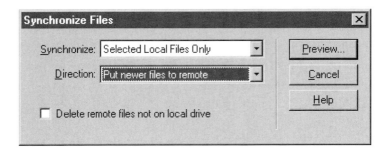

2 From the Synchronize drop-down menu, choose the method you prefer—the entire site or the selected files.

3 From the Direction drop-down menu, select which site you want the new files copied to:

- Put Newer Files to Remote Uploads local files with more recent modification dates than the corresponding remote files.

- Get Newer Files from Remote Downloads remote files with more recent modification dates than the corresponding local files.

- Get and Put Newer Files Transfers the most recent versions of all files to both the remote and local sites.

4 The Delete option checkbox offers different options depending upon your selection in the Direction drop-down menu. By selecting Put Newer Files To Remote, the Delete option removes any remote files not found on the local site. By selecting Get New Files From Remote, the Delete option removes any local files not found on the remote site. If you don't want any files deleted, leave the Delete box unchecked.

FIGURE 14-5

The Synchronize dialog box allows you to single out files you don't want to take action on.

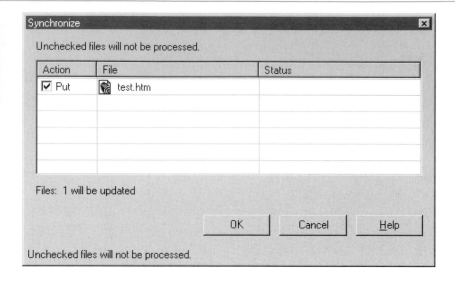

5 Click Preview to display the Synchronize dialog box, shown in Figure 14-5. Dreamweaver examines the remote and local sites and displays the files that require action. If no synchronization is necessary, Dreamweaver displays an alert to inform you.

6 In the Synchronize dialog box, deselect any file you don't want Dreamweaver to delete, put, or get by clicking the checkbox in the Action column.

7 Click OK to begin synchronizing your files. The Synchronize dialog box will change to reflect the status of the affected files. The OK and Cancel buttons become Save Log, which you can press to create a text file of the file transfer information, and Close, which closes the dialog box.

USING CHECK IN AND CHECK OUT

When you're the only person working on a site, you don't have to worry about other people going into the files and making changes, but if you're part of a team it's a whole new ball game. What you need is *source control*—some method of preventing people from overwriting each other's work. Dreamweaver has a very effective Check In/Check Out system that lets members of a team know who is working on a specific file at any given time.

With this system enabled, any file you check out shows a green check mark next to it in the Site window. Files checked out by other members of your team will have a red check mark. The best part is that the name of the person currently working on the file is also shown, and when clicked, launches your e-mail program so you can tell the other developer to hurry it up.

To keep your copy of the local site from getting messed up, Dreamweaver makes the files on your local site that you check back in read-only and puts a little lock icon next to them. This means you can't edit them without checking them back out again and prevents you from making any changes to a file while other team members have it checked out. The thing you need to be aware of, though, is that Dreamweaver does *not* make checked-out files on the remote server read-only, so if someone transfers a file to the server with a different program, the files can get overwritten.

CONFIGURING DREAMWEAVER'S CHECK IN/CHECK OUT SYSTEM

Provided you've set up the remote server information for a given site, setting up Check In/Check Out is easier than falling out of bed.

To Set CHECK IN/CHECK OUT OPTIONS:

1 In the Site window, select Define Sites from the Current Site pop-up menu, or choose Site | Define Sites from the menu bar.

2 In the Define Sites dialog box, choose the site for which you want to enable Check In/Check Out options and click Edit.

3 In the Site Definition dialog box, click Remote Info in the Category list, and check Enable File Check In And Check Out. The Check Out Files When Opening option appears, checked, as do the Check Out Name and Email Address fields (see Figure 14-6). Check Out Files When Opening automatically checks out a file when you double-click it in the Site window.

4 Enter a check-out name and e-mail address. Your check-out name appears as a link in the Site window next to files you've checked. When team members click the link, their e-mail application opens a new message with your e-mail address in the To field. The Subject field will display the corresponding file and site name.

FIGURE 14-6

The Remote Info category panel changes when you enable File Check In and Check Out.

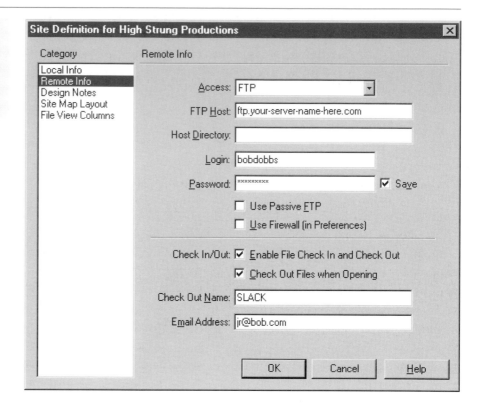

CHECKING FILES IN AND OUT

Once you've enabled Check In/Check Out, you'll notice two appropriately named buttons added to the Site window toolbar. At this point, checking files in and out is no more difficult than using the Get and Put buttons was.

To Check FILES IN OR OUT:

1 Select the files you want to check out. It makes no difference if you select them in the Remote Site Panel or Local Site Panel.

2 Click the Check In or Check Out button (refer to Figure 14-2). Alternatively, you can select the same commands from the Site menu or the context menu.

3 As with Get and Put, the Dependent Files dialog box is displayed. Select Yes to include the dependent files, and No to leave them behind.

If you check out a file, but decide you don't need it, or if you have made changes to it you don't want to keep, you can undo the check out by selecting Undo Check Out from the Site menu, or by right-clicking the file and selecting the same command from the context menu. Your local copy of the file becomes read-only again, and any changes you made are discarded.

USING DESIGN NOTES

Design Notes are the electronic equivalent of Post-Its. They can be used to track the status of a file in development, to leave a message for the next person checking out the file after you've finished with it, or just for notes to yourself so you won't forget the killer idea you had at 4:00 A.M. when you couldn't keep your eyes open any longer.

You can attach notes to any file type within your site, including images and multimedia files, as well as page templates.

To Add DESIGN NOTES TO A FILE:

In the Site window, select a file and double-click in the Notes column, or right-click on the file and select Design Notes from the context menu. This displays the Design Notes dialog box (see Figure 14-7).

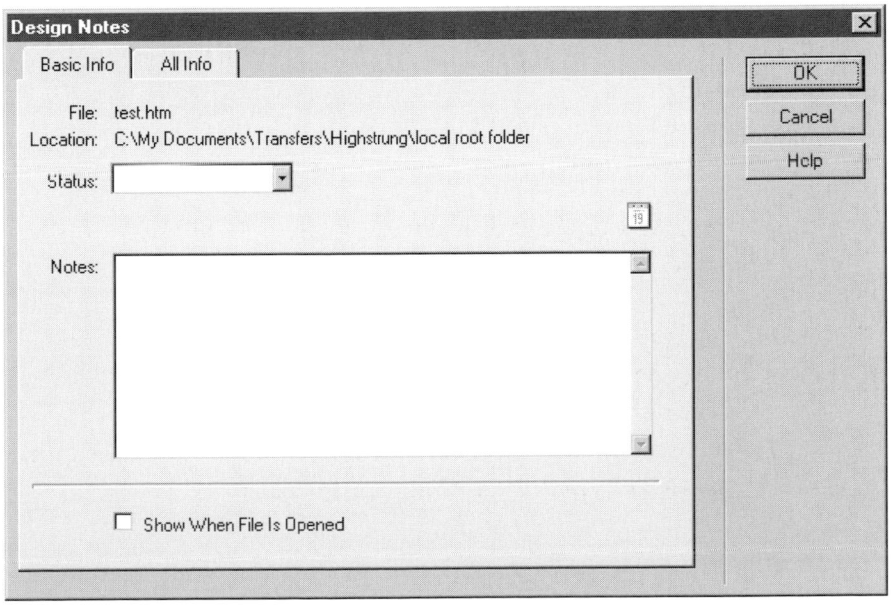

FIGURE 14-7

The Design Notes dialog box is the interface in which you enter notes, as well as read them.

2 In the Basic Info tab, make a selection from the Status drop-down menu and enter comments into the Notes text field. Click the calendar icon to insert the current date. Check Show When File Is Opened to have the note displayed every time the file is opened.

3 Use the All Info tab to create your own name/value pairs—for example, enter Author in the Name field and enter your name in the Value field (see Figure 14-8).

4 Click OK to close the dialog box.

You'll now see a Design Note icon beside the file in the Notes column. You can double-click the icon at any time to read or edit the note.

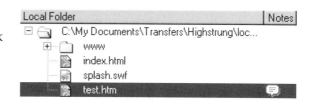

Design Notes are saved to the local site in the same location as the file they belong to. They are kept in a folder called _notes which is not visible in the Site window. The note's file name is taken from the corresponding file and given an *.mno* extension. For example, if you attached a note to an image file named tricycle.gif, the note file would be named tricycle.gif.mno. However, if you happen to delete or rename the image file outside of Dreamweaver, the note file would still remain within your

FIGURE 14-8

Name/value pairs are just a "this equals that" construction. Use them to elaborate on topics not covered in the Basic Info tab.

local site files, and unless you went browsing through your local site folder with an application like Windows Explorer, you'd never see it. Fortunately, Dreamweaver provides a method for cleaning up your Design Notes files so you don't have to worry about them piling up.

To Delete UNASSOCIATED DESIGN NOTES FILES:

1 In the Site window, select Define Sites from the Current Site pop-up menu, or choose Site | Define Sites from the menu bar.

2 In the Define Sites dialog box, choose the site for which you want to enable Check In/Check Out options and click Edit.

3 In the Site Definition dialog box, click Design Notes.

4 Click the Clean Up button in the upper-right corner. Dreamweaver informs you it is about to delete any Design Note not associated with a file. Click Yes to continue or No to stop.

If you delete a file in the Site window with an associated Design Notes file, the Design Notes file is deleted as well.

Beyond the Basics

Well, then, you've reached the last chapter. With any luck, if I've done my job well, you've learned something along the way. They say it's possible to have too much of a good thing. As far as learning is concerned, I think that's bunk— we never stop learning. At least, we never should stop learning. The choice is really up to us.

Personally, I hope finishing this book develops in you a serious appetite for more. The more you learn about Web development, the better your Web sites will be. Of course, the better your Web sites are, the better the Web becomes as a whole, and if you take a look at the majority of what's out there you'll agree this can only be a good thing.

What I want to do in this chapter is familiarize you with Dreamweaver's Help tools and then direct you to some of the resources available on the Internet, not only for Dreamweaver information, but for HTML, JavaScript, and other technologies as well.

USING DREAMWEAVER HELP RESOURCES

Macromedia doesn't just want you to buy their software and leave it at that. They want you to become skillful in its use, and hopefully enjoy yourself in the process. With these goals in mind, they've created one of the best software Help interfaces you may ever find. But that's not the half of it. Included with your Dreamweaver installation are guided tours, tutorials, and lessons to aid you on your journey.

THE DREAMWEAVER HELP INTERFACE

To access Dreamweaver Help, simply select Help | Using Dreamweaver from the menu bar. Instead of being part of the application itself like most Help sections, it is a standalone, HTML-based system displayed in your Web browser (see Figure 15-1). The files it accesses are placed in the Dreamweaver directory on your local hard drive when you install the software. It is, in effect, a Web site in its own right. This "site" is frames-based, with a narrow left frame housing the navigation, and a larger main frame to the right in which the content is displayed.

Dreamweaver Help provides both a table of contents and an index (see Figure 15-2), each of whose entries are links that display their pertinent information in the main frame. You can also search for information via a Java-enabled search window, as shown in Figure 15-3.

> **TIP** The Help interface relies heavily upon JavaScript, as well as upon Java. Be sure you're using Internet Explorer 4.0 or Netscape Navigator 4.0, or higher, with both these technologies enabled.

FIGURE 15-1

Macromedia's Dreamweaver Support Center Web site can be accessed by clicking the Macromedia Dreamweaver 4 graphic at the top of the left frame.

FIGURE 15-2

Click the letter corresponding to the topic you're looking for, then scroll through the entries provided and click to display it in the main frame.

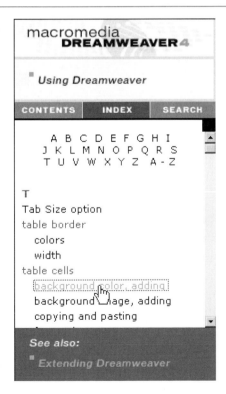

FIGURE 15-3

Enter the topic you're looking for and click the List Topics button.

THE DREAMWEAVER TUTORIAL

Included in the Help section is a tutorial that teaches you the Dreamweaver basics by guiding you through the construction of a site for an imaginary adventure travel company. You'll create a local site using a folder of predefined content that comes with the Dreamweaver installation.

The Tutorial folder, found inside the Dreamweaver folder on your hard drive, includes sample images, HTML documents, and Macromedia Flash content to be added to pages you create in completing the exercises.

To Begin THE TUTORIAL:

1 Select Help | Using Dreamweaver from the menu bar, or press F1. This opens the Dreamweaver Help interface in your Web browser, shown previously in Figure 15-1.

2 From the table of contents in the left frame of your browser, click Dreamweaver Tutorial to display the subject headings for this section. Click the individual subject headings to see them displayed in the main frame of your browser.

3 Follow the steps outlined in the tutorial to build a sample site utilizing the documents, images, and multimedia files provided.

TAKING THE GUIDED TOUR

Dreamweaver's Guided Tour is a combination of text descriptions and movie clip examples that together help demonstrate the basic concepts underlying Dreamweaver's development process.

To View THE GUIDED TOUR:

1 Select Help | Guided Tour from the menu bar.

2 In the resulting window, shown here, click the title of the tour you want to view.

3 Use the buttons along the bottom to navigate forward, back, or Home. Throughout the tour, you will see buttons depicting a movie camera. Click these to launch animated sequences demonstrating different parts of the Dreamweaver interface in action.

INTERACTIVE LESSONS

Macromedia provides seven interactive lessons, each focusing on a particular capability of Dreamweaver (see Figure 15-4). There are sample pages with all the necessary content required to complete each lesson.

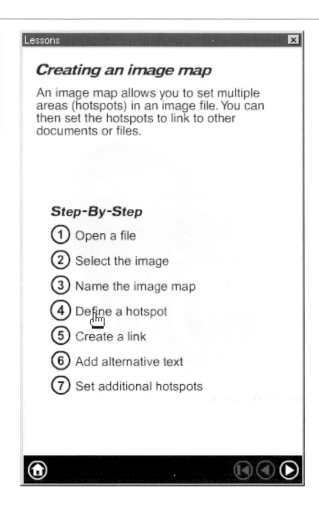

Lessons ☒

Creating an image map

An image map allows you to set multiple areas (hotspots) in an image file. You can then set the hotspots to link to other documents or files.

Step-By-Step

1. Open a file
2. Select the image
3. Name the image map
4. Define a hotspot
5. Create a link
6. Add alternative text
7. Set additional hotspots

To Access THE INTERACTIVE LESSONS:

1 Select Help | Lessons from the menu bar.

2 Choose the lesson you want in the resulting window.

WEB DEVELOPMENT RESOURCES ON THE NET

When I first started developing Web sites, there was no such thing as a WYSIWYG HTML editor. It was just me, my text editor, a browser, and a whole lot of trial and error. JavaScript was an iffy proposition at best. Style sheets? Ha! Didn't have 'em! Okay, before I begin some proverbial "forty miles to school in the snow, walking uphill both ways" sad tale of woe, let me settle down and get to the point before it escapes me.

Before there was a ton of great software and mountainous tomes on this subject at my local bookstore, the only place to find information about Web development was the Web itself—either through my favorite search engine or by deconstructing good Web sites whenever I found them. I still highly recommend both practices. What follows is a collection of starting points for gathering information about HTML, JavaScript, and general Web design practices. The greatest thing for me about the Internet is that one site always seems to lead to another, and then another, and another—thus "surfing," right? I've yet to come away empty-handed when trying to locate something useful about a computer-related topic using the Web. I hope these examples prove useful.

THE WORLD WIDE WEB CONSORTIUM

The World Wide Web Consortium was founded in 1994 by Tim Berners-Lee, the creator of HTML and the Hypertext Transfer Protocol (http://). The Consortium develops and maintains the technical specifications for HTML and related technologies. This site can tell you everything you could ever possibly want to know about what HTML is, its history, and its future.

▶ http://www.w3c.org/

WEBMONKEY

Webmonkey is "tutorial central" for the budding Web designer. Here you can find award-winning articles and commentary that cover nearly every Web design topic you can think of. What I believe Webmonkey is probably most famous for is their "Monkey See – Monkey Do" HTML teaching tool (see Figure 15-5). The tutorial gives you the skinny on a basic HTML tag and the design concepts that employ it, and then provides you with a split browser window with a layout to mimic on one side, and an input area on the other to enter your code. When you're ready, click the go button to display what your code produced and you'll see if you've got the concept down.

▶ http://hotwired.lycos.com/webmonkey/

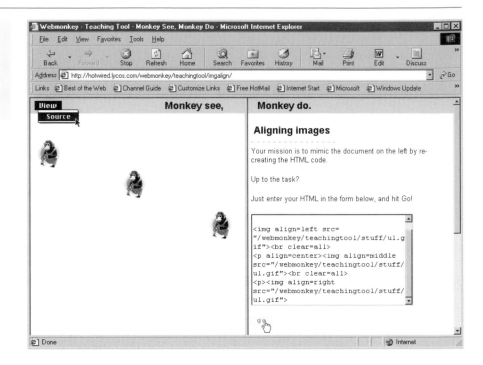

DEVELOPER SHED

"A site created by Web developers for Web developers," Developer Shed offers forum discussions, tutorials, and industry news related to HTML, JavaScript, CGI scripting, and more. They strive to be the most comprehensive resource available, serving the needs of the beginner and expert alike.

▶ http://www.devshed.com/

THE MACROMEDIA DREAMWEAVER SUPPORT CENTER

Last, but far from least, I mention the Dreamweaver Support Center. This is where Macromedia's commitment to their users is most evident. The site provides you with documentation, bug reports, technical notes, tutorials, and more.

▶ http://www.macromedia.com/support/dreamweaver/

To Code or Not to Code: HTML and the Wonders of WYSIWYG

So here you are, armed with a computer, one of the best Web design tools on the market, and a copy of this book. You're raring to go, but there is one small thing that concerns you: you don't know the first thing about HTML, or if you do, you don't think you know enough. These are not insurmountable problems. This appendix offers a brief description of what HTML is, how Dreamweaver implements HTML as you develop sites, and how you can use Dreamweaver as a teaching tool to learn HTML as you work. Is it really important that you learn HTML?

As stated, Dreamweaver is one of the best Web design tools available, and one of its greatest advantages is that it gives the user quick and easy access to the source code of the documents it creates. The reason being that even with the best tool in the world there are going to be times when you'll still want to tweak a Web page's code manually. This certainly doesn't mean you can't make really great Web sites in Dreamweaver without knowing HTML, only that it behooves you as a creator of Web content to learn the basic language underlying every Web page on the Internet.

WHAT'S IN A WEB PAGE?

When you're sitting at your computer looking at a Web page, what is your browser showing you? It's simply text-based content laid out using HTML code. The code is a set of instructions that tells your Web browser what font the text should be in, what colors should be used, where images should be placed, where links should direct you, and so on. This is not to say there isn't or can't be a high level of complexity to a Web site, only that in the end it is all HTML. So until something bigger and better comes along, the Hypertext Markup Language will be the language your Web browser speaks in and the format of any document you create using Dreamweaver.

How does the Hypertext Markup Language work? HTML consists of a set of *tags* used to tell your Web browser how the contents of a page should be displayed. Say you have a word that needs to be italicized. In order for the Web browser to display that word in italics, it needs to be *marked up* with the appropriate HTML tags—in this case, `<i></i>`. These tags would sit on either side of the word in question: `<i>Italics</i>`, with the end result looking like this: *Italics*. All the structural parts you find in a Web page, such as paragraphs, bulleted lists, tables, or images, are called *elements*, and these elements are all created using HTML tags.

Sometimes tags will have *attributes*. Tag attributes are used to apply an even greater level of control over an element. A good example would be the `<font>` tag. By itself, it will do nothing, but by adding a number of attributes to it, such as `<font face="Arial" size="2" color="blue">`, you've gained almost the same level of control over your text that you'd expect to have with any word processor. So there you have it. In a nutshell, an HTML document is made up of elements, those elements are defined with HTML tags, and the tags themselves can possess attributes that further modify an element.

THE HTML DOCUMENT

There are three primary components to any Web page without which a page couldn't even be displayed. These are the opening and closing `<html></html>` tags, which tell the browser what type of document it's viewing. The Head and Body elements of the document are between these tags. Figure A-1 shows the source code for a new blank document created in Dreamweaver displayed in the Code Inspector. You can also view source code by clicking the Code View button or the Design And Code View button on the Document window toolbar.

THE HEAD ELEMENT

The Head element of an HTML document serves to maintain pertinent information about the Web page, such as its name, any keywords or descriptions for search engines to consider, or the character set the page should be displayed in. This information is divided between the `<title></title>` and `<meta>` tags.

FIGURE A-1

View the source code using the Code Inspector window.

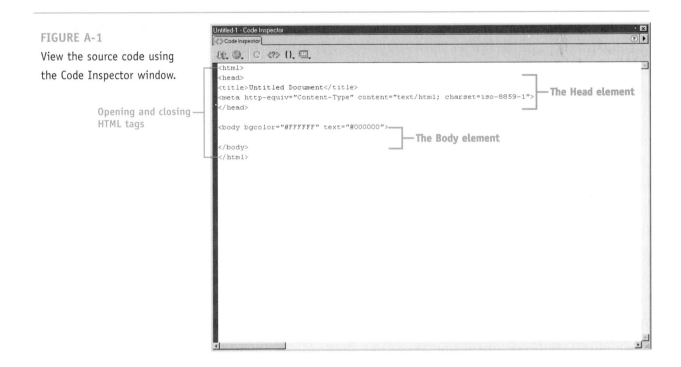

Anything written between the opening and closing `<title></title>` tags will be displayed on the browser's title bar when viewing the page. `<meta>` tags are used for document keywords and descriptions of the page's content, among other things. In pages that employ scripting, any global declarations and subroutines that need to be defined before the page loads are placed in the Head as well. Figure A-2 shows an example of the Head element in a sample Web page. Observe the separate `<meta>` tags. The `name` attribute defines the purpose of the tag. For example, `name="Description"` tells you this tag will provide a short description of the page or site. The `content` attribute supplies the text for that description.

THE BODY ELEMENT

This is where it all happens. Everything you see when viewing a Web page consists of elements housed between the `<body></body>` tags of an HTML document. The attributes for the Body tag control the document's margins, what the background color of the page will be, the default color of text, what colors links will have in their various states, and what background image should be used, if any. Figure A-3 shows the Body tag with its various attributes defined.

BRINGING IT ALL TOGETHER

We've talked a bit about HTML and discussed the basic outline of an HTML document, but nothing works quite as well as seeing something in action. By looking at a Web page and seeing the code it takes to make it, any mystery that might be

---

FIGURE A-2

The Head element

```
<head>

<title>Dreamweaver 4 Virtual Classroom</title>

<meta name="Author" content="Robert C. Fuller">

<meta name="Keywords" CONTENT="Dreamweaver, Macromedia, Virtual Classroom,  Web Development,
Osborne, McGraw-Hill">

<meta name="Description" CONTENT="Dreamweaver 4 Virtual Classroom, by Robert Fuller & Laurie
Ulrich, is a wonderful book that EVERYBODY should buy! HONEST!">

<meta http-equiv="Content-Type" content="text/html; charset=iso-8859-1">

</head>
```

FIGURE A-3

The attributes of the Body tag

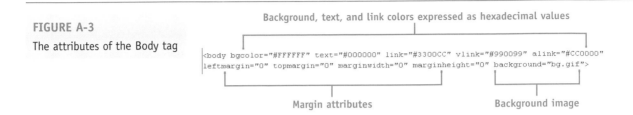

Background, text, and link colors expressed as hexadecimal values

```
<body bgcolor="#FFFFFF" text="#000000" link="#3300CC" vlink="#990099" alink="#CC0000"
leftmargin="0" topmargin="0" marginwidth="0" marginheight="0" background="bg.gif">
```

Margin attributes   Background image

left should begin to fade. HTML is not terribly hard to learn, and Dreamweaver can be a very good place to start that process. Figure A-4 shows a very basic Web page. Figure A-5 shows its associated source code.

From looking at this example, the things we've discussed so far should be fairly easy to pick out. You'll notice that every tag has both an opening and closing form. In most cases, the closing tag is a repeat of the opening tag proceeded by a forward slash (/). See how the paragraphs are enclosed between the <p> and </p>? Look at the beginning of the paragraph and find the opening font tag. You can see the face attribute, which tells the browser to use a font from a particular font family, and the size attribute, which indicates how large the font should be.

FIGURE A-4

A simple HTML document viewed in Design view

FIGURE A-5

The same document displayed
in Code view

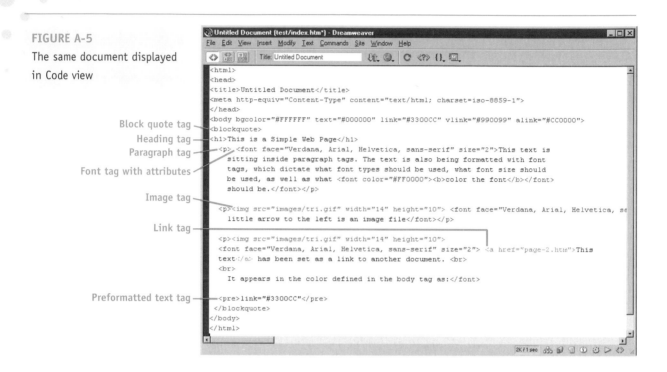

Block quote tag

Heading tag

Paragraph tag

Font tag with attributes

Image tag

Link tag

Preformatted text tag

Immediately following the second <p> tag is an image source tag (<img src=...>),
which is used to insert a graphic into a document. When using an image tag,
you always have to list the path to the image if it's not in the same directory on
the server the HTML document is in. It's always a good idea to keep your images
in their own directory as part of maintaining an organized file structure. In this
case, the image is inside another directory called *images*, and the image file's name
is *tri.gif*.

The third paragraph contains a link that uses the anchor tag, <a>. The primary
attribute for the anchor tag is *href*, which stands for hypertext reference. In the
simplest terms, this tag says, "Please use whatever falls between these opening
and closing anchor tags to reference this other page." It can be text as shown,
or you could insert an image source tag just as easily.

As you can see, HTML has a very friendly syntax and reads almost like English.
Most tags are simply single-letter representations of the elements they stand for or
are no more complex than a syllable or two. This is not to insinuate that HTML
can't produce some grand constructs, but rather to remind you that HTML was
designed to be straightforward and easy to comprehend. As you learn more and

begin designing your own pages (and maybe start deciphering some of your favorite sites to see how they work), your understanding and abilities will grow. The efforts you make to learn more will be rewarded in the quality and complexity of the sites you'll be able to produce.

> **TIP** If you want to take a look at the source code of your favorite Web site, select View | Source from the menu bar in Internet Explorer or View | Page Source in Netscape Navigator.

HTML AND THE WYSIWYG EDITOR

Now that we've covered a brief explanation of HTML, and looked at a few examples of tags and their implementation, let's look at what Dreamweaver does for you in your development of Web content. If you've never seen the acronym WYSIWYG (pronounced "wizzy-wig"), it stands for What You See Is What You Get. Dreamweaver would be considered a WYSIWYG tool because you use it to lay out Web pages in a graphic environment instead of coding them manually. What this means is that Dreamweaver will allow you to open a document window and start typing away just as you would in a word processor, seeing your formatting right on the screen. You can insert images, text, and many other complex structural elements and see them almost exactly as they would appear in the finished Web page, all while Dreamweaver is simultaneously generating the appropriate HTML code for your document.

DREAMWEAVER AS HTML TUTOR

As stated at the start of this chapter, much of the power of Dreamweaver comes from the seamless integration of its visual and text editing environments. For the HTML novice, this is a boon. It becomes a simple matter to enter content, view its source code, and then deconstruct your creation.

New in this version of Dreamweaver is the Reference Palette (shown in Figure A-6). By viewing the source code, highlighting a tag, and pressing the Reference button on the menu bar, the Reference palette is invoked. Here a full description of the tag as defined in *HTML: The Definitive Guide*, by Chuck Musciano and Bill Kennedy, published by O'Reilly & Associates, is available to the user, including any author bias (which can make for some fun reading!). By clicking on the Description drop-down menu, you can also access descriptions of the associated

FIGURE A-6

The Reference Palette

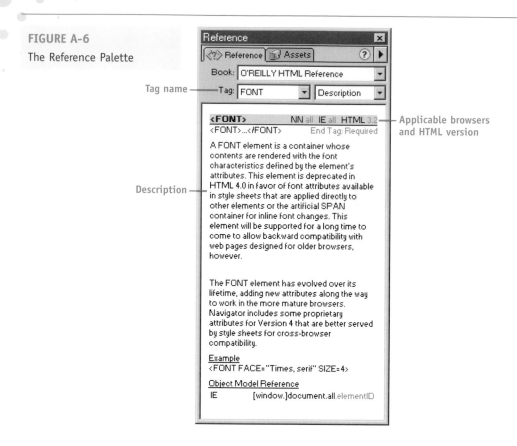

Tag name

Description

Applicable browsers
and HTML version

attributes for the tag. The palette displays the opening and closing syntax for the
tag, whether a closing tag is necessarily required, which browsers recognize the
tag, and which version number of HTML the tag is from. Armed with this feature,
even HTML beginners should be able to advance at breakneck speed.

Macromedia Fireworks: The Basics

Fireworks is the premier image editor that comes bundled with Dreamweaver if you've purchased the Dreamweaver/Fireworks Studio. Fireworks allows you to create button graphics, navigation bars, image rollovers, and animations, and to retouch photos—basically, to create and edit any type of graphic you can think of. If you've purchased the Dreamweaver/Fireworks Studio and installed both applications, Fireworks is assigned as the default image editor for manipulating images from inside Dreamweaver.

Fireworks creates images in the .PNG file format, the newest addition to the rather short list of acceptable Web graphic formats. Originally, .JPG and .GIF images were the only formats Web browsers were capable of displaying. The .PNG format (pronounced "ping") has recently been accepted by the W3C (World Wide Web Consortium), and the latest versions of both Internet Explorer and Netscape can display .PNG images successfully, although older browsers will not. Fortunately, you can export Fireworks graphics, optimizing them in both the .JPG and .GIF formats.

THE FIREWORKS INTERFACE

In the latest versions of its software, Macromedia strives for a level of consistency across its application interfaces. In Fireworks, as in Dreamweaver, you will see tabbed panels and inspectors, each serving as drawing and editing tools or providing options for controlling how the tools work.

> **TIP** Toolbox buttons with triangles in their lower-right corner mean there are related tools available. Select and hold the button, or click directly on the triangle to see the button's selection of tools.

The main elements of the interface are as follows:

▶ **Menu bar** Select the menu names to view their list of commands. As with Dreamweaver, many have keyboard equivalents. Use the Window menu to select which interface elements are visible.

▶ **Toolbox** Similar to Dreamweaver's Objects Panel, this panel groups Fireworks' predominant drawing and manipulation tools (shown here). The tools enable you to create shapes and lines, paint, fill, erase, move, resize, and select elements of your images. Place your cursor over any tool to display its name.

▶ **Toolbar** Running directly below the menu bar, the toolbar offers the standard Open, Save, Print, and Clipboard tools, as well as buttons for viewing palettes and changing which tab is active on displayed palettes. If you do not see the toolbar, select Windows | Toolbar | Main. This will open the toolbar in a floating position. You can dock it to any side of the image window by dragging it until it snaps into position.

▶ Floating palettes The four floating palettes, shown in Figure B-1, contain a number of individual tabs for modifying tool and file attributes. You can use the floating palettes to select a brush size for the tool you're using, pick textures or picture fills for a shape or area you've drawn, and control the layers within your image, for example.

▶ Image window This window is the primary workspace for Fireworks, as shown in Figure B-2. Whenever you open an existing image, or create a new one, the image appears here.

FIGURE B-1

The Fireworks floating palettes

FIGURE B-2

Create and edit your images in the Fireworks image window.

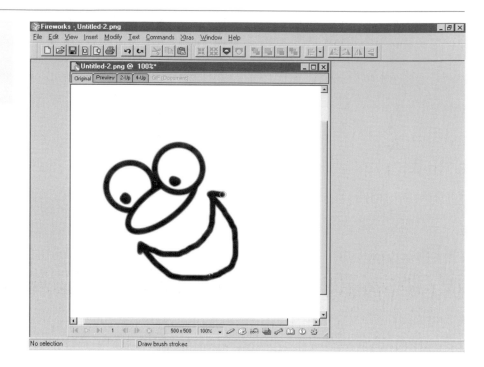

CREATING WEB GRAPHICS

To create a Fireworks graphic, you must open a new image window, and then use the drawing and editing tools to complete the image.

To Create A NEW IMAGE:

1 Select File | New from the menu bar. This displays the New Document dialog box.

2 Enter the width, height, and resolution you want for the new image. You can select pixels, inches, or centimeters as the default unit of measure.

3 Select a canvas color. You can select a custom color, use a transparent background, or stick with the default white.

4 Click OK to confirm your settings and close the dialog box. The new untitled image window opens.

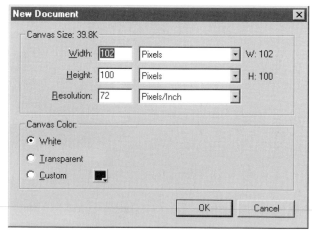

With the new blank image window prepared, you can begin drawing your image. Use the Toolbox to draw shapes and lines, paint, and type text (see Figure B-3).

You can view your graphic in four ways: in its original state, as a preview of its optimized online state, or in two split-screen forms—2-Up shows the original and one optimized image which you can then adjust to see the effect of different optimization settings, and 4-Up offers three independently adjustable preview images, as shown in Figure B-4.

MANIPULATING LINES AND SHAPES

You can select your stroke and fill colors with the Toolbox color tools as you draw lines and shapes. Depending on which part of the drawing is selected (a shape or a line), the fill or stroke color tool will be activated.

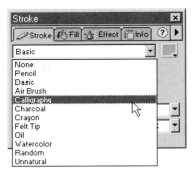

You can also change the way the paintbrush and pencil tools work, choosing from a variety of Stroke options.

FIGURE B-3
A graphic in progress

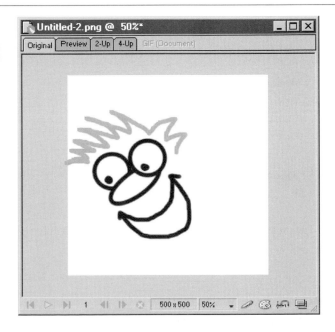

FIGURE B-4

The 4-Up view lets you check three different optimization settings against the original.

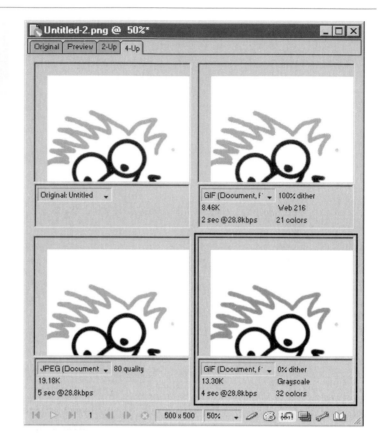

USING TEXT IN AN IMAGE

Add text to your images by clicking the Text tool and then clicking inside the image where you want the text to appear. This displays the Text Editor dialog box (Figure B-5), where you select the font, color, style, size, and alignment of the text.

You can also control the horizontal and vertical spread of your text, and smooth the edges of your text by applying various anti-aliasing settings. The default is Smooth which, as the name implies, softens the edges of most fonts.

SAVING FIREWORKS FILES

By default, Fireworks saves graphics in .PNG format. If you choose Save or Save As from the File menu, you can simply save your file by giving it a name and choosing a folder and drive on which to store it. You can, of course, export files to more common Web formats.

FIGURE B-5

The Text Editor dialog box lets you see just what your text will look like before it's inserted.

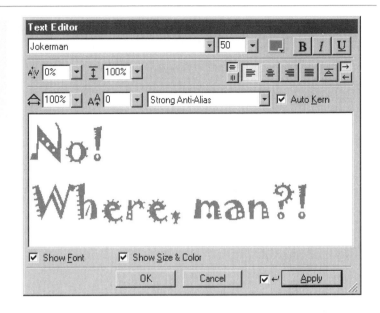

To Export YOUR IMAGE TO GIF OR JPG FORMAT:

1 Choose File | Export Preview. This displays the Export Preview dialog box, as shown in Figure B-6.

2 On the Options tab, click the Format drop-down list to select a file format in which to save the file.

3 To export only part of an image, use the Export Area button found along the bottom of the dialog box, as shown here, to crop to the desired region.

Export Area button

> **TIP** If you want to save the Fireworks original image, including all the separate layers and settings you chose through the palettes, you can do so, giving the file the same name as the JPG or GIF version you exported. By retaining this version of the file, you make it easier to make edits in the future. For example, if you create and export an image containing text, and later discover the text is misspelled or needs to be changed, you can quickly edit the original version of the file and then re-export it, replacing the first export.

4 Click the Export button to open the Export dialog box (see Figure B-7), where you can choose where to save your file and what to call it. The image will be saved in the format you chose in the Export Wizard dialog box.

5 Click the Save button. The original image remains open in the Fireworks window.

FIGURE B-6

The Export Preview dialog box provides a range of options for saving your image.

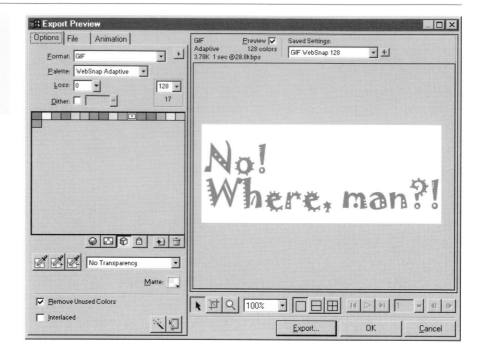

FIGURE B-7

Use hyphens and underscores instead of spaces in file names. Stick with lowercase characters, as well.

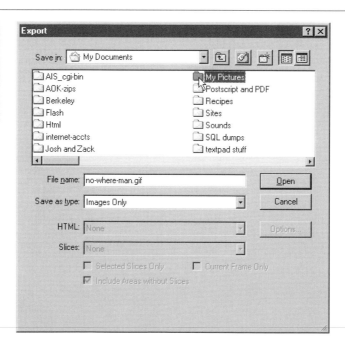

THE TIP OF THE ICEBERG

This extremely basic overview only provides an inkling as to the wide range of Fireworks' possibilities, but with this introduction you should be able to get started building images for your Web pages. Fireworks has an extensive set of tools that go beyond the intention of this appendix. If you plan to use Fireworks as your primary image creation and manipulation tool, take advantage of the online help and other documentation provided with the software. The information is thorough, accurate, and easy to navigate.

Index

Note: Page numbers in *italics* refer to illustrations or charts.

nested lists, 57
> *See also* lists

nested tables, 115, *116*
> *See also* tables

nesting framesets, 153
> *See also* frames

nesting layers, 171-172

nesting tables, Layout view, 119

Netscape Navigator, plug-ins, 226-228

New Document dialog box, Fireworks image editor, *330*

New Editable Region dialog box, templates, *282*

New Style dialog box, CSS (Cascading Style Sheets), *187*, *198*

nicknames, assigning to favorite assets, 278

NoFrames screen, accommodating older browsers and frames, 165

notes, Design Notes, 307-309

null links, Behaviors Panel, 238-240

O

Objects Panel, 14-15
> button palettes, 14
> Draw Layer button, *168*
> Draw Layout Cell button, 119
> Draw Layout Table button, *117*
> Insert ActiveX button, *229*
> Insert Applet button, *232*
> Insert Email Link button, *87*
> Insert Flash button, 217
> Insert Form button, *130*
> Insert Hidden Field button, 139
> Insert Navigation Bar button, 93, 94
> Insert Plugin button, *226*
> Insert Radio Button button, 135
> Insert Shockwave button, 217
> Layout View button, 117
> predefined framesets, 152-153

onAbort event handler, Behaviors Panel, *240*

onAfterUpdate event handler, Behaviors Panel, *240*

onBeforeUpdate event handler, Behaviors Panel, *240*

onBlur event handler, Behaviors Panel, *240*

onChange event handler, Behaviors Panel, *241*

onClick event handler, Behaviors Panel, *241*

onDblClick event handler, Behaviors Panel, *241*

onError event handler, Behaviors Panel, *241*

onFocus event handler, Behaviors Panel, *241*

onHelp event handler, Behaviors Panel, *241*

onKeyDown event handler, Behaviors Panel, *241*

onKeyPress event handler, Behaviors Panel, *241*

onKeyUp event handler, Behaviors Panel, *241*

onLoad event handler, Behaviors Panel, *241*

onMouseDown event handler, Behaviors Panel, *241*

onMouseMove event handler, Behaviors Panel, *242*

onMouseOut event handler, Behaviors Panel, *242*

onMouseOver event handler, Behaviors Panel, *242*

onMouseUp event handler, Behaviors Panel, *242*

onMove event handler, Behaviors Panel, *242*

onReadyStateChange event handler, Behaviors Panel, *242*

onReset event handler, Behaviors Panel, *242*

onResize event handler, Behaviors Panel, *242*

onScroll event handler, Behaviors Panel, *242*

onSelect event handler, Behaviors Panel, *242*

onSubmit event handler, Behaviors Panel, *242*

onUnload event handler, Behaviors Panel, *242*

Open Browser Window action, Behaviors Panel, 252-254

Open To Source Of Link option, Site Map, 90

opening
> Frames Panel, 154
> Site window, 27

opening files, Site window, 31

ordered lists, 53
> *See also* lists

overflow, layers, 177

P

<p> and </p> tags, HTML paragraphs, 45

Page Properties dialog box
> frames, *164*
> hyperlinks color, 84, *85*
> templates, 287
> text color, *52*

page titles
> adding to framesets, 163
> Site Map and HTML, 37-39

paragraphs, 45-46
> *See also* text
> <p> and </p> tags, 45

password fields, 134
> *See also* forms; text boxes

pasting. *See* copying and pasting

pathnames, hyperlinks and, 82-83

percentage widths, Insert Table dialog box, 100, *101*

physical text styles, 58-59

pixels
> clipping areas and, 178
> layers and units of measurement, 173

planning, Web site design, 20

Play Timeline action, Behaviors Panel, 262-263

plug-ins (Netscape Navigator), 226-228
> *See also* ActiveX controls; multimedia elements
> adding to Web pages, 226
> customizing, 226-227
> Insert Plugin button, *226*
> overview, 226
> troubleshooting, 227-228

point-to-file icon for creating hyperlinks, 83, *84*

Popup Message action, Behaviors Panel, 254

INTERNATIONAL CONTACT INFORMATION

AUSTRALIA
McGraw-Hill Book Company Australia Pty. Ltd.
TEL +61-2-9417-9899
FAX +61-2-9417-5687
http://www.mcgraw-hill.com.au
books-it_sydney@mcgraw-hill.com

CANADA
McGraw-Hill Ryerson Ltd.
TEL +905-430-5000
FAX +905-430-5020
http://www.mcgrawhill.ca

**GREECE, MIDDLE EAST,
NORTHERN AFRICA**
McGraw-Hill Hellas
TEL +30-1-656-0990-3-4
FAX +30-1-654-5525

MEXICO (Also serving Latin America)
McGraw-Hill Interamericana Editores S.A. de C.V.
TEL +525-117-1583
FAX +525-117-1589
http://www.mcgraw-hill.com.mx
fernando_castellanos@mcgraw-hill.com

SINGAPORE (Serving Asia)
McGraw-Hill Book Company
TEL +65-863-1580
FAX +65-862-3354
http://www.mcgraw-hill.com.sg
mghasia@mcgraw-hill.com

SOUTH AFRICA
McGraw-Hill South Africa
TEL +27-11-622-7512
FAX +27-11-622-9045
robyn_swanepoel@mcgraw-hill.com

**UNITED KINGDOM & EUROPE
(Excluding Southern Europe)**
McGraw-Hill Publishing Company
TEL +44-1-628-502500
FAX +44-1-628-770224
http://www.mcgraw-hill.co.uk
computing_neurope@mcgraw-hill.com

ALL OTHER INQUIRIES Contact:
Osborne/McGraw-Hill
TEL +1-510-549-6600
FAX +1-510-883-7600
http://www.osborne.com
omg_international@mcgraw-hill.com

LEARN DREAMWEAVER FASTER!

MORE VIDEO LESSONS FROM ROBERT FULLER AND BRAINSVILLE.COM

Dear Friend,

Thank you for buying this book. I hope that you found it useful and enjoyed the CD-ROM full of video lessons.

There were too many great Dreamweaver topics to cover on one CD, so I created the **Dreamweaver CD Extra**, a second CD covering key areas like these:

Creating Flash Elements
Use Dreamweaver to produce eye-catching Flash animations

Text and Links
Format these essential Web site elements swiftly and easily

Styles and Tables
Tools and techniques for making your pages look the way you want

Easy Access to HTML
Work "under the hood" with the language of the Web

Extending Dreamweaver
Go beyond the basics and improve Dreamweaver's capabilities

...And more! The complete contents are listed at www.Brainsville.com.

The lessons on the **Dreamweaver CD Extra** use the same easy-to-follow video presentation style as the CD you already have. I'm right there on your screen, talking to you about Dreamweaver in the same practical, understandable way.

The **Dreamweaver CD Extra** is an essential tool for learning Dreamweaver. Check it out at www.Brainsville.com.

Best Wishes,

Robert Fuller

Name: Robert Fuller
Project: Dreamweaver CD Extra